ANTI-NATURALISM

BROADWAY PLAY PUBLISHING INC.

357 W 20th St., NY NY 10011
212 627-1055

ANTI-NATURALISM

First printing: September 1989
ISBN: 0-88145-056-1

Book design: Marie Donovan
Word processing: WordMarc Composer Plus
Typographic controls: Xerox Ventura Publisher Professional Extension
Typeface: Palatino
Printed on acid-free paper and bound in the USA.

CONTENTS

A NOTE FROM THE PUBLISHER

REALISM, NATURALISM, AND ANTI-NATURALISM

I use the words "realism" and "naturalism" interchangeably. I know there is a distinction, but as many times as I have looked it up, the difference seems too narrow to worry about. An "anti-naturalistic" play, to me, is a creative work that quite obviously couldn't be taking place in this world as we know it.

The American naturalistic/realistic play is stuck in a dreary dead-end that is piled high in kitchen sinks and trailer parks, mired in self-indulgent autobiography. In no way am I rejecting the place in the theater of realism or naturalism. I am not going to deny the power of much of the writing of Beth Henley, David Mamet, Marsha Norman, August Wilson, or Lanford Wilson. Realism, in the right hands, gives us some of our most memorable dramas. Of the younger generation of writers, William Mastrosimone's CAT'S PAW, Tom Dulack's DIMINISHED CAPACITY, Richard Lees' RIGHT OF WAY, and Alan Bowne's SHARON AND BILLY are some of the most riveting pieces of theater I have ever read.

But realism only works in certain types of plays. For me, the real test for playwrights is how they let their imagination go. By telling the audience "this is not going to be a realistic play," all preconceived expectations must be cast aside. The playwrights have thrown down the gauntlet, daring us to come into this world they have created.

This is not to say that I love every play that employs non-naturalistic devices. Too often, a playwright will be content to throw a cacophony of images or crazy characters at the audience, yet never tie the whole thing together in any way. In this sense, I am a traditionalist: I believe there has to be some sort of "linear progression" in a play. Without some form of logical development, there is no tension to a play, and so the audience rapidly loses interest. All the plays in this anthology, despite their use of non-naturalistic techniques, have obvious linear progression.

TECHNIQUES OF ANTI-NATURALISM

Two of the playwrights in this collection—Eric Overmyer and Dan Therriault—express themselves through the use of heightened language. To read any play by one of these two gifted writers is to revel in poetry and in an overwhelming imagination. Their earlier plays—NATIVE SPEECH and IN A PIG'S VALISE by Eric Overmyer, and BATTERY and FLOOR ABOVE THE ROOF by Dan Therriault—are heady battles with the English language. One is continually awed by the verbal pyrotechnics. Of course, that is not all these talented writers give us. ON THE VERGE travels through space and time, and THE WHITE DEATH turns into a new wave/noir whodunit.

All the plays in this anthology instantly plunge the audience into a surreal world. Except for THE WHITE DEATH, all are "journey" plays. With each ensuing scene, the protagonists encounter totally unfamiliar people, objects, and events. They become farther and farther removed from any world we recognize. By defying expectations of what would happen in "reality", each playwright makes his characters face situations that have never happened before; they are explorers across uncharted realms of the imagination. This is what appeals most to me about non-naturalistic plays, and why they continue to fascinate me.

PANTHEON OF LIVING AMERICAN PLAYWRIGHTS

Arthur Miller has to be at the top of the list of living American playwrights, whatever one's opinion might be of what he's written in the last twenty years. One has to toss Neil Simon in up there, too, with the same proviso. Then, one gets to a separate-but-equal level, where stand my triumvirate of active American playwrights: David Mamet, Sam Shepard, and Lanford Wilson. Each of them has an incredible range to their oeuvre. But beneath them, whom do we have? Few other playwrights have significant bodies of work to be adequately judged. Many have shown promise, but few have been able to live up to the expectations that their first plays aroused.

For my money, Craig Lucas, Richard Nelson, and Eric Overmyer all have to be counted as challengers to the Big Five mentioned in the paragraph above. Each has at least four full-length plays upon which he can be judged. The growth and range that they display with each new play is exhilarating.

As for Keith Reddin, Daniel Therriault, and Mac Wellman, if their next plays continue the promise of their earlier ones, then they, too, are most definitely challengers.

ORIGINAL PRODUCTIONS

A little should be said about some of the producing organizations that were (and in many cases still are) involved with these playwrights:

Center Stage, in Baltimore, made Eric Overmyer an Artistic Associate four years ago. They have supported him both financially and with first-rate professional productions of his plays. This is the sort of family a writer needs so he won't be enticed by that siren, Hollywood. Stan Wojewodski,

Center Stage's Artistic Director, is to be commended and emulated by other theater managers.

Likewise, Playwrights Horizons, under André Bishop, has grown to become, arguably, the primary theater in America for new plays. In addition to producing two of Keith Reddin's plays, they also have given us plays by both Craig Lucas and Richard Nelson. They supported Eric Overmyer for a few years while he was their Literary Manager.

It is a sad comment on the New York theater that a group as creative and innovative as The Production Company no longer exists. In the eight years they operated, they premiered all of Craig Lucas' plays, each time directed by their Artistic Director, Norman René. Luckily, this creative pair continues to work around the country, notably at South Coast Rep, and are, in the words of Lee Melville of Drama-Logue, "...the most insightful theater team since Prince and Sondheim."

A list of the theaters that have premiered Richard Nelson's plays reads like a *Who's Who in the American Theater.* As it happens, BAL was produced in his hometown, at the Goodman Theater, where it was directed by someone who has gone on to even greater fame: Gregory Mosher.

HARM'S WAY was produced at LaMama ETC. If Joseph Papp is the King of the American Theater (deposing Bernie Jacobs and Jerry Schoenfeld of the Shuberts), then Ellen Stewart is uncontestedly the Queen. No theater person has done more to foster peace and understanding around the world than Ellen Stewart. It is to her credit that she let George Ferencz (incidentally, the original director of Daniel Therriault's BATTERY) direct Mac Wellman's surreal Western in the cavernous Annex space.

Daniel Therriault's THE WHITE DEATH is an anomaly among these plays. Its only professional production has been in Equity Waiver in Los Angeles, by the same group that originally produced BATTERY there.

Patterns start to emerge when one looks at the theaters and people associated with these playwrights. A finite number of theaters and directors are promulgating the works of this new generation of playwrights. Obviously, there is no organized movement going on here. But, ten or fifteen years from now, when many of the playwrights in this collection are recognized as being in The Pantheon, these interconnections will be pointed out as important influences in the American theater.

DISCLAIMER

This anthology is this publisher's personal manifesto. None of these playwrights has expressed any particular antipathy to realism or naturalism; nor have they ever professed to be part of any larger movement.

July 1989 Christopher Gould, Publisher

RECKLESS

Craig Lucas

ABOUT THE AUTHOR

Craig Lucas also is the author of MISSING PERSONS, BLUE WINDOW, PRELUDE TO A KISS *(Broadway Play Publishing, 1989)*, and THE SCARE, all originally directed by Norman René. The two are responsible for conceiving and developing MARRY ME A LITTLE, an evening of trunk songs by Stephen Sondheim. They have collaborated on a film of BLUE WINDOW for *American Playhouse*, and are currently making a second film, LIFETIME COMPANION. Mr. Lucas has received the George and Elisabeth Marton Award, the L.A. Drama Critics' Award, a Drama-Logue Award, Guggenheim and Rockefeller grants, and play commissions from South Coast Repertory and American Playhouse. His musical play, THREE POSTCARDS, which he co-authored with composer/lyricist Craig Carnelia, was selected as Best Musical of 1986-87 by the Burns Mantle Theater yearbook. He has written two opera texts with composer Gerald Busby, COUSIN LILLIE and ORPHEUS IN LOVE. A graduate of Boston University where he studied with poet Anne Sexton, Mr Lucas is a company member of Circle Repertory and a member of the Dramatists Guild.

This play is dedicated to Daniel Clarke Slautterback

RECKLESS originally was produced (in an earlier version) by The Production Company, Norman René, Artistic Director; Abigail Franklin, Managing Director, at Theatre Guinevere, in New York City, opening on 11 May 1983. The cast, in order of appearance, was as follows:

RACHEL FITSIMMONS .... Lori Cardille
TOM FITSIMMONS .... Timothy Wahrer
LLOYD BOPHTELOPHTI .... W.T. Martin
POOTY .... Maureen Silliman
ROY .... James Bormann
BERNADETTE HANDS* .... Suzanne Henry
TRISH HAMMERS .... Susan Blommaert
FIRST through SIXTH DOCTORS .... Patrizia Norcia
TIM TIMKO .... James Dupont
TALK SHOW HOST .... James Dupont
DR. HELEN CARROLL .... Suzanne Henry
A MAN WITH POOR POSTURE* .... James Bormann
MAN IN SKI MASK .... Timothy Wahrer
WOMAN PATIENT .... Susan Blommaert
TOM JUNIOR .... Timothy Wahrer

*Roles cut from present version.

Director .... Norman René
Set design .... James Wolk
Costumes .... Steven L. Birnbaum
Lights .... Debra J. Kletter
Production stage manager .... Bill McComb

CHARACTERS

RACHEL
TOM
LLOYD
POOTY
ROY
TRISH
FIRST DOCTOR
TIM TIMKO
SECOND DOCTOR
THIRD DOCTOR
FOURTH DOCTOR
FIFTH DOCTOR
FIRST DERELICT
SECOND DERELICT
SIXTH DOCTOR
TALK SHOW HOST
DR. HELEN CARROLL
MAN IN SKI MASK
WOMAN PATIENT
RECEPTIONIST
TOM JUNIOR
Voices of various announcers and newscasters

RECKLESS *can be performed with as few as seven actors.* TOM, TOM JUNIOR, *and the* MAN IN SKI MASK *are doubled, as are the* FIRST *through* SIXTH DOCTORS.

A solitude ten thousand fathoms deep
Sustains the bed on which we lie, my dear;
Although I love you, you will have to leap;
Our dream of safety has to disappear.

W.H. Auden

Scene One

(The glow of the television. RACHEL, *at the window, in her nightgown;* TOM *in bed.)*

RACHEL: I think I'm more excited than they are. I really do. I think we just have kids so we can tell them all about Santa Claus and have an excuse to believe it all ourselves again. I really do. They are so excited. I remember that feeling so clearly. I didn't think I could ever sleep. And I remember pinching myself and pinching myself to stay awake so I could hear the reindeers' footsteps, you know? I wanted to believe it so badly. I think that was the last year I did.... Oh, God.... Is it still snowing? Why don't you turn the sound up?

*(*TOM *shakes his head, stares at the screen.)*

RACHEL: Oh, it's coming down like crazy. You can hear it, can't you, when it gets deep like this? It just swallows up all the sound and you feel like you've been wrapped up in the hands of a big, sweet, giant, white...monster. Good monster. He's going to carry us away into a dream. My family always had champagne first thing before we opened our presents — I mean, in the morning, you know. I always loved that. I felt like such an adult having champagne and I remember saying to my mother that the bubbles in the champagne looked like snow if you turned your head upside down. I remember thinking I wanted to live in Alaska because it always snowed and Santa was up there, so it must always be Christmas.... You're my Santa Claus. And our two elves. I'm having one of my euphoria attacks. I think I'm going to be terminally happy, you'd better watch out, it's catching. Highly contagious.... What's the matter? Just sleepy?

*(*TOM *nods.)*

RACHEL: Can we listen for a second, I won't stay up all night, I promise. *(She switches on the TV.)*

ANNOUNCER'S VOICE: —as they raise their small voices in joyous celebration once more. *(The Vienna Boys Choir is heard singing.)*

RACHEL: Oh, God, look at those faces. I feel so sorry for Jeanette and Freddie sometimes. These things happen for a reason, I know, but.... I always think if something happened to us I'd want them to raise the boys.

ANNOUNCER'S VOICE: This is David Harbinger from Vienna.

SECOND ANNOUNCER'S VOICE: And in a bizarre note this Christmas Eve: An Albanian woman fled across the border into Yugoslavia where it is said she gave birth to a two-headed child today. Both mother and son are reported to be in stable condition. According to spokesmen, the woman is either unwilling or unable to speak. So far there has been no explanation for her flight. Well, whoever's dreaming of a white Christmas doesn't have to dream tonight. Weatherman Sheldon Strafford has the story.

RACHEL: *(Overlapping)* Isn't that awful?

*(*TOM *has begun to cry.)*

THIRD ANNOUNCER'S VOICE: Bill, we thought this low pressure front might never move out, but as you can see it finally has and tiny tots and snowmen should be playing together in the streets by dawn.

RACHEL: *(Continuing over TV)* What's the matter?... Oh, honey, it's just the news, come on, it's not real. We'll turn it off, see? It's gone. *(She switches off TV.)* Don't be upset on Christmas. Everything's great, I'm here and everything's fine.

TOM: I took a contract out on your life.

RACHEL: What do you mean? Life insurance?

TOM: A contract on your life.

RACHEL: That is the sickest joke, I'm sorry. I don't care what's bothering you, you could just come out with it—

TOM: All right, listen to me—

RACHEL: You get these idiotic ideas of what's funny—

TOM: I want you to listen to me if you've never listened to me in your life—

RACHEL: It's Christmas Eve!

TOM: In five minutes a man's going to break through the bay windows downstairs. I'm sorry this is happening this way, it's a stupid solution and we should have talked it out, but it's done and he'll be here in less than five minutes. I want you to put on your coat and some slippers, you can climb out this window over the garage and run over to Jeanette's. When he's gone I'll call you and we can talk about it.

RACHEL: *(Overlapping)* Tom Fitsimmons, I know you and I think this is really off the mark, I'm sorry. Fun is fun.... I'm going to sleep in the other bedroom.

TOM: *(Grabbing her)* Rachel! Listen to me now if you want to live!

RACHEL: You're hurting me.

TOM: I paid this man, he's a professional, I cannot take it back. All right, look: *(He produces a handgun.)* This is a .38. It has no bullets. It's staged to look like he broke in and I pulled a gun and he killed you—a thief—an accident. I'm sorry, you can't be here, we'll talk it all out in a little while when he's gone.

RACHEL: You're frightening me.

TOM: I'll tell him you went to stay with your mother. He has his money, he can go. Tell Jeanette we had a fight, it doesn't matter, I'll call you when he's gone.

RACHEL: This is so mean.

(The sound of glass shattering below. RACHEL *climbs out the window.)*

TOM: Go! He won't see you! Stay in the dark! Keep in the shadows!

Scene Two

*(*RACHEL *at a pay phone in her robe and slippers. Snow.)*

RACHEL: Jeanette? Rachel. Merry Christmas.... No, everything's great, but listen, would you and Freddie mind taking a little spin down here to the Arco station at Route 3 and Carl Bluestein Boulevard? No, no, nothing like that, I just came outside.... Oh, isn't it? It's beautiful, uh-huh, listen, Jeanette, Tom took a.... Tom.... It's so ridiculous. He took a contract out on my life.... A contract?...Uh-huh. Right. And, I mean, the man broke in downstairs so I thought I'd better go out of the house, so I climbed out over the garage and I was afraid to ring your bell, because you have all those pretty lights and I was afraid he might be following my tracks in the snow—

*(*LLOYD *approaches in the darkness.)*

RACHEL: —and so I thought maybe you'd just zip down here and we'd all have some eggnog or something, what do you say?...Jeane—? No.... No, I know, I am, I'm a kidder.... But—Merry Christmas to you too, Jeanette, please don't....

*(*JEANETTE *has hung up.* RACHEL *turns, sees* LLOYD, *screams.)*

RACHEL: AAAAAAGH! NO, MY GOD! PLEASE!

LLOYD: *(Overlapping her, backing up)* Hey. Hey.

RACHEL: Oh, I'm sorry. Did you want to use the phone? Please, go right ahead.

LLOYD: I'm just trying to find a gas station.

RACHEL: This is a gas station, right here, you found one. For GAS! Oh, not on Christmas Eve, maybe up on the turnpike.... Merry Christmas.

LLOYD: Merry Christmas. You need a lift?

RACHEL: No. Yes. No.

LLOYD: It's no problem.

RACHEL: No. Thank you.

LLOYD: You're sure?

RACHEL: No, thank you. I mean, yes—I....

LLOYD: Come on, hop in.

Scene Three

(In the car)

RACHEL: Thank you.

LLOYD: Better?

RACHEL: Yes.

LLOYD: Where you headed?... Some night.

RACHEL: Yes. Yes. Christmas. I love Christmas.

LLOYD: Yeah.

RACHEL: Snow.... You have a family?

LLOYD: No. Well, you know.... You?

RACHEL: No.... No, no. *(Her wedding ring)* Oh this? This is just costume. I just wear this, see? *(Tosses the ring out the window)* Good-bye! That felt wonderful. Maybe you should just let me off up at the, uh.... Well, I can get off anywhere. Oh, you wanted to get gas. Where do you live?

LLOYD: Springfield.

RACHEL: Springfield.... The field of spring.

LLOYD: You and your husband have a fight or something?

RACHEL: I'm not married. You married?... You have a girlfriend.

LLOYD: Just Pooty.

RACHEL: Pooty... Pooty.... My son does the cutest thing. I was married before. He's four and a half. My son has custody—my father—oh God. My son is four and a half, my husband has custody, my father is dead. And he does this thing—there are two boys, but Jeremy's just three. But Tom—Tom

Junior, not my husband, Tom Senior—Tom Junior is always firing everybody, you know, if he doesn't like what you're doing. He'll say to his babysitter who is usually my friend Jeanette who can't have kids of her own because of this thing in her—uterus—he'll say to Jeanette, you know, um, "You're fired, Jeanette!" You know? Just because she wants to put him to bed or something. And just today he fired me. I mean, on Christmas Eve. I said, "You're gonna fire your own mother?" "That's right," he said, "You're fired!" So.

LLOYD: Now you're fired.

RACHEL: Now I'm fired. What does Pooty do? Is that her name?

LLOYD: Pooty.

RACHEL: What does she do?

LLOYD: She works.

RACHEL: Oh, that's good. Do you work? *(He nods.)* Same place Pooty works? *(He nods.)* Now how did I know that? Not me, I've never worked. *(Pause)* Did you tell me your name?

LLOYD: Lloyd.

RACHEL: Lloyd.

LLOYD: Bophtelophti.

RACHEL: Bophtelophti. Isn't THAT an interesting name. I'm—Mary Ellen Sissle. Is my maiden name.

LLOYD: Nice to meet you.

RACHEL: Don't let go of the wheel! Nice to meet you, too. My father always said, "Don't interfere with the driver whilst the vehicle is in motion." You think I'm escaped from an institution, don't you?

LLOYD: Are you? *(She laughs.)* What's so funny?

RACHEL: Nothing, I'm sorry, I just suddenly saw.... I mean, me in my house-dress and my slippers out in the snow.

LLOYD: Oh, it's cool.

RACHEL: Yes, it was. I've always wanted to do something like that, you know? Run away in the middle of the night in your slip and your slippers with some strange man who would ruin your reputation and disappoint your parents terribly and disappoint your friends and just make you really happy. Well, I think we get these ideas from rock-and-roll songs, actually.

LLOYD: Right.

RACHEL: Which is why I would never really do anything like that except here I am. But, no, I mean, this isn't really like that, I just meant running away and becoming.... Well, I don't know what I thought I'd become. But running away. And here I am.

LLOYD: Here you are.

RACHEL: On my way to....

LLOYD: Meet Pooty.

RACHEL: Meet Pooty.... *(Pause)* Lloyd?

LLOYD: Yeah?

RACHEL: Do you think we ever really know people? I mean, I know we know people....

LLOYD: You mean really.

RACHEL: But really.

LLOYD: You mean KNOW them.

RACHEL: Do you think?

LLOYD: Well... I don't know.

RACHEL: I don't know either. I mean, I suppose I know lots of people.

LLOYD: Sure you do.

RACHEL: And you know lots of people.

LLOYD: Pooty.

RACHEL: We live our lives and we know lots of people and.... I don't know what I'm saying. D'you get a Christmas tree? *(He nods.)* That's nice. "Oh, Christmas tree! Oh, Christmas tree...." *(She stops singing, near tears.)*

LLOYD: It's all right.

RACHEL: I know....

LLOYD: The holidays can be tough sometimes.... You see your parents?

RACHEL: Not since they died....

LLOYD: You'll spend Christmas with us.

Scene Four

(Living room)

RACHEL: Don't wake her.

LLOYD: Oh, she'll be glad to meet you. *(He goes off.)*

RACHEL: I love your house.... Be calm....

LLOYD: *(Back)* She'll be out in a sec.

RACHEL: This is so Christmasy.

LLOYD: How 'bout a rum toddy?... Comin' right up! *(He goes off again.)*

RACHEL: This is so lovely....

LLOYD: *(From off)* Glad to have the company.

(POOTY enters in her wheelchair.)

RACHEL: Surprise! Hello, Rachel—Mary Ellen! Rachel Mary Ellen, the Rachel is silent. Nice to meet you. This is so nice. I hope I'm not, you know. I feel.... Well, actually, my house burned down and Lloyd was kind enough to say I could stop in. You know, stop up. So, I'm, uh, not....

(No reaction. LLOYD returns.)

LLOYD: You have to keep your face towards her so she can read your lips.

RACHEL: Oh, she's deaf. You're deaf! I'm sorry, not that you're deaf, but.... I just LOVE your house.

(LLOYD signs for POOTY.)

LLOYD: The one and only Pooty-Poot-Pooter.

RACHEL: Yesssss.

LLOYD: *(Spelling the name)* Mary Ellen Sizzler.

RACHEL: Well. Did you slip on the ice, it looks like.

LLOYD: She's paraplegic.

RACHEL: Parapalegic! Oh, parapalegic.

LLOYD: Paraplegic.

RACHEL: I have to keep my face this way, don't I?... Um.... Tell me, Pooty—

LLOYD: I'm just gonna check on the toddies. *(He goes out again.)*

RACHEL: —what kind of name is that? Your name. It's so unusual. YOUR NAME!

(POOTY jots on a piece of paper.)

RACHEL: *(Reads)* "Pooty." Uh-huh. You know, I was just saying before....

(LLOYD returns with two glasses.)

LLOYD: She talk your ear off?

RACHEL: Thank you.

LLOYD: Pooter Bear.

RACHEL: Aren't you having any?

LLOYD: Never touch the stuff. Cheers.

RACHEL: Cheers. Sure there isn't any poison in here?

(She smiles, drinks. LLOYD *and* POOTY *confer in sign.)*

RACHEL: Mmmmm.... Isn't that beautiful the way you do that?

LLOYD: All right, everybody, have a seat. Time to open presents.

RACHEL: I'll watch. This'll be fun.

LLOYD: *(Handing her a gift)* Merry Christmas. From us. Open it.

RACHEL: But I didn't get anybody anything.

LLOYD: Go on.

RACHEL: Oh, I think this was meant for someone else. This is so strange. *(Opens the package; it's a shower massage.)* Look! Aren't you both so nice? Thank you.

LLOYD: You like it?

RACHEL: Ohhh, LIKE it?

LLOYD: Okay, who's next?

RACHEL: Wait, okay, I know what I want to do. Now I'm sorry I didn't get a chance to wrap this, but.... *(Gives* POOTY *her necklace)* Merry Christmas! Isn't this fun? I'll put it on.

LLOYD: She says you didn't have to do that.

RACHEL: Of course I didn't have to do that. You didn't have to ask a woman in her slippers to come spend Christmas with you either. I could be a mass killer. I could be anybody.... I could be anybody.

Scene Five

RACHEL: *(On the telephone)* Jeanette? Yes, Happy New Year, how are you? I'm great. So how was your Christmas, what did you get?... What? Oh, right now? Oh, I'm just up at my cousin's, you know. Of course I have a cousin, what do you mean you didn't know I had a cousin? Everybody has cousins. Where? I don't know, Jeanette, right up route—what difference does it make? But—no, I'm fine. Jeanette. Do I sound fine? Do I sound fine? Well. Oh shoot, here comes my bus, but listen, do me a favor? No, I will, but—I can't, Jeanette, but would you look in on the boys for me? When you get a chance? You will? Thanks, but listen, they're closing the doors, I've got to go. Okay. Bye, Jeanette! *(She hangs up.)*

Scene Six

(Living room)

LLOYD: Earth to Mary Ellen?

RACHEL: Hm?

LLOYD: Hungry?

RACHEL: No, thanks. Oh, I'll cook, how's that? What would you like?

LLOYD: What do you make?

RACHEL: Whatever you want, just name it. It's yours.

LLOYD: Whatever we want?

RACHEL: Whatever you want.

LLOYD: *(After conferring in sign with* POOTY*)* Well, we've discussed it.

RACHEL: Uh-huh?

LLOYD: And we both want you to stay here.

RACHEL: For dinner?

LLOYD: For as long as you like.

RACHEL: Oh no, I couldn't.

LLOYD: Why?

RACHEL: Well, I mean, I could, but I can't.

LLOYD: Well?

RACHEL: No. Thank you, though. Very much.

LLOYD: Why can't you?

RACHEL: Because.

LLOYD: Because why?

RACHEL: Because.

LLOYD: Because why?

RACHEL: Lloyd.

LLOYD: I'm serious.

RACHEL: Because I have to get a job, I have to get some shoes, I can't just move in.

*(*POOTY *exits.)*

LLOYD: Why not?

RACHEL: Pooty, come on!

LLOYD: She can't hear you, she's deaf.

RACHEL: Thank you, Lloyd, I'm having enough trouble as it is.

LLOYD: Well?

RACHEL: Because.

LLOYD: Because why?

RACHEL: This is the way children talk.

LLOYD: So?

RACHEL: So? So's your old man. Just because.

(POOTY returns with her lap filled with shoes.)

RACHEL: And what is this? Shoes. Oh God, I love you both so much, I do. Why are you doing this?

LLOYD: Because.

RACHEL: And where ARE we, anyway? Where is Springfield?

LLOYD: We've got an atlas.

RACHEL: I mean, do you people even have identification? My mother may not even let me play with you. She's very fussy, you know.

(LLOYD opens the atlas.)

LLOYD: Here.... Hold on....

RACHEL: I believe you.

LLOYD: Springfield. If you lived here you'd be home by now.

RACHEL: *(Holding the book)* Look how big the world is: It's all in this book.... Oh, Lloyd.... I would love to stay here, you know that. I would love to start my whole life right here at this second.

LLOYD: Why can't you?

RACHEL: Because. I'd have to get a job.

Scene Seven

(The office. TRISH at a computer terminal; ROY and RACHEL standing.)

ROY: Hands Across the Sea is a not-for-profit, humanitarian foundation.

RACHEL: *(To TRISH) Hi.*

ROY: This does not mean we get away with murder.

RACHEL: Uh-huh.

ROY: Any of us. We all work very long, very hard hours for very little pay. Trish Hammers, this is our new clerk, Mary Ellen Sissle.

RACHEL: How do you do?

ROY: Americans lead soft, sheltered lives, I'm sure I don't need to tell you.

RACHEL: No.

ROY: We are barely cognizant of the human misery as it exists on this planet today, under our very noses too.

RACHEL: Really.

ROY: If I could pay you less than minimum wage I would, believe me. Medical research, building a school in a foreign desert with illiterate, unskilled, underfed ignoramuses.... Well, it's expensive. Clinics, halfway houses, physical therapy labs where Lloyd and Pooty work—

RACHEL: Right.

ROY: Adult education programs, drug rehabilitation.... These are your insurance forms. Fill these out and give them to Mr. Seakins. Then ask Trish for some documents to process, she'll explain how you do that. Any other questions come straight to me.

RACHEL: Great.

ROY: So, enjoy.

RACHEL: I will, thanks.

ROY: Welcome aboard.

RACHEL: Thank you.

(He goes out.)

RACHEL: He seems nice. *(She sits; her chair collapses.)* Whoops! I'm going to need insurance. Do you know how I, uh...? *(No response)* Never mind, I got it. *(Adjusts seat)* So how was your Christmas? You see your family?

TRISH: I'm not a big fan of Christmas.

RACHEL: Oh. Parents put coal in your stocking one year or something?

TRISH: My parents were killed when I was six months old.

RACHEL: Oh, I'm terribly sorry.

TRISH: Why? You didn't do it.

RACHEL: No, I know. *(Realizing her chair has sunk down again)* Oh, God, I thought I was getting shorter. Is there another chair do you know?... *(Headshake)* This is fine. *(Starts to fill in forms)* Who's Mistress Eakins? I'm sorry, I'm supposed to take this to Mistress Eakins, do you know where she is?... Mistress Eakins? Do you know what I'm talking about?

TRISH: No.

RACHEL: Mistress Eakins, I think he said.

TRISH: Mr. Seakins.

RACHEL: Oh. I thought he said Mistress Eakins. I thought that was kind of a strange name, but mine is not to reason why, mine is just.... So where is he? Mr. Seakins.

TRISH: I'll give it to him.

RACHEL: No, I don't mind.

*(*TRISH *takes the forms from* RACHEL.*)*

RACHEL: Well. So do you have any kids or anything?

TRISH: No.

RACHEL: No family?

TRISH: Nope.

RACHEL: Brothers or sisters? *(*TRISH *shakes her head.)* Wow, you get your own screen and everything, huh?

TRISH: All right. I'd like you to take the white sheets, transfer everything onto the green sheets, and staple them together. File everything in alphanumerical order in the cabinets marked "Hardcopy". After that we'll go through the storeroom and if there's time I'll show you where the microfilm records are kept.

RACHEL: Great.

Scene Eight

(Living room)

LLOYD: So how was it?

RACHEL: *(Signing to* POOTY *throughout)* It was great.

LLOYD: You liked Trish?

RACHEL: Oh, yeah. Now she's in charge of what again?

LLOYD: All the budget.

RACHEL: Oh.

LLOYD: And she's pretty convinced she doesn't need an assistant, either.

RACHEL: Oh, really? Well.

LLOYD: She'll loosen up.

RACHEL: *(To* POOTY*)* So then she does the payroll?... How do you say payroll, Lloyd?

LLOYD: I don't know, ask her.

RACHEL: No, come on.

LLOYD: Spell it. I'll be out in the woodshed if anybody needs me.

RACHEL: You're just trying to turn me into a deaf girl, I know.

LLOYD: *(As he exits)* I can't hear you!

*(*POOTY *and* RACHEL *sign for a moment.)*

RACHEL: She does. She seems kind of tightlipped.

POOTY: She is. Now, listen, he can't know. *(*RACHEL *is dumbfounded.)* It would break his heart.... I'm sorry I didn't say anything before.

RACHEL: Oh, listen...you know.

POOTY: When I lost the use of my legs a friend drove me up here to Springfield to take a look at this place where they worked with the handicapped. I watched the physical therapists working with the patients and there was one. I remember he was working with a quadriplegic. I thought he was the most beautiful man I'd ever seen. A light shining out through his skin. And I thought if I couldn't be with him I'd die. But I knew I would just be one more crippled dame as far as he was concerned, so my friend helped to get me registered as deaf and disabled. I used to teach sign language to the hearing impaired. I thought if I were somehow needier than the rest I would get special attention. I realized soon enough: Everyone gets special attention where Lloyd is concerned. But by then it was too late. He was in love with me, with my honesty. He learned to sign; he told me how he'd run away from a bad marriage and changed his name so he wouldn't have to pay child support. He got me a job at Hands Across the Sea and I couldn't bring myself to tell him that I had another name and another life, that I'd run away too, because I owed the government so much money and wasn't able to pay after the accident. I believe in honesty. I believe in total honesty. And I need him and he needs me to be the person he thinks I am and I am that person, I really am that person. I'm a crippled deaf girl, short and stout. Here is my wheelchair, here is my mouth.

RACHEL: I'm not judging you.

POOTY: When he goes out I babble. I recite poetry I remember from grade school. I talk back to the television. I even call people on the phone and say it's a wrong number just to have a conversation. I'm afraid I'm going to open my mouth to scream one day and....

(She does; no sound. LLOYD *returns with fresh-chopped kindling.)*

LLOYD: Keep it down in here. How's it going?

RACHEL: Great. It's pretty good.

LLOYD: I'm sorry, I didn't hear you.

RACHEL: It's pretty good, I say.

LLOYD: I still can't hear you.

RACHEL: I said it's—

LLOYD: WHAT?

RACHEL: Oh.

(She signs. He signs and goes out again.)

POOTY: He was the first person who ever heard me. Really heard me. And I never had to make a sound. You mustn't ever tell him.

RACHEL: I won't. I think people who love each other, whatever way they love each other, nobody should say it's right or wrong. *(Pause)* Do you think Lloyd...? I mean, do you think he would ever...hurt you? I mean, not hurt you, but....

POOTY: Want to?

RACHEL: Want to, say.

POOTY: Sure. It wouldn't be love, would it?

RACHEL: Would it?

POOTY: Why?

RACHEL: Oh, I don't know.

POOTY: Did someone try to hurt you?

RACHEL: Oh, no, no, no, no.

POOTY: Who tried to hurt you?

RACHEL: Nobody.

POOTY: You can tell me.

RACHEL: Tom wouldn't do anything like that. He wouldn't.

POOTY: Who's Tom?

RACHEL: *(Overlapping)* Forget I mentioned it. Really. *(Beat)*

POOTY: I think you should talk to someone about this, don't you?

Scene Nine

*(*DOCTOR*'s office)*

DOCTOR: Go on.

RACHEL: Well, I don't know. There's really no problem.

DOCTOR: No?

RACHEL: No. I don't know....

DOCTOR: What are you thinking?

RACHEL: I don't know. About Christmas, I guess.

DOCTOR: Do you feel like telling me about it?

RACHEL: Well, last Christmas? Christmas Eve? My husband Tom is all tucked into bed like a little kid and our two boys are in their beds, I've just tucked them in, and I tell Tom how perfect it all seems, I've never been so happy, which is true. And.... Well, my father was allergic to dogs, you know, and Tom didn't like puppies, so I never said anything about wanting a puppy, but I was thinking about it. And I was looking out into the snow and talking about Alaska or something, but I was thinking about how people in books and movies are always getting puppies on Christmas and you never see anybody having to clean up the....

DOCTOR: Shit.

RACHEL: Or get hit by cars. You always see them with a big red bow and the kids are smiling and—but I didn't say anything, I was just thinking it. I didn't want Tom to feel guilty if he hadn't gotten me a puppy which I knew he hadn't because he hates them, so it was just a private little something I was thinking about and that's all I needed really was to think about it and rub its little imaginary ears. And we were watching the news, I remember, and suddenly I realize Tom's upset. So naturally I assume he knows I really want a puppy, so I go to comfort him, because I don't care about it, really, if it's going to make him unhappy, I don't even mention it, I just give him a big hug and tell him it's Christmas and be happy and he says he's taken a contract out on my life.

DOCTOR: This upset you.

RACHEL: Maybe I'm overreacting. Or he's kidding, which I think he must be. But anyway, I wind up spending Christmas with this man I meet at the Arco station and his girlfriend who is crippled and deaf, she says, you know, with hand signals until suddenly she just turns to me and starts saying how she had to pretend she was deaf to get the attention of this man we're all living with who's changed his name and run away and she's changed her name and I've changed my name and we're all working in the same place and she's telling me all these secrets and all of a sudden she says, "Why don't you talk to a psychiatrist?"

DOCTOR: And here you are.

RACHEL: Here I am.

DOCTOR: When did you have this dream?

Scene Ten

(The office)

TRISH: I'm going to have to take an early lunch today, Mary Ellen.

RACHEL: Okay.

TRISH: So if you'll hold down the fort.

RACHEL: Anything I can do for you on the computer or anything?

TRISH: No, thanks.

RACHEL: Well, anytime you want to teach me.

TRISH: I think you probably have enough work to keep you busy.

*(*TRISH *goes out.* RACHEL *looks around, then moves over to* TRISH*'s seat.* LLOYD *enters.)*

LLOYD: Hi.

RACHEL: Hi.

LLOYD: Mind if I join you?

RACHEL: No. Have a seat.

LLOYD: Learning Lotus?

RACHEL: No, what's that?

LLOYD: Oh, that's the software.

RACHEL: What's software?

LLOYD: Oh, that's what tells the computer what to do.

RACHEL: Oh.

LLOYD: I don't even know if that's what we use.

RACHEL: You know? In all the months I've been here Trish has never shown me how to do anything except file and take care of the storeroom and stuff like that.

LLOYD: Well, give her time.

RACHEL: Yeah. I guess. She has no family.

LLOYD: Yeah.

RACHEL: She says.

LLOYD: What do you mean?

RACHEL: I don't know. Just for all we know she could have ten families and a trail of broken hearts behind her, right? Who knows?

LLOYD: What else have you and Pooty been discussing?

RACHEL: Nothing.

LLOYD: Anything you'd like to ask me personally?

RACHEL: Oh, I wasn't even thinking about that.

LLOYD: Yes, I left my family, no, they don't know where I am—

RACHEL: No, I wasn't asking any of this.

LLOYD: *(Overlapping)* No, I don't pay child support, no, Bophtelophti is not my real name—

RACHEL: Please, Lloyd.

LLOYD: My real name is Boyd T. Theophillo....

RACHEL: The past is irrelevant. It's something you wake up from.

LLOYD: I walked out on a woman with multiple sclerosis and two children, one of them brain damaged, because I was too drunk to see him playing in the snow and I ran over him with the snow blower. I left them with no money and no way to feed themselves, moved as far away as I possibly could, changed my name, took the cash I'd stolen from the savings account to pay for the kids' education and put myself through school, so that I could become a physical therapist and work with multiple sclerosis victims and the occasional brain-damaged child with resultant motor-skill difficulties, none of whom held the slightest interest for me other than to remind me of what I could never escape as long as I live. And let's see. I married a nice crippled, deaf girl and I don't drink anymore. The past is something you wake up to. It's the nightmare you wake up to every day.

RACHEL: Well, these things happen for a reason, I believe that, I'm sorry, I do. And you're not helping anybody by punishing yourself. Why don't you pay back the money and say you're sorry?

LLOYD: It was thirty-five thousand dollars.

RACHEL: So? Big deal. People win that on game shows.

Scene Eleven

(TV studio)

ANNOUNCER: And here's your host, Tim Timko!

TIM: Okay, here we go, how does this game work, where are we? Oh, yes, it all comes back to me, like last night, who was that girl? Okay, enough of that, it's good to be back, let's see who's here.

(Houselights)

TIM: Remember, all you need's a mother, a wife, and the crazy idea that you could tell the difference. Looks like an awful lot of bag ladies slipped in here. How're we all doin'?

(Crowd response)

TIM: Anybody want to play this thing? What's it called? Your Brother's Wife? Your Sister's Best Friend's Mother-in-Law?

(Sign lights up. RACHEL, LLOYD, *and* POOTY *are in the audience, dressed as the solar system with cardboard and papier-mâché constructions over their heads.)*

TIM: "Your Mother or Your Wife." Ah! Wait. *(He makes his way over to the oddly costumed trio.)* Wait, wait a minute, I know what I like and don't tell me now, you folks are dressed as the solar system, aren't you?

LLOYD: That's right, Tim.

TIM: This looks like the planet Earth down here.

LLOYD: That's my mother, Tim.

TOM: Mother Earth.

LLOYD: Right.

TIM: I'll bet your world revolves around your sun, too, doesn't it. What's your name, Sir?

LLOYD: Lloyd.

TIM: You have a last name, Lloyd?

LLOYD: Bophtelophti.

TIM: Where're you from, Lloyd?

LLOYD: Springfield?

TIM: Springfield? Massachusetts? *(To* RACHEL*)* And you must be the little lady.

LLOYD: That's right, Tim.

RACHEL: Venus.

TIM: Ah. "On touch of."

LLOYD: That's right.

TIM: Well, you've met our requirements, Lloyd.

LLOYD: I should tell you, Tim, my mother is deaf. But my wife speaks sign language.

TIM: So she can translate. Okay. Come on up and get set to play "Your Mother or Your Wife"!

(Music, applause. LLOYD, RACHEL, *and* POOTY *are led onstage.)*

TIM: All right, correctly identify which of these lovely ladies answered each of three scintillating questions supplied by our studio audience made up entirely of Nobel Prize Laureates by the way— *(To someone in the audience)* What, you don't believe me? Get him out of here. And you can win yourself up to twenty thousand dollars, Lloyd, and a chance to play for our grand prize.

ANNOUNCER: Tim, the Bophtelophtis will be playing for a grand cash total of one hundred thousand dollars.

TIM: A hundred grand. Are you ready for our glass booth?

LLOYD: I guess so, Tim.

TIM: Then take him away.

*(*LLOYD *is led offstage.)*

TIM: Never to be heard from again. *(To* RACHEL and POOTY) Good evening, ladies.

RACHEL: It's great to be here, Tim!

TIM: You're going to translate.

RACHEL: That's right.

TIM: No funny business. Anybody here speaks deaf, keep an eye on these two. All right, Venus, first question.

RACHEL: Okay.

TIM: Would you say that Lloyd is more like a Ping-Pong ball or a paper clip? Mmmmm.

RACHEL: I'll say a Ping-Pong ball.

TIM: Any particular reason?

RACHEL: He bounces around a lot?

TIM: He does? Okay. Mom? Is Lloyd more like a Ping-Pong ball or a paper clip, would you say? Two 'P's...

(RACHEL *and* POOTY *confer in sign.)*

RACHEL: She says a paper clip.

TIM: Because?

RACHEL: Because he holds the family together.

TIM: Awww, that's—disgusting. No, I'm just teasing you. Question number two: Mom first this time. If Lloyd were a salad dressing, what flavor would he be? If blank were a salad dressing....

RACHEL: She says blue cheese.

TIM: He's getting a little moldy? But okay, Venus?

RACHEL: I'll say blue cheese.

TIM: Blue cheese it is. Ladies, third question: If you could choose between your husband leaving you for another woman or, in Mom's case, her son leaving her for another mom...? *(Looks to the control booth)* Guys, this question doesn't make sense. What's he gonna do, get another mother?... Judges say fly with it. All right—between your husband leaving you for another woman or staying together, knowing he doesn't love you, Venus, which would it be...?

RACHEL: I'd have to say another woman.

TIM: Another woman. Mom? Between losing your son to another mother or knowing he didn't love you. All right, fair enough.

RACHEL: She says another mother.

TIM: 'M' is for the many ways. Ladies, for our grand prize: Who does Lloyd love most, you or Mom?

RACHEL: His mother.

TIM: And Mom? This should be interesting.

(RACHEL *and* POOTY *confer.* POOTY *points to* RACHEL.*)*

TIM: And she says you! Okay, we'll be right back with the three happy Boopy-Boppies after this word from the good folks at Nu-Soft. Don't go away.

(Lights change; LLOYD *is escorted onstage.)*

ANNOUNCER: We're going right on. Ten seconds.

TIM: *(To* RACHEL*)* Say your name for me.

RACHEL: Bophtelophti.

TIM: Bophtelophti.

(Lights restore.)

ANNOUNCER: Five, four, three.... Rolling.

TIM: And we're back with the Bophtelophtis from Springfield, Massachusetts. Bophtelophti, is that Polish?

RACHEL: Yes, T—

LLOYD: *(Simultaneously)* No, well, it's—

RACHEL: It's....

LLOYD: Welsh, actually.

RACHEL: Welsh and Polish.

TIM: Welsh and Polish. How long've you been married?

LLOYD: Ten....

RACHEL: Years.

TIM: Ten years. Any kids so far?

LLOYD: No.

RACHEL: But....

LLOYD: We're hoping, Tim.

TIM: Well, good luck to you. Because you're gonna need it! Okay, here we go, round two, Lloyd, for five thousand dollars: When asked if you reminded them of a paper clip or a Ping-Pong ball, who said "paper clip" and I quote, "Because he holds the family together." Your mother or your wife?

LLOYD: Boy.... My mother?

*(*RACHEL *hops up and down and claps.)*

TIM: Right you are if you think you are, Lloyd.

LLOYD: Okay.

TIM: For ten thousand dollars, when asked what type of salad dressing you reminded them of, who said "blue cheese"? Your mother or your wife?

LLOYD: That's my favorite.

TIM: Nobody's interested in your personal life, Lloyd. No, take your time.

LLOYD: I'll say both.

TIM: Both it is for a quick ten grand! All right, for twenty thousand dollars and a chance to lose it all, Lloyd: Which... wait, let me get this straight. Which of the women in your life said they would rather lose you to another woman, wife or mother as the case may be, than believe you to be unhappy in their home. Mother Earth or the Venus de Milo, Lloyd. Lose you to another woman....

LLOYD: Both?

TIM: Both it is! Congratulations, Lloyd Bophtelophti from Warsaw, Wales, you've just won twenty thousand dollars and a chance to go away before you ruin your marriage.

LLOYD: No, we want to keep going.

TIM: Remember, if you miss this one, we keep it all, Lloyd, but you do go home with a free home version of your mother and your wife.

LLOYD: We'll play.

TIM: He says he'll play. All right, no eye contact now, no help from the studio audience please, Lloyd, for one hundred thousand dollars IN CASH, we asked your mother and your wife: Who does Lloyd love the most? Who said—keep breathing, Lloyd—you love your wife the most? Your mother, your wife, or your mother AND your wife, it could be both. Don't think too hard, Lloyd.... Your mother, your wife, or your mother and your wife.... I'm sorry, we're running out of time, we'll have to have an answer, Lloyd.

LLOYD: My mother.

TIM: Your mother!

(Lights flash. Audience screams. RACHEL, LLOYD, *and* POOTY *express their enthusiasm.)*

TIM: For one hundred thousand dollars, Lloyd Bophtelophti from Springfield, you've said the magic word, take the money, be happy, this is Tim Timko saying good night, we'll see you next week with your mother, your wife, your mistress, whoever else you got out there....

ANNOUNCER: *(Under)* For tickets to "Your Mother or Your Wife" write your name and address on a postcard and mail it to, "Your Mother or Your Wife", Box 1224, New Hope Station, New York, New York....

(His voice fades.)

INTERMISSION

Scene Twelve

(The office)

TRISH: How much?

RACHEL: A hundred thousand dollars.

TRISH: You're kidding.

RACHEL: I'm not.

TRISH: That's....

RACHEL: Incredible, isn't it?

TRISH: It's incredible.

RACHEL: It's incredible. And you know what the moral is?

TRISH: What's the moral?

RACHEL: You can't be afraid.

TRISH: No.

RACHEL: These things happen for a reason, I keep saying it. I mean, we're all so afraid to take chances and what have we got to lose? We're all going to be dead in a hundred years anyway.

TRISH: This is true.

(Pause)

RACHEL: Trish?

TRISH: Uh-huh?

RACHEL: Remember when I first came here?...Wow, it's almost a year ago now, isn't it?

TRISH: That's right.

RACHEL: You didn't really like me, did you?

TRISH: Oh.

RACHEL: No, come on, it's all right.

TRISH: Well, I don't always warm up to people right away.

RACHEL: Oh, I know. But I think it's also because you thought I just wasn't smart enough to handle anything very complicated, didn't you?

TRISH: No.

RACHEL: Well, I decided to take the bull by the horns anyway, and I've sort of been teaching myself about the computer.

TRISH: You have?

RACHEL: When you go to lunch. Look. I got this book on Lotus and I learned how to call up the menu and the file directory and everything.

TRISH: Great.

RACHEL: And I even figured out about the separate accounts you have filed that don't appear on the main index. You know, like the one that's attached to the Christmas fund as a footnote.

TRISH: How'd you figure that out?

RACHEL: Well, I was just, you know—I was trying to figure out what the password was and I was playing around with anagrams and stuff and your name spells "Shirt", I'm sure you know, because you used it for the footnote file.

TRISH: Good for you.

RACHEL: Yeah. My dad and I used to like to play word games and things when I was little.... Anyway.... You're not mad, are you?

TRISH: No, why should I be mad?

RACHEL: Oh, I don't know. Actually, some of the math doesn't add up, either, but....

Scene Thirteen

(DOCTOR's office)

DOCTOR: In the dream....

RACHEL: Uh-huh.

DOCTOR: You pretend to be the wife and Pooty.... Pooty?

RACHEL: Right.

DOCTOR: Pooty is an unusual name.

RACHEL: Mm-HM.

DOCTOR: Pooty pretends to be the mother. *(Pause)* Do you think there's any significance to that?

RACHEL: No. I mean, you can't go on the show unless you have a mother and a wife. That's just the way the game works, and Lloyd doesn't have a mother. So—

DOCTOR: But Pooty is the wife and you are not a member of the family at all, unless we say that you are the adopted child.

RACHEL: Right. But Pooty's deaf. I mean, she's not, but it was just easier to make her seem like a mother since she wouldn't have to talk and she's in a wheelchair.And it worked. I mean, we won the money and Lloyd paid back his ex-wife, so....

DOCTOR: I know you haven't wanted to talk about your parents. Rachel, and we agreed you don't have to until you feel you're ready. The loss of our parents is the greatest single trauma of our adult lives. But I also believe that our dreams are a way of telling ourselves what we think we mustn't know, our secret wishes and fears, written in code like an anagram where all the letters are jumbled, but the secret is there.

RACHEL: Like an anagram.

DOCTOR: Right. *(Pause)* Why do you think you picked Your Mother or Your Wife?

RACHEL: Oh, they picked us. I mean, we just sent in the postcard.

DOCTOR: Whose dream are we discussing?

RACHEL: Nobody's. I'm sorry I didn't say that before. I thought that was part of the therapy, to talk about everything like it was a dream. It's not a dream. I'm sorry, I was confused. Sorry.

(Pause)

DOCTOR: Would you like to see another therapist?

RACHEL: No.

DOCTOR: Is that what you're telling me?

RACHEL: Not at all.

DOCTOR: There's nothing shameful in that. I won't be angry with you. Sometimes it's a good idea to shop around, try different types of therapies.

RACHEL: I know.

DOCTOR: I honestly think it's time, Rachel, that you try to think about what it is in the loss of your parents that is so difficult to share with me.

(Pause)

RACHEL: My mother was run over by a school bus when I was six. My father died of a heart attack the year I married Tom.

DOCTOR: Thank you, Rachel. *(Pause)* Rachel? Did you ever wish—not really mean it—just wish that your mother would go away? Did you think that you were responsible for what happened?

RACHEL: She was run over by a school bus.

DOCTOR: And then what happened?

RACHEL: I lived with my father.

DOCTOR: Until you were how old?

RACHEL: Nineteen.

DOCTOR: And then?

RACHEL: I married Tom.

DOCTOR: And your father died.

RACHEL: Of a heart attack.

DOCTOR: What is a heart attack? Isn't it a broken heart?

Scene Fourteen

(Living room. LLOYD *and* POOTY *are dressed as Santa and a reindeer.)*

LLOYD: Ho, ho, ho!

RACHEL: Wait. Okay. Before we open presents—I love it!—I just want to say something, both of you. A year ago when I first came here and you both took me in...that was probably the nicest thing anybody ever did for me. You've taught me the true spirit of giving and Christmas; you've made me part of your family, you know? And...you're just the best family that anybody could ever ask for.

(Doorbell)

LLOYD: Aw, who the hell is that?

(He opens the door. TOM *stands there, holding a bottle of champagne and a large gift box.)*

TOM: Is Rachel Fitsimmons here?

LLOYD: No, I'm sorry, there's no one here by that—

TOM: Rachel? It's Tom.

RACHEL: Oh, hi, how've you been?

TOM: May I come in?

RACHEL: Sure. Oh sure. Lloyd, Tom—Tom, Lloyd.

LLOYD: How do you do.

RACHEL: Lloyd, Pooty—Pooty...Tom.

TOM: *(Indicating the champagne)* This was, um, I found this sitting on the step. It says, "From Santa".

RACHEL: Uh-huh.

TOM: Nice to meet you all.

RACHEL: Pooty is deaf. And Tom is my husband.

TOM: How've you been, Rache?

RACHEL: Great. You?

TOM: I saw you on TV.

RACHEL: Uh-huh.

TOM: I almost didn't recognize you.

RACHEL: Oh.

TOM: You had a....

RACHEL: Planet.

TOM: On your....

RACHEL: Face.

TOM: Right. I thought maybe you'd remarried.

RACHEL: No.

TOM: That was....

RACHEL: Pretend.

TOM: TV. Right. *(Pause. He indicates gift box.)* I brought you something.

RACHEL: Oh.

TOM: It's something you've always wanted. And I'm sorry I didn't give it to you before. There isn't anything I can say, Rache. I keep trying to find the right words. Something that could make...take away... take it away. It. There, you see, all I have to do is say it and there it is. What I did. The thing I can't ever take back. It. I can't live without you, Rache. And I can't live with—with it. I can't, but I'm just so afraid to die, Rachel, I'm afraid.

RACHEL: No one's going to die.

TOM: Well, we're all going to die.

RACHEL: Not right now, please.

TOM: I'm so sorry, Rachel.

RACHEL: Why don't we have some of this champagne? Lloyd, would you get some glasses, please?

(LLOYD *goes off.)*

RACHEL: Oh, Tom, it was very nice of you to bring the champagne, that means a lot to me.

TOM: It was just sitting on the step.

RACHEL: Oh, well, it was nice of someone then, wasn't it? *(The gift box)* What's this? Is this for me?

TOM: Uh-huh.

RACHEL: You brought this? I can't think what it could be.... Does anybody mind?

(POOTY *signs.* RACHEL *unwraps the package.)*

TOM: The boys said if I brought you that maybe you'd come home. They're with Jeanette and Freddie for the weekend.

RACHEL: Oh, how is Jeanette?

TOM: Everybody sends their love. We all miss you.

RACHEL: *(Looks in the box)* Tom!

TOM: You like him?

RACHEL: Oh, he's so sweet.

TOM: You can name him whatever you want.

RACHEL: He's so beautiful. Look! Tom, thank you. *(She holds up a stuffed animal puppy.)*

TOM: And you don't have to clean up after him.

RACHEL: I know. Look, everybody!

LLOYD: *(Returned with the champagne and a glass of milk for himself; he pours.)* Cute.

RACHEL: Oh, thank you.

TOM: You're welcome.

LLOYD: How 'bout some champagne? Everybody like champagne? Poot? *(Hands them their glasses)*

TOM: Thanks.

RACHEL: Awww.

LLOYD: Drink up.

TOM: Please comes home, Rache. We miss you.

RACHEL: Cheers! *(She clinks her glass against* TOM*'s, overemphatically, and her glass shatters.)* Whoops! Oh God.

LLOYD: That's okay, I'll get you another one.

RACHEL: Thanks.

*(*LLOYD *goes off.)*

RACHEL: *(To* TOM *and* POOTY*)* Oh, go ahead, please. I'm fine.

TOM: *(To* POOTY) Cheers.

*(*POOTY *signs the word for "cheers". They drink.* LLOYD *returns with another glass and pours.)*

LLOYD: Here you go.

RACHEL: Thank you, Lloyd. Cheers.

*(*TOM *bends forward in sudden discomfort.* POOTY *emits a small noise.)*

TOM: Is there a bathroom?

LLOYD: Poot?

*(*RACHEL *holds her glass, untasted, watching as* TOM *and* POOTY *double over in pain.)*

TOM: Ow!

POOTY: Lloyd!

*(*LLOYD *is stunned.)*

TOM: Jesus! Aaaagh!

POOTY: Lloyd!

TOM: Aaaaaaaa!

POOTY: AAAAAAAAAAAAAAAAAA!

(They die.)

Scene Fifteen

(The car. RACHEL *drives.* LLOYD *in his Santa suit.)*

RACHEL: Calm.... Calm.... Okay. Did I miss my exit? Okay. Lloyd? Okay. Okay, if we call the police—did we? Are we calling the police? Did we? No, I remember, okay. We could. Here's the thing: We didn't. We called the ambulance, okay. We called the ambulance. Why didn't we call the police? Because. They'll think we did it. Why will they think we did it? Because we didn't call the police. No, our fingerprints were on the bottle. "So what?"

"What do you mean 'So what?' Why did you leave your family? Why do you have assumed names? What are you hiding?" "Nothing." "Uh-huh. Where'd you get all this cash in hundred-dollar bills?" "Oh, we won it on a game show." "What game show?" "Your Mother or Your Wife." "Is this your mother?" "No." "Is this your wife?" "No." Turnpike!... Is this the right ramp? Lloyd? *(Looks in rearview mirror)* I think those people are following me. Are those the same people? No, wait, Tom brought the champagne! That's right. Tom brought the champagne. "We're all going to die," remember? *(She reads road sign.)* West. We're all going to die. Just take a look over your shoulder and tell me if those are the same people.... No! No, it was sitting on the step, that's right, remember? From Santa. Or he was lying. All right, wait. Wait. Maybe it was just a bad bottle. Maybe—maybe— They're following me. Don't turn around. Look like you're having a good time. Uh-huh! Uh-huh! Really!... Oh God. *(She turns on the radio.)*

ANNOUNCER: The mellow sound of Nat King Cole. Gone before his time. It's 10:00 A.M. Christmas morning. Let's hope Santa left something special under your tree. In the news—

(She turns off the radio.)

RACHEL: Wait a minute! Santa! Santa. Sat—na. At—sna. At—san. Tas—na. As—nat. Santa, Merry Christmas from Santa.... Sat—na. Sat—an. Satin. Satin. *Satan*! Merry Christmas from Satan! Oh God. Christ's birthday, Merry Christmas from Satan, Lloyd! That's horrible. Why is this happening? Why is it always Christmas? I love Christmas. I always used to say I wanted to live in Alaska because they had snow all year round and Santa was up there, so it must always be Christmas.... Oh Lloyd. They won't feel any more pain from now on, I know they won't. No more pain from now on, all right, Santa Claus? I'll drink to that.

Scene Sixteen

(Night. Snow. RACHEL *is still driving.* LLOYD*, in his suit, staring.)*

RACHEL: Toopy.... P.... Oop. Oopy. Toopy. Poot. Pyoot. Ypoot. Ytpoo. It. It.... Toopy. Two Ps. Two.... Y-po-to. Toy—po. Poy sounds like boy. Two boys! I have two boys. *(Pause)* I don't even know what state we're in, do you? *(Sees road sign)* Wait, can you read that?...Spring...*field*. Springfield!?!? Is that what it said? How can we back in Springfield— *(Reads)* Ohio! Springfield, Ohio, thank you, God! Springfield, Ohio... *(Sighs with relief)* Oh God. Who would ever want to live in Springfield, Ohio? *(She has a revelation.)* NOBODY.

Scene Seventeen

(A seedy hotel room; LLOYD *remains in his Santa suit.)*

RACHEL: Lloyd, I know we can be happy here, I just know we can. Who would ever think to look for us in Springfield, Ohio! Nobody. Why would we ever want to go back to Springfield? We wouldn't, you see, we wouldn't! And the lady at the real estate agency said there's one in every state. Fifty Springfields. So we don't have to stay here if we don't like it. We don't have to do anything. We can go anywhere, we can be anybody. We can go from Springfield to Springfield. How many people ever get a chance to do that in their whole lives?... Lloyd... I know I can't take her place. But she'll always be right here. You're what keeps her memory alive. But you have to keep yourself alive. You have to *eat* something. And we have to get you out of that suit. We're lucky to be alive, I mean, we could have had some of that champagne. Well, you don't drink, but.... Let's pick names. What do you like? How about Jessie? I'll be Jessie or you be Jesse and I'll be Mrs. Mancini. I can find a new doctor. You know, it's a good idea to shop around, try different types of therapies—

LLOYD: SHUT UP! SHUT THE FUCK UP PLEASE! COULD WE HAVE ONE—TINY—MOMENT OF SILENCE IF IT ISN'T TOO MUCH TO ASK FOR? PLEASE?

(Pause)

RACHEL: I'm sorry.

LLOYD: What?

RACHEL: I said I'm sorry.

LLOYD: I can't hear you.

(Pause)

RACHEL: I said....

(Pause. RACHEL *signs "I'm sorry.")*

Scene Eighteen

(Another DOCTOR*'s office)*

SECOND DOCTOR: Do you have nightmares, Mrs. Mancini?

RACHEL: No.

SECOND DOCTOR: Phobias?

RACHEL: No.

SECOND DOCTOR: Eczema? Asthma?

RACHEL: No.

SECOND DOCTOR: Do you take drugs?

RACHEL: No.

SECOND DOCTOR: Alcohol?

RACHEL: No.

SECOND DOCTOR: Are you an alcoholic?

RACHEL: No.

SECOND DOCTOR: Would you say you're chronically depressed?

RACHEL: No.

SECOND DOCTOR: Or unfulfilled in any way?

RACHEL: No.

SECOND DOCTOR: Have you ever tried to kill yourself?

RACHEL: No.

SECOND DOCTOR: Is it difficult for you to make a decision?

RACHEL: No.

SECOND DOCTOR: Are you sure?

RACHEL: Mm-hm.

SECOND DOCTOR: Do you have trouble sleeping?

RACHEL: No.

SECOND DOCTOR: You sleep too much?

RACHEL: No.

SECOND DOCTOR: Dietary difficulties?

RACHEL: No.

SECOND DOCTOR: Overeating?

RACHEL: No.

SECOND DOCTOR: Undereating?

RACHEL: No.

SECOND DOCTOR: Is sex a problem for you, Mrs. Mancini?

RACHEL: No.

SECOND DOCTOR: Does that embarrass you, my asking?

RACHEL: No.

SECOND DOCTOR: Do you ever have any trouble relating to new people?

RACHEL: No.

SECOND DOCTOR: Telling the truth?

RACHEL: No.

SECOND DOCTOR: Is shyness a problem for you?

RACHEL: No.

SECOND DOCTOR: Do you have something that you're ashamed of?

RACHEL: No.

SECOND DOCTOR: A speech defect?

RACHEL: No.

SECOND DOCTOR: What's the problem, Mrs. Mancini?

*(*RACHEL *shrugs.)*

Scene Nineteen

(Another hotel room)

LLOYD: You know what I feel like having?

RACHEL: What?

LLOYD: You know what I really feel like having?

RACHEL: What?

LLOYD: You know what I really feel like having right now?

RACHEL: What?

LLOYD: Champagne.

Scene Twenty

(Another DOCTOR*'s office)*

THIRD DOCTOR: You're not from Alabama.

RACHEL: No.

THIRD DOCTOR: Now how did I know that?

RACHEL: You see, two Christmases ago, my husband Tom.... Well, we've lived in Springfield before.

THIRD DOCTOR: Oh, you have.

RACHEL: Twice. And I have two sons, too, actually. And my husband tried to kill me twice, too.

THIRD DOCTOR: Your husband? Tried—

RACHEL: *(Overlapping)* Two Ps!...Pooty.... My first shrink said that Pooty was an unusual name. And she said—

THIRD DOCTOR: Oh, you've been in therapy before?

RACHEL: Twice. But.... Okay: How long do you think a person could live if they drank nothing but champagne and they didn't eat anything? Just out of curiosity.

THIRD DOCTOR: Well....

RACHEL: Does a month seem like a long time? To you.

Scene Twenty-one

(Another hotel room)

LLOYD: Here's a question.

RACHEL: Nope.

LLOYD: Do you remember asking me if we ever really know anybody?

RACHEL: Not until you eat something.

LLOYD: You remember that?

RACHEL: *(Unpacking groceries)* Do you hear me?

LLOYD: You asked me if I thought we ever really knew anybody.

RACHEL: You are going to eat something if it kills me.

LLOYD: And I've thought about it.... And I would have to say....

RACHEL: You don't have to taste it.

LLOYD: My considered opinion would be....

RACHEL: Just smell it.

LLOYD: No. No way.

RACHEL: Croissants, Lloyd!

LLOYD: Not on your life.

RACHEL: Look, paté.

LLOYD: No dice.

RACHEL: Just open your mouth and take one bite.

LLOYD: Ixnay.

RACHEL: Strawberries.

LLOYD: Nope.

RACHEL: Ice cream.

LLOYD: Uh-uh.

RACHEL: It's pistachio.

LLOYD: No way, José.

RACHEL: Lloyd, you can't—

LLOYD: Forget about it.

RACHEL: Soup. Soup!

LLOYD: No chance.

RACHEL: You can't survive on champagne alone, it's an old saying.

LLOYD: No, no, a thousand times no.

RACHEL: I need you now.

LLOYD: Nyet.

RACHEL: Please.

LLOYD: Non.

RACHEL: You can't live on wine.

LLOYD: Nein.

Scene Twenty-two

(Another DOCTOR*'s office)*

FOURTH DOCTOR: This is very important, Cheryl. We've talked about the birth scream. It is a terrible shock to be torn away in a shower of blood with your mother screaming and your home torn open and the strange doctor with his rubber hands slapping you with all his might and the cold light piercing the dark, the warm beautiful wet dark, the silent murmuring safe dark of Mummy everywhere and Daddy, everything is one and everything is sex and we are all together for eternity and we are happy and nothing ever passes through your mind but good thoughts until suddenly this squeezing is going on around you and everyone is pushing and pulling and cold steel tongs pinch your skin and pull you by the top of your head and you don't want to go, no, you don't want to leave your home where you're always floating and your mother's heart is always beating for something unknown and cruel where people are cold and you're stinging now, everything is breaking, it makes you want to scream, Cheryl, makes you want to scream the scream of all ages, scream of the greatest tragedy of all time and your mummy is screaming and your daddy is screaming and now all the doctors are screaming and everything's blinding you and you're torn away and they're hitting you and they throw you up in the air and you open your eyes and your mother is covered in blood and you scream, Cheryl, scream, scream, SCREAM, Cheryl, SCREAM, *SCREAM*!!! *(Pause)* All right, we'll try it again.

Scene Twenty-three

(Another DOCTOR*'s office and another hotel room)*

LLOYD: Not all champagne is champagne. They call it champagne. Sure, they call it champagne. I'll tell you what is interesting about champagne. Pain. It is pains-takingly made. They take great pains.

FIFTH DOCTOR: Say I am a decent human being.

RACHEL: I am a decent human being.

FIFTH DOCTOR: Say I deserve to be loved.

RACHEL: I deserve to be loved.

FIFTH DOCTOR: Now repeat everything after me. I was put on this earth to love and be loved.

LLOYD: Great pains, believe me.

FIFTH DOCTOR: I was put on this earth...

RACHEL: I was put on this earth to love and be loved...

FIFTH DOCTOR: I am whole when I am alone and I am part of everything.

FIFTH DOCTOR:	LLOYD:
Mrs. Bophtelophti? I said I am whole when I am alone and I am part of everything.	And it is only in the region of Champagne where champagne is made.

RACHEL: Uh-huh.

FIFTH DOCTOR: And I would like you to repeat that.

RACHEL: Wait a minute.

FIFTH DOCTOR: What?

RACHEL: Wait a minute!

FIFTH DOCTOR: What?

RACHEL: You know what? Things just happen. People die. And bus drivers don't always look where they're going, even if they should, even if they're driving a school bus. Even if you love somebody they can still take a contract out on your life. And if you try to help somebody because they've been kind to you when you needed them, they can STILL refuse to eat and drink nothing but champagne, chamPAGNE, that's all they'll drink, and if you ask them to please, PLEASE take off their Santa Claus suit, just when they go out, just when you go to the store, they won't. So? Things just happen!

Scene Twenty-four

(Another hotel room. LLOYD *moans in the glow of the television.)*

RACHEL: I'm here. Shhhh. I'm here, here we go. Mother's milk. *(Produces two bottles of champagne)* It's your Christmas present, all right? I couldn't think what else to get you. I'm sorry. I got you two bottles. We're going to have a festive Christmas, just the two of us. It's our anniversary, too, remember? Don't you want to listen to the news?... Where's the knob? Did you pull out the knob?

(She takes the knob from him. He tries to remove a champagne cork, but is too weak.)

RACHEL: It's the one night in the year they save up all the good news. Don't you want to hear it? I'll help you with that, just a sec. Look. Doesn't that woman look like Trish Whatshername from Hands Across the Sea. Hammers. *(Putting in the knob)* My God! Lloyd, look! *(Sound comes on.)*

ANNOUNCER: —refused to comment, but local spokesmen say Ms. Hammers may have embezzled as much as a half a million dollars in her more than twenty years as an accountant for the humanitarian organization.

RACHEL: *(Under)* Oh my....

ANNOUNCER: David Harbinger spoke with Roy Morgrebi, president of the northeast chapter of Hands Across the Sea in Springfield.

RACHEL: There's Roy! Lloyd!

ROY: It just boggles the mind, you know. Very sweet girl.

SECOND ANNOUNCER: Would you say this is something we should all begin to be wary of? Donating money to charity—

ROY: No.

SECOND ANNOUNCER: —which will end up somehow in private hands?

ROY: Definitely not. I feel this is an isolated case, one hopes, and obviously we intend to institute tighter controls.

FIRST ANNOUNCER: Police are still looking for the two alleged accomplices in last year's Christmas killing here in Springfield. More news after this word.

RACHEL: *(Over the fading sound of a commercial)* They think we did it! Lloyd! They think we did it.... She tried to poison us! And it wasn't Tom! It wasn't Tom at all!... Lloyd, we've got to go to the police, because WE DIDN'T DO IT! Don't you see? Okay! Okay! Say goodbye to Springfield!

*(*LLOYD *is dead.)*

RACHEL: Say goodbye . . .

*(*LLOYD *slumps forward.* RACHEL *grabs him by the shirt, shakes him, lets him fall.)*

Scene Twenty-five

(A shelter. RACHEL, *the* SIXTH DOCTOR, and two DERELICTS *in front of the television.)*

TV ANNOUNCER: Street people they're called and Anne Lacher-Holden has the story.

FIRST DERELICT: *(Overlapping)* Shit on the floor, shit on the floor and you know it!

SIXTH DOCTOR: *(Overlapping)* This is us, don't you want to listen?

WOMAN ANNOUNCER: In the summertime they seem to be everywhere, but where do they go in the winter? It is in shelters like this one, in storefronts all over the city where the needy, the cold, and hungry, come for food and comfort. How many of these people would starve to death if not for the efforts and dedication of individuals like Dr. Mahalia Maden.

SECOND DERELICT: Dr. M & M's!

WOMAN ANNOUNCER: Doctor, how many years have you been running this shelter?

SIXTH DOCTOR'S VOICE: Six years this Christmas, Anne.

WOMAN ANNOUNCER: And where do you get your funds?

SECOND DERELICT: *(Under)* Steal it.

SIXTH DOCTOR'S VOICE: Well, money's a funny thing, you know. A lot of people want to help save the whales, but tell them they can help save a human being....

WOMAN ANNOUNCER: That's right. What kind of people stay here and where do they come from?

SIXTH DOCTOR'S VOICE: All over. We have bank presidents, writers, you name it.

WOMAN ANNOUNCER: What brings them here?

SIXTH DOCTOR'S VOICE: Life's been reckless with these people, Anne. Some more than others. Often they carry no identification whatsoever, it's difficult.

WOMAN ANNOUNCER: I see.

SIXTH DOCTOR'S VOICE: We have one of our people, I guess you could say she's our mascot. She came to us our first night six years ago on Christmas Eve—no idea who she was, no name, we thought she was deaf. I'll be darned if a few weeks ago she didn't start to talk in her sleep. Talks a blue streak.

WOMAN ANNOUNCER: Really?

SIXTH DOCTOR'S VOICE: Who's to say these people can't lead normal, healthy lives again.

WOMAN ANNOUNCER: You say they can. Doctor, it's been a pleasure talking with you. I'm Anne Lacher-Holden with Street Beat.

SECOND DERELICT: I'm bored.

ANNOUNCER: Thank you, Anne. Coming up we'll take a look at a woman who claims she's Santa Claus. And Marge von Bargen will—

(SIXTH DOCTOR *switches off the television.)*

FIRST DERELICT: Shit on your floor and you know it!

(DERELICTS *disperse.)*

SIXTH DOCTOR: *(To* RACHEL*)* No more secrets now, Eve. The whole world knows you can hear me and you know you hear me, because you spoke to me last night. Look at me: I asked you what was wrong and you said you were afraid and you were not asleep, Eve, so don't try that with me now. Your eyes were open and you answered me. Look at me: You answered me. What did you say? Everyone's afraid, Eve, I'm afraid. What did you say? A man in a ski mask who follows you when you leave here. Why does he follow you? Whose face is he hiding, Eve? Whose face? Behind the mask.... I have bad dreams too, Eve. I wake up in the middle of the night, too, and want someone to hold me. I remember what I did to someone once and can never, never undo. Because you can never give back a life. But I made a pledge to myself that I would try. And I went to school and I studied to be a doctor and I swore to myself that I would scrimp and save and deny myself and do anything, Eve, if I could give one person back their life. And six years ago on Christmas Eve we opened the doors here. Who do you think was the first person to walk in off the street and join us? Eve.... Do you want to know my dream? That someday you'll trust me. And tell me all your dreams, all the good ones, so I can help you make them all come true. That's my dream.... The TV people gave me some tickets to a talk show. Would you like that? A talk show? How does that sound?

Scene Twenty-six

(TV studio)

HOST: And we're back with Dr. Helen Carroll, author of *Stand Up Straight*. Doctor, before the break you were saying—

HELEN: Sit up straight, David.

HOST: Sorry.

HELEN: Doesn't that feel better?

HOST: Yes, actually, it does.

HELEN: You look better and you feel better. You don't have to be tall to feel tall. Feeling tall in a state of mind.

HOST: Sounds like a song, doesn't it?

HELEN: Napoleon was tall.

HOST: Ah-hah.

HELEN: All right, everybody, sit up straight in your chairs. I want you to look out as if you're the tallest person in the room, proud. Shoulders back, don't slouch, slouch is for grouches. Don't slump, slump is for grumps. Pull this little string from the top of your head, uuuuup! All right, here's what we're talking about, come on.

*(*HELEN *approaches front row of the audience. Monitor reveals* RACHEL *and* SIXTH DOCTOR *seated.* HELEN *addresses* RACHEL.*)*

HELEN: Stand up. Stand up!

SIXTH DOCTOR: No, she can't, really—

HELEN: Oh, she'll be fine. Come on.

SIXTH DOCTOR: She really shouldn't—

HELEN: Come on. *(Pulls* RACHEL *to her feet)* That's right, now turn around, look at the audience. There! Look at that face. Isn't she lovely?

(Applause)

HELEN: There. Now what have you got to scrunch down in your chair for, hm? No one's going to shoot you. This is what I call the I'm Not Really Here Type, David. All right now, watch. *(To* RACHEL*)* Shoulders back. I'm going to give you a copy of my book and I want you to read it. Chin up. That's right. Eyes straight ahead.

*(*RACHEL *sees something at the back of the theater.)*

HELEN: Now tell us all your name in loud clear tones.

*(*RACHEL *shakes her head.)*

HELEN: Do you have a name?

RACHEL: No.

HELEN: You don't? What do you mean—?

SIXTH DOCTOR: *(Overlapping)* Good, Eve!

RACHEL: NOOOOO!

(At the same time, a MAN IN A SKI MASK *has screamed from the aisle of the theater.)*

MAN: DEVIL WOMAN!

(He rushes the stage, pointing a handgun at RACHEL.*)*

HOST: Look out! Somebody!

(The gun goes off. RACHEL *ducks and* DR. HELEN CARROLL *is mortally wounded. Pandemonium.)*

HOST: Look out. My God! Doctor! DOCTOR!

RACHEL: NO! NO! NO!! NO!

(The HOST *and* DR. CARROLL *disappear. The* SIXTH DOCTOR *has rushed to* RACHEL*'s side.)*

Scene Twenty-seven

(The action is continuous. RACHEL *repeats the word "no" over and over again, struggling to break free from the* SIXTH DOCTOR.*)*

SIXTH DOCTOR: Yes! Yes, Eve, yes! Yes! Look at me, yes, you spoke, yes, yes, yes. You spoke. Look at me. You spoke. Eve, yes, say yes. Say yes. Shhhh, I'm here, close your eyes, I'm here, yes, you spoke. Yes, and I was wrong.

There was a man. You were so right, there was a man and I was wrong, I'm sorry, Eve, I was wrong. There was a man and he was trying to hurt you, but he's gone now.

(RACHEL *has quieted down.)*

SIXTH DOCTOR: We'll never know why he was trying to hurt you. The important thing is you spoke out loud and people heard you and I heard you and YOU heard you, Eve. You heard you. You. Eve. If you can tell yourself what you want, you can have it. I swear to you. I used to drive a school bus. Did you know that? I drove a school bus. And how many bus drivers do you think become doctors, Eve? None. Not at all. EXCEPT THE ONES WHO DO. All right, Eve, close your eyes. I want you to imagine a place. I want you to imagine the most beautiful place in all the world. I don't want you to think about what anybody said you could or couldn't do. I want you to dream, Eve. I want you to imagine a time of year—your favorite time of year, the weather that gives you goosebumps—the right temperature, the right light in the sky, the right smell in the air. I want you to imagine someone standing there, Eve. Someone who makes people feel good about themselves and does all the things you ever wanted to do and has all the things you ever wanted to have. I want you to imagine that person standing there in that place at that exact time of day doing exactly what that person would be doing...Eve...if that person....

Scene Twenty-eight

(An office)

RACHEL: Yes?

WOMAN PATIENT: That's the end.

RACHEL: You wake up?

WOMAN PATIENT: I wake up.

RACHEL: And how do you feel?

WOMAN PATIENT: Happy.

RACHEL: The dream makes you feel happy?

WOMAN PATIENT: Yes.

RACHEL: I'm afraid we're going to have to stop here, Sharon.

WOMAN PATIENT: But what does it mean?

RACHEL: What does what mean?

WOMAN PATIENT: Why am I happy?

RACHEL: Does there have to be a reason?

WOMAN PATIENT: I don't know.

RACHEL: You're happy.

WOMAN PATIENT: Yes.

RACHEL: You feel happy now?

WOMAN PATIENT: Yes. Oh. That's what it means. It means I'm happy.

RACHEL: Yes.

WOMAN PATIENT: It means I'm happy.

RACHEL: It could mean that.

WOMAN PATIENT: It means I'm happy. Thank you.

RACHEL: Don't thank me, thank yourself.

WOMAN PATIENT: *(With* RACHEL*)* "Thank yourself." Well... Merry Christmas.

RACHEL: You too, Sharon.

WOMAN PATIENT: I'll see you next week. *(She leaves.)*

RECEPTIONIST: *(Pokes her head in)* Doctor, there's a student here from the University of Alaska waiting to see you. They called while you were in your session to say he was coming over.

RACHEL: Send him in, thanks.

RECEPTIONIST: *(To the offstage student)* You can go on in. There you go.

(She exits as TOM JUNIOR *enters.)*

TOM JR.: Doctor?

RACHEL: Yes, I'm— *(Her throat catches.)* Sorry, there's something caught in my throat. I'm sorry if I kept you waiting.

TOM JR.: *(Extending his hand)* Tom Fitsimmons.

RACHEL: Tom. Won't you, please.... Have a seat, Tom. Please. Anywhere.

(He sits in the only chair.)

RACHEL: What's the problem? What can I do for you? Take your time, relax, Tom, what's the story?

TOM JR.: I, uh.... I was just trying to get some sleeping pills and they said I would have to, uh....

RACHEL: I see.

TOM JR.: You look really familiar.

RACHEL: I do?

TOM JR.: You look really familiar. Where do I know you from...?

RACHEL: Why do you think you're having trouble sleeping, Tom? Are you? Having trouble?

TOM JR.: I know who you look like.

RACHEL: Your mother.

TOM JR.: Yes.

RACHEL: That's the transference, Tom. The patient projects an image onto the parent. Onto the....

TOM JR.: It's incredible.

RACHEL: But you say you feel you need something, is that right?

TOM JR.: No, but like I've only seen pictures of her, but you really do. I mean, you're a lot older.

RACHEL: Of course.

TOM JR.: But still, I mean, it's...incredible.

RACHEL: Good.... Tom, what is all this about sleeping pills? Is that what you need?

TOM JR.: Sort of.

RACHEL: Why?

TOM JR.: I can't sleep. But I mean, it's just for this week. I mean, next week I'll be fine, so it doesn't have to be very many.

RACHEL: Why is it just this week?

TOM JR.: Because.

RACHEL: Does it have something to do with Christmas...?

TOM JR.: You know, I really feel better now that we've talked. I really do. I don't think I need sleeping pills at all, it's incredible, thank you.

RACHEL: Sit down.

TOM JR.: I'm serious.

RACHEL: Sit down, Tom. What is it about Christmas?...Some people think that the things you're afraid to think about are the things which eventually destroy you. And that if you talk about them, as painful as that is, it helps them to go away.

TOM JR.: I'm not afraid to think about them.

RACHEL: Then what is it? You think I won't believe you?

TOM JR.: Maybe.

RACHEL: Why don't you try me?

TOM JR.: My mother... the one....

RACHEL: Right.

TOM JR.: Ran away like on Christmas.

RACHEL: How old were you?

TOM JR.: Four.

RACHEL: Go on.

TOM JR.: So the next year our father, you know, leaves us with friends, so—he says because he's going to bring our mother back, because.... I don't know.

RACHEL: You have brothers and sisters?

TOM JR.: One brother. Younger. And instead he gets killed.

RACHEL: Your—?

TOM JR.: Father. By... well, it probably had something to do....

RACHEL: I'm listening.

TOM JR.: It may have had something to do with this whole...scandal. Anyway, he died. And they said our mother was involved, but they never were able to find her. And so we were raised, you know, by—my brother and I—by these neighbors and they were really nice. And then...my brother disappeared when he was twelve and we didn't hear anything for a long time. And then he called and said he'd found this woman in California and she was gonna pay or something and... I guess he just freaked out and he shot this lady on some talk show right around Christmas time.... I don't know. I mean, they didn't convict him, but... I kind of thought I'd get away, you know? Alaska seemed like the place.

RACHEL: It is.

TOM JR.: Not really. They have Christmas here too.

RACHEL: You have no memories of your mother, Tom?

TOM JR.: No. Oh, yes, I do—one. But I mean, I think I dreamed it. I mean, I don't know. I think I dreamed it.

RACHEL: What is the memory?

TOM JR.: Well, it's Christmas.

RACHEL: Uh-huh.

TOM JR.: And, um, she's like reaching up, putting something up.

RACHEL: On the tree.

TOM JR.: Uh-huh. Or something. And she's really...she's really happy. Everything's bright and she's all in a glow and she looks right at me and says, "How's that?"

RACHEL: "How's that?"

TOM JR.: Like that. And I don't know. I just said it, you know?

RACHEL: What?

TOM JR.: Lousy, you're fired. I was just kidding.

RACHEL: Of course.

TOM JR.: But... sometimes it seems like that was the start of everything. It's like I hurt her feelings or something and she left and my father left and my brother left.... I keep feeling like if I could just go back to that—time. And she would turn to me, you know, all lit up and say, "How's that?" I'd say, "Beautiful, Mom." You know.

RACHEL: Uh-huh.

TOM JR.: Because it was like for one second I wanted to spoil everything. Everybody was too happy and I was too excited. But I would take it back. I would take it all back, because I didn't mean it.

RACHEL: Of course you didn't mean it.

TOM JR.: No, but I can't. It's like I can't wake up. I just know—I feel if I could just wake up, we'd all be there around the tree and my mom and dad would take care of me. And I keep pinching myself and pinching....

RACHEL: Trying to wake up.

TOM JR.: Yes. I just keep wishing—

RACHEL: Yes.

TOM JR.: —for....

RACHEL: Someplace where it's always Christmas.

TOM JR.: Yes. How do you know?...Oh, I see, now you become my mother.

RACHEL: How's this time for you, Tom? Is this is all right?

TOM JR.: Fine. Are we through?

RACHEL: Tomorrow at this time?

TOM JR.: Fine.

RACHEL: And the day after?

TOM JR.: Great. Wait, that's Christmas.

RACHEL: Would you rather not?

TOM JR.: No. You work on Christmas?

RACHEL: I love my work. And try to hold off the sleeping pills for a while, all right?

TOM JR.: Sure.

RACHEL: Tomorrow then?

TOM JR.: Great.

RACHEL: Tom?... I'm sorry I kept you waiting.

TOM JR.: Oh, no problem. Oh, I see. Right. Right. Well.... Tomorrow.

*(*TOM *goes.* RACHEL *moves to the window as* "I'll Be Home for Christmas" *plays and snow falls. The lights fade.)*

END

BAL

Richard Nelson

ABOUT THE AUTHOR

Richard Nelson's other plays, which include SOME AMERICANS ABROAD, PRINCIPIA SCRIPTORIAE *(Broadway Play Publishing, 1986)*, BETWEEN EAST AND WEST *(Broadway Play Publishing, 1989)*, AN AMERICAN COMEDY, THE RETURN OF PINOCCHIO, RIP VAN WINKLE OR THE WORKS *(Broadway Play Publishing, 1986)*, CONJURING AN EVENT, and THE KILLING OF YABLONSKI, have been produced by such theaters as the Mark Taper Forum, Yale Repertory Theatre, The Empty Space, Goodman Theatre, Playwrights Horizons, The Second Stage, The Double Image, and The American Place, as well as by the Royal Shakespeare Company and the Hampstead Theatre Club in London, and by numerous theaters in Europe. He has translated and adapted Moliere's DON JUAN *(Broadway Play Publishing, 1989)*, Goldoni's IL CAMPIELLO, Beaumarchais's THE MARRIAGE OF FIGARO, Chekhov's THREE SISTERS, Brecht's JUNGLE OF CITIES and THE WEDDING, Erdman's THE SUICIDE, and Fo's ACCIDENTAL DEATH OF AN ANARCHIST, and is the author of the book for the Broadway production of the musical CHESS.

Nelson has received two Obie awards, a Guggenheim Fellowship, a Rockefeller Playwriting Grant, a Playwrights USA Award, and two National Endowment for the Arts playwriting fellowships—the most recent being one of the NEA's first two-year grants—as well as a *Time Out* London Theatre Award and a Giles Cooper Award.

BAL is for Marty Kapell and Jennifer Tipton

BAL was first presented by The Williamstown Second Company in the summer of 1979, directed by Martin Kapell.

BAL was produced subsequently by The Goodman Theatre, Gregory Mosher, Artistic Director, on 6 March 1980, with the following cast:

BAL	Jim Belushi
JOHNNY	Cosmo White
SOPHIE	Caitlin Clarke
JOHANNA	Lora Staley
DUSZAK	Del Closea
EMILY DUSZAK/FEMALE SINGER	Patricia Hodges
PLANTER/CRAP-PLAYER	Michael Saad
ZEIGLER/PRIEST/CRONY	John E. Mohrlein
YOUNG WOMAN	Ellen Crawford
MAN/MAN WITH FISHING POLE	Dennis Kennedy
YOUNG MAN	Leland Crooke
MAN WHO ACTS LIKE BEAST/WAITER	Daniel Cooney
MAN WHO ACTS LIKE BEAST/BOSS	Ron Dean
GUEST	Belinda Bremner
Director	Gregory Mosher
Costumes	Dunya Ramicova
Lights	Jennifer Tipton

Scene One (a)

(A field. Night. BAL *(thirties) and* JOHNNY *(early twenties) lie on their backs looking at the stars. Johnny has a notepad. Music in the distance. Pause.)*

JOHNNY: I took your advice and talked to Johanna. *(No response)* My girl?

BAL: Oh. And...?

JOHNNY: And nothing. We talked. Or rather she did. She claims it has nothing to do with me, and if she were to go to bed with anyone, it would certainly be with me. But right now, she has a lot of things to figure out about herself. She says, she wants to know who she is before getting too involved in anything.... I don't know. I can wait, if that's what she wants; that is, if I have to. But Jesus Christ, I don't know. What do you think, Bal? She's only sixteen.

BAL: What do I think? *(*JOHNNY *nods.)* I think many things, Johnny. One moment this. The next something else. Some of my thoughts are pretty stupid. Some are fantastic. Some have changed my life. Others have bored me to tears. I think a lot of things. Bal does. *(Short pause—looks back at the stars)* Is it wrong to want to feel?

JOHNNY: *(Opening up his notepad, set to write)* Go ahead, Bal, I'm listening.

BAL: *(Continuing his thought)* I mean, in a certain way, I wish we didn't know what we know, or maybe that what we knew we found out was wrong. How I would love to look up at the stars and the moon and say—"What fools we were to think that we were spinning; to think that we were on an earth which revolves." I would love to pity the poor scientists. I would love to once again believe that we were at the center of things, that all moved around us. Then I wouldn't feel like I was missing something. Then I wouldn't be bothered by not being able to feel us moving. If we are spinning, is it really wrong to want to feel it? And if I can't feel it, I'd rather not know we were moving at all.

JOHNNY: Beautiful, Bal.

BAL: *(Getting up)* That's enough of that for tonight.

JOHNNY: I can hardly wait to finish this profile. The notes I've already submitted, you can't imagine what a stir they've created. My editor's even talking about a cover, Bal.

BAL: Listen. *(We hear the music in the distance.)* That party won't last forever. Come on, I need a drink. *(He starts to go.)* I want to feel myself spinning.

Scene One (b)

*(*DUSZAK*'s dining room. Music. Food. Drink.* DUSZAK, *a wealthy businessman;* EMILY DUSZAK, *his attractive wife;* ZIEGLER, *an employee;* PLANTER, *a servant;* YOUNG MAN; YOUNG WOMAN *and* MAN *(guests). Also* JOHNNY *and* BAL, *who sits at a table and eats.)*

DUSZAK: Planter, another bottle of Bordeaux!

PLANTER: Yes, Mr. Duszak. *(Hurries out)*

DUSZAK: I can tell, Ziegler, that you think Old Duszak's being a bit extravagant.

ZIEGLER: I wasn't thinking anything of the kind, Sir. Though there are but four or five bottles of Bordeaux left in the cellar.

DUSZAK: I know perfectly well what is and what is not in my own cellar, Ziegler. So there are only four or five bottles of Bordeaux left. The question is, Ziegler, *why* are they left?

ZIEGLER: Why, Sir?

DUSZAK: Because I have been hoarding them. And why have I been hoarding them, Ziegler?

ZIEGLER: Why, Sir?

DUSZAK: For a reason, that's why. And what sort of reason am I suggesting, Ziegler?

ZIEGLER: What, Sir?

DUSZAK: For a *very good* reason, that's what. Ziegler, man has reasons for what he does. He has a mind. He thinks. He reasons. I am a man. I have a mind, I think. So I have my reasons!

ZIEGLER: I'm sure you must, Sir.

DUSZAK: *And* if I have my reasons for hoarding my Bordeaux, then it is fair to assume that I have my reasons for uncorking it as well. Ziegler, man thinks. Man has new thoughts. Man changes his mind. And man finds new reasons! And what sort of reasons must a man find to change his mind?

ZIEGLER: I give up, Sir.

DUSZAK: Very good reasons, that's what!!

ZIEGLER: Makes sense, Sir.

DUSZAK: And what could be a better reason than.... *(Waves his arms, pointing out the room)*

ZIEGLER: Than what, Sir?

DUSZAK: *(Yelling)* Mr. Bal!!!

EVERYONE: *(Stopping their chit-chat and toasts)* To Mr. Bal!!!

BAL: Pass the sausage plate, please. *(He eats.)*

YOUNG WOMAN: *(Slightly drunk)* Mr. Duszak, would you tell us again how you found our guest of honor?

MAN: *(To* YOUNG MAN*)* I love this story, don't you?

*(*YOUNG MAN *and* MAN *go back into conversation.)*

DUSZAK: You can't want to hear it *again!*

(Everyone is back to their chit-chat, no response. Short pause.)

DUSZAK: But if I must, I must.

EMILY: *(Passing out sausages)* Go ahead, dear. You speak so well.

DUSZAK: Well, I know when my arm is being twisted. Man resists. But man overcomes his resistance. And man grows! So, to begin at the beginning, it was Johnny here who first brought Mr. Bal to my attention. Johnny.

JOHNNY: *(Taking a sausage from* EMILY*)* Well, my generator had gone on the whosits. I called the repair shop and Mr. Bal was sent to fix it. He arrived late in the afternoon, around five or half past, and as I wrote that night in my journal, my first impression of him was one of, and I quote: "A man who remembers his dreams, a man who knows, and a man who lives."

*(*YOUNG MAN *applauds.)*

ZIEGLER: *(To* YOUNG MAN*)* Shut up, we're not finished with the story yet.

DUSZAK: *(To others, who only casually listen)* You notice how my secretary, Mr. Ziegler, says "we" when he means me. How odd to express such participation when only a moment ago he was questioning whether Mr. Bal was worthy of such a celebration.

EMILY: *(To* ZIEGLER*)* No!

ZIEGLER: I wasn't saying....

DUSZAK: Of course you weren't saying. You never say. You insinuate. That's all you ever do. That's your type, Ziegler. In this world there are those who insinuate and those who....

ZIEGLER: Who what?

DUSZAK: I forget. *(Grabs his glass)* To Mr. Bal!

EVERYONE: *(Stopping their chit-chat for a moment to toast)* Mr. Bal!

BAL: Is there any mustard?

*(*PLANTER*, who has returned with the wine, runs out after mustard.)*

DUSZAK: But to continue with our story. Johnny here kept talking about this remarkable young mechanic he had met. In fact, you could say that every third word out of Johnny's mouth was "Bal."

JOHNNY: Bal this. Bal that.

DUSZAK: The "ideas" of Bal. The languages that this Bal knew. The books that this man, Bal, had read.

JOHNNY: I drove you crazy, Mr. Duszak.

BAL: *(Eating)* But you couldn't help yourself.

DUSZAK: Johnny drove me crazy. But he kept saying he couldn't help himself.

*(*ZIEGLER*, a little drunk now, drops a glass, which shatters.)*

DUSZAK: Control yourself, Ziegler. *(Back to the story)* Last week I would have sworn I knew every single educated man left in our district. So you can imagine how incredulous I was. But still one never really knows does one?

ZIEGLER: Never.

DUSZAK: Man is curious, he questions, he explores! So I felt it almost my duty to meet with this young mechanic, named Bal, and quiz him. And we subsequently met for the first time at Johnny's. And believe me when I say this, but I pulled no punches. I mean, bushes, in my opinion, were not made to be beaten around, if you catch my meaning. So I wanted to know right from the start whether I was wasting my time. So I said to Mr. Bal, I said—

JOHNNY: "True hope is swift, and flies with swallow's wings; Kings it makes gods, and meaner creatures kings."

DUSZAK: And Mr. Bal, without so much as a breath, replied—what did you reply, Mr. Bal?

BAL: *(Reaching for more sausages, with his mouth full)* Richard the Third, Act Five, Scene Two.

DUSZAK: What more is there to say!! To Mr. Bal!!

EVERYONE: *(Toasting)* Mr. Bal!

*(*EMILY *gives her husband a kiss as others applaud the end of the story.)*

JOHNNY: *(To* BAL*)* Are you enjoying yourself? You've been terribly quiet. *(*BAL *knocks over a glass.)* You're not drinking too much, are you, Bal?

BAL: Man eats. Man drinks. Man vomits.

ZIEGLER: *(To a guest, holding his stomach)* EXCUSE ME. *(Hurries out)*

BAL: Ziegler is a man.

DUSZAK: *(Pushing* JOHNNY *aside)* Excuse me, Johnny. Mr. Bal, I just wanted to tell you—before you get the wrong idea, I just wanted to tell you that if it were only up to me, I would, of course, say: "Of course. A man of your talents deserves the top." I would say that, Mr. Bal. And I would mean it, too. But it is not up to me.

BAL: *(Trying to stare at* EMILY*)* It's not up to you.

DUSZAK: That's correct. There are other employees, there's seniority, there'd be jealousy. But you're a man of the world, you know how these things work. They take time.

BAL: I know how things work.

DUSZAK: So I will come right to the point then. That's the sort of man I am, Mr. Bal. You'll soon learn that working for me.

BAL: I'll learn.

DUSZAK: So here is what I have in mind. I'm thinking—why not bring Mr. Bal in as a foreman. A foreman, Mr. Bal, it's not the top, but it sure beats being a mechanic. Foreman, I am thinking—foreman....

BAL: And I'm thinking that you are blocking my view.

DUSZAK: What? Oh, of course. This is not the time to talk shop. *(Backs off)* We'll talk later. We'll talk. Don't worry, when I say we'll talk....

BAL: We'll talk.

*(*DUSZAK *moves away;* EMILY *comes by with a tray.)*

PLANTER: *(To* YOUNG WOMAN*)* My uncle once had a barber who spoke ancient Greek.

EMILY: *(To* BAL*)* You're very quiet. I hope we haven't put you off. *(He just stares at her.)* Johnny tells me you might be looking for a new apartment.

BAL: Who isn't?

EMILY: Do you really live in an attic, Mr. Bal?

BAL: Is that what Johnny says? *(He drinks.)*

EMILY: He says there rats and awful smells from the street. And he says you never lock your door or close a window. Is that wise, Mr. Bal, not to lock your door? *(No response; he stares.)* Johnny says you love fresh air. *(He stares.)* He says you've written books yourself which you've burned. He says that you told him those books were written only for you. *(He stares.)* He says, Mr. Bal is the most fascinating person he has ever met. *(*BAL *holds his head, feeling a bit dizzy.)* My husband owns a few buildings and I'm sure you could get into one if you'd like.... See, I think about creature comforts. I think a person's surroundings are very important, don't you?... I'm scared of rats myself.... Maybe I should get you some coffee, Mr. Bal.

BAL: I would like that. I enjoy watching you walk.

*(*EMILY *leaves.)*

YOUNG MAN: I'll ask him. I'm not afraid to ask him.

PLANTER: Then ask him. No one's stopping you.

YOUNG WOMAN: He is just a mechanic after all.

PLANTER: And he's just been sitting there.

YOUNG WOMAN: If you won't, then I will....

YOUNG MAN: No. I'll do it. I said I'll do it, so I will. *(Goes up to* BAL*)* Mr. Bal.... *(*BAL *turns to him.)* Uh....

YOUNG WOMAN: Mr. Bal, we were all wondering, since you have been so... quiet. You have been very very quiet.

YOUNG MAN: Hardly said a word all night, Mr. Bal.

YOUNG WOMAN: Hardly a....

PLANTER: And now that you've had the chance to get to know us...well, we'd sort of like to....

YOUNG MAN: We'd be very interested in....

YOUNG WOMAN: We want to get to know....

ALL THREE: You!

ZIEGLER: *(Who has just returned and heard this)* Speech! Speech!

EVERYONE: Speech! Speech!

(Commotion settles down. Pause. Everyone looks at BAL.*)*

BAL: You want to know what's on my mind? What I'm thinking? *(Everyone nods.)* I see. Just give me a second or two to collect myself. *(Pause, everyone waits, then finally—)* I'm thinking—sausages. Good sausages. I'm thinking I wonder when was the last time I had sausages like.... But, you know, I can't remember when it was. I'm thinking how I can't remember. I'm thinking, how it must have been a long time ago. *(Short pause)* I'm thinking, on the whole, you are probably pretty decent people. Helpful. Nice. You know. I'm thinking on the other hand that you are also assholes. And I'm thinking I will most probably ridicule you like crazy in the days to come. That sort of thing.... I'm thinking I can't eat another sausage. I'm feeling bloated. I'm thinking how can I use you. A job. An apartment. How can I take advantage. Something along those lines.... What else? Uh, I'm thinking I shouldn't have drunk as much as I have. I feel sort of dizzy. I'm concerned about being sick to my stomach. I'm afraid of embarrassing myself. I'm wondering if I will be constipated in the morning.... I'm thinking—am I speaking out of turn, saying all this? Will they resent me? Then—will I care? And what else? (EMILY *comes in with the coffee.)* Oh yes. There is one more thing. The wife over there. What's your name?

EMILY: *(Confused by the silence of the party)* Emily.

BAL: I am feeling this strong urge to get on top of her. I am. I'm feeling that. And I'm also thinking that I will try to keep her in mind, I will try to think of her, the next time I masturbate.

(Long silence as the lights fade.)

Scene Two (a)

(A rowdy bar. Tables. Noise. JOHNNY, EMILY, *and* JOHANNA *[*JOHNNY*'s young girlfriend] sit at one table.* EMILY *is crying,* JOHNNY *and* JOHANNA *are uncomfortable. At another table,* BAL *is telling a funny story to the* TWO MEN WHO ACT LIKE BEASTS. *They laugh wildly.)*

JOHANNA: Emily are you okay? *(*EMILY *nods, though keeps crying. To* JOHNNY:*)* I just don't understand how you could bring me to such a revolting place. I thought I knew you, Johnny, but now I'm beginning to wonder.

JOHNNY: Bal thought we'd enjoy seeing something besides the ends of our own noses, Johanna. He thought we should see the hairs in our noses and the warts on the human face.

JOHANNA: How pretentious! This Mr. Bal of yours is just a con man. He's making a fool out of you, Johnny.

JOHNNY: If that's what he's doing, then I'd rather be a fool than a snob. Admit it, maybe you're not enjoying yourself now, but in a day or two you'll be boasting like crazy about having seen all this.

JOHANNA: Five minutes more. That's all. Then I'm going home with or without you.

JOHNNY: Five minutes! Fine. Five minutes to teach you that there's a world beyond your turned-up nose!

(Laughter from BAL *and the* TWO MEN. BAL *wanders over to* EMILY*; he holds an almost empty bottle.)*

BAL: *(To* EMILY*)* Do you have any more cash? This bottle's about had it.

JOHNNY: *(Reaching into his pocket)* Bal, here's some.... *(*BAL *gestures for him to put away his money.* BAL *continues to stare at* EMILY.*)*

EMILY: What were you talking about with those men?

(Pause. BAL *takes her purse.)*

BAL: *(Finally)* You. *(Horse-laughter from the* TWO MEN. EMILY *suddenly grabs her purse and hugs it.)*

JOHANNA: *(Standing)* I'm sorry, but I'm leaving....

EMILY: *(To* JOHANNA*)* Please, no! *(*JOHANNA *stops.)*

BAL: *(To* EMILY*)* You seem to have almost a sexual attachment to that purse. *(To* JOHNNY*)* You know I once had the same kind of thing with an old brown wallet. Kept patting it. Especially in crowds. Even when I had no money. So it wasn't just that I was patting it to feel secure. I think it was more because the wallet was soft leather. *(Turns back to* EMILY*)* I was telling those two men there what you are like. I mean, your positions; what you moaned. I also told them something else, what was it? Oh right, I remember. I told them how you taste. I let them smell my fingers....

*(*EMILY *cries.)*

JOHANNA: *(To* JOHNNY*)* Stop him!

JOHNNY: Bal....

BAL: Johnny, she asked. She did ask.

EMILY: *(Crying)* You're disgusting!

BAL: That doesn't tell me anything I don't already know. But on the other hand, I'm always fascinated by how other people see me. No matter what they say, that I'm cruel or terrific, doesn't much matter. What I like is that they are talking about me and giving me another point of view from which I can relate to me. That makes me feel in touch with myself.

*(*EMILY *bursts out crying; she tries to hit* BAL, *but he catches her blows. The* TWO MEN *come closer to watch.)*

JOHANNA: *(*JOHNNY *gestures to her for them to leave.)* We can't leave her!

BAL: *(To* EMILY*)* Now look what you've done—you've drawn a crowd. A man stands next to a woman who's sobbing. People will begin to draw conclusions, Emily. And it's the man who will be fingered as the guilty party. And once he begins to feel their hostile stares, he'll want to crawl away and hide. Emily, you've made me feel like I want to crawl away and hide. You have, Emily. *(Screams at her)* You!!!... You've made me feel guilty.

EMILY: I don't know what I ever saw in you!

JOHANNA: He's just sick!

BAL: *(To* JOHANNA*)* Mmmmmm. I too can make judgments of other people. For example, I find her boring. But the moment I make such a judgment, I find myself judging the judgment. Was it "boring" I really meant to say, or was it "tiresome"? That kind of thing.

EMILY: *(Breaks away from* BAL*)* This is a nightmare!

BAL: Now there you have another thing I find people always doing. I see them relating one experience to another—just as you did there with "nightmare" and our situation here—but I wonder if what in fact people really should be doing is trying to precisely articulate for themselves just one experience at a time. Do you see what I mean? But as I'm sure you noticed, I did the very same thing with your purse and my patting my wallet. So who am I to say?

EMILY: Stop him! What are you doing to me?!!!

BAL: What? You don't know? I'm abusing you, Emily. I am being very cruel, even vicious. I am being a bastard. All that is quite clear to me, isn't it to you? *(To* JOHNNY*)* She asked.

*(*EMILY, *crying, moves to leave. The* TWO MEN *suddenly grab her, and attempt to hug and kiss her. She fights and screams.* JOHANNA *screams.* JOHNNY *hesitates, first looking at* BAL, *then at the* TWO MEN; *then he tries to pull them off* EMILY. JOHANNA *helps. She picks up a small chair and tries to hit them.)*

JOHANNA: Get off her! Get the fuck off her!! Fuck you! Fuck you! Fuck you!

(Suddenly the TWO MEN *stop and simply walk away.* EMILY *cries;* JOHANNA *hugs her;* JOHNNY *breathes heavily.)*

JOHNNY: Bal, why didn't you try to stop that?

BAL: *(Yells)* Because I started that!! Boy are you thick. Emily's been hanging around my neck for a week, I'm sick of her.... I find that despicable of me, don't you?

JOHANNA: *(Hugging* EMILY*)* She's cut herself. You ought to be ashamed of yourself.

BAL: I am.

JOHANNA: Come. We'll wash it out.

JOHNNY: Bal, what's gotten into you?

BAL: *(Grabs* JOHANNA*'s hand)* Your hands are shaking, are your legs shaking too? *(She pulls away.)*

JOHNNY: *(To* JOHANNA*)* He's usually not like this.

EMILY: *(To* JOHANNA*)* He isn't.

JOHANNA: I'm sure.

JOHNNY: It's the whiskey.

JOHANNA: Yes.

EMILY: It is. It's the whiskey.

JOHANNA: Yes.

EMILY: You don't think I'd go with a man who ALWAYS acted like that, do you?

*(*EMILY *and* JOHANNA *leave in the direction of the bathroom.)*

BAL: You're right. It is the whiskey.... And when it's not the whiskey, then it's my upbringing. And when it's not my upbringing, then it's my environment. When it's not my environment, then it's something else. My schooling maybe. Or how about my diet?... Do you have any cash, I want another bottle.

JOHNNY: Bal, I think you've had enough.

BAL: So do I. *(Calls)* Waiter! Another bottle!

Scene Two (b)

(Bathroom of the bar. JOHANNA *looks at the shoulder of* EMILY*'s dress.)*

EMILY: It's ripped, isn't it? It's ruined.

JOHANNA: It's on the seam.

EMILY: It's ripped. He ripped it.

JOHANNA: It's on the seam.

EMILY: I'll never wear it again. I can't.

JOHANNA: Only if you don't want to.

EMILY: I don't. I can't *(Suddenly)* I'm drugged! That's how he got me here. Don't you see? He slipped something into a drink. Who'd have thought. I mean, who would ever have thought. You can't blame me, I'm drugged! *(Turns to* JOHANNA*, no response)* No. But I wish I were. I wish I were something. If not drugged then I wish I had a mental illness. I wish I were out of my senses....

JOHANNA: I have a safety pin in my pocketbook. *(She leaves.)*

EMILY: "I have a safety pin in my pocketbook." Go to hell. *(She tries to see the rip but can't. She takes off her dress, wears only a slip. Looks at the rip.)* It's on the seam.

*(*JOHANNA *returns with her pocketbook, starts to pin the dress.)*

EMILY: So I like sex, so shoot me.

JOHANNA: You don't have to explain.

EMILY: I don't, do I? That's a good one. I'll have to remember that. So I don't have to explain. Just who are you to say that to me?!!! *(She cries, covering her face with her dress. Pause.)*

JOHANNA: Emily? *(No response)* Emily, look, I'll make a little confession of my own. *(*EMILY *looks up.)* I'll bet that if I didn't watch my step, I too could find myself falling for this Mr. Bal. *(*EMILY *looks at her.)* See, you shouldn't blame yourself. It could happen to anyone.

EMILY: You're lying aren't you?

JOHANNA: No.

EMILY: You're just trying to make me feel better, aren't you?

(Pause)

JOHANNA: Yes.

EMILY: You're lying?

JOHANNA: Yes.

EMILY: Good. Bal wouldn't give you the time of day. I'd hate to see you disappointed.

Scene Two (c)

(The bathroom. EMILY, *alone, putting on her make-up.)*

EMILY: Bastard. Son of a bitch. Slime. Shit.

*(*JOHANNA *enters.)*

JOHANNA: Emily?

EMILY: I'm not upset.

JOHANNA: Johnny says if you want to, you could come out now.

EMILY: Nothing happened. Why should I be upset?

JOHANNA: We'll make sure you get home all right. Johnny and me.

EMILY: Rise—that's what I always do. That's how I was brought up. Rise above the stench, hold your nose, and lift your head.

JOHANNA: Bal says he is sorry.

EMILY: For what? Nothing happened.

JOHANNA: He's been dancing. He's put on almost a show. He's very funny. Bal is.

EMILY: Rise. *(Stands up)*

JOHANNA: He even tried to get Johnny to get up and dance. But he'd have no part of that.

EMILY: I'm holding my nose. See. That's how I was brought up. *(Leaves)*

JOHANNA: *(After a pause, looks in the mirror)* Whoa. I haven't danced like this in ages. *(Fans herself; stops)* Even my legs are shaking.

Scene Two (d)

(Bathroom. EMILY *and* JOHANNA *enter talking. Both out of breath from dancing.)*

JOHANNA: I think I liked it best when we didn't know who we were supposed to be dancing with. Then I wasn't thinking so much. Then I wasn't trying to be so good at it. I could just sort of let go. *(She giggles.)*

EMILY: Then do. *(Takes off her shoes)* I shouldn't have worn these shoes.

JOHANNA: Do what?

EMILY: Let go. Abandon yourself. Feel the breeze on your cheeks. You're old enough. You told me yourself Johnny's almost begged you.

JOHANNA: He has, but I couldn't. I've thought too much about it. I want to wait until I'm done thinking about it.

EMILY: Flower, woman, flower!

JOHANNA: No.

EMILY: That means yes.

JOHANNA: Maybe.

EMILY: That really means yes. Johnny's not so bad. You'll like it. You'll love it.

JOHANNA: Maybe.

EMILY: You want some advice?

JOHANNA: No.

*(*EMILY *rubs her feet; dance music grows in the background,* JOHANNA *dances; stops.)*

EMILY: *(Looks up at* JOHANNA, *obviously thinking)* So I like sex....

*(*JOHANNA *turns to* EMILY.*)*

JOHANNA: *(Innocently)* So shoot me. *(They laugh.)*

Scene Two (e)

(Bathroom. JOHANNA *alone.)*

JOHANNA: *(To herself)* Mother, Father, close your eyes. And sleep well tonight. I'm grown up. And that can't be helped. *(Recites)*
"Although I joy in thee,
I have no joy of this contract to-night,
It is too rash, too unadvis'd, too sudden,
Too like the lightning, which doth cease to be
Ere one can say it lightens."
How I hated it when Mr. Peters made the whole class memorize that.
(Recites) "This bud of love, by summer's ripening breath,
May prove a beauteous flower when next we meet.
Good-night, good-night! as sweet repose and rest
Come to thy heart as that within thy breast!"
(Short pause) Thank you, Mr. Peters. Thanks. *(Leaves, calling)* Johnny! Johnny!

Scene Three (a)

*(*BAL*'s attic. Bed.* JOHANNA *in bed, covering herself with the covers.* BAL *sits on the edge of the bed.)*

JOHANNA: I don't believe what I've done. How did this happen?

BAL: First, I unbuttoned your blouse, then I stuck your hand inside my pants.... *(*JOHANNA *covers her ears.)* You asked me a question.

JOHANNA: I'm confused. This room. I don't even know where I am.

BAL: You can start by blaming your sweetheart, Johnny. If that boy could hold his liquor, he wouldn't have passed out and left me to take you home.

JOHANNA: Then why didn't you?! Why didn't you just take me home?!!

BAL: It must have been the whiskey.

JOHANNA: They'll notice. Everyone will notice. I can't go back there. I can't. *(Quickly turns to* BAL*)* Bal, I love you. Let's go away, Bal. Dear, come. I'll write home. After we're settled, my parents can come and visit. They'll see I did the right thing. I'll show them. They'll forgive and forget. Where's my blouse? *(Hysterical)* Where's my blouse?!!! *(*BAL *has been sitting on it. He hands it to her.)* Well—pack! What are you waiting for? Pack!!!!

BAL: The only place I'm going is into the bathroom. I want to wash myself.

JOHANNA: What?!! You have to go with me! *(Short pause)* I want that!!! *(She collapses; to herself.)* God, what was I thinking of. Go away with... I'd sooner die. I'd sooner slit my wrists. No one will know. I don't look so different. Do

I? Do I?!! And who's going to find out? I'm not going to tell anybody. I'm not going to tell a soul. And you won't either, will you? *(Short pause)* Will you?!!!

BAL: I never know what I'm going to do. Only what I've already done, Johanna.

JOHANNA: Promise me!!! *(No response)* Promise me!!!!!!

BAL: As a matter of fact, knowing me as I do, once I see my best friend Johnny's face, I'm probably not going to be able to resist telling. Just out of curiosity, I suppose. To see his reaction. I wish I could promise, Johanna. I really wish I could. No, that's not true. I'm past the point of wishing. I never wish, anymore. Do you want to hear something funny? I hate wishing wells. I do. I detest them. I find them loathsome. It's true. There's something I'll bet you didn't know about me. *(Pause)* I'm not a very good person, Johanna.

JOHANNA: *(Hysterical, screams)* Noooooooooooooo!!!!!!! *(She runs out. Long pause.)*

BAL: *(Sincerely, to himself)* I feel very guilty.

Scene Three (b)

(The attic. BAL *and the* CRAP-PLAYER *have just finished a game of crap.)*

CRAP-PLAYER: *(At the window)* They're still dredging the river for that poor girl.

BAL: *(Counting out money)* Johanna.

CRAP-PLAYER: So you did know her.

BAL: Who told you I did? *(No response)* I knew her boyfriend. *(Handing him the money)* Here's eighty, I'll give you the rest on Friday. You don't have to count it.

CRAP-PLAYER: *(Counting the money)* My landlady saw her jump. That was fortunate.

BAL: Because she called the police?

CRAP-PLAYER: No, because now she has something besides me to talk about. One more game? *(*BAL *shakes his head, gets a cigarette.)* Just want to give you a fair shake. Never know when your luck will turn.

BAL: No such animal as luck.

CRAP-PLAYER: No?

BAL: No. If I roll a poor game, there are reasons.

CRAP-PLAYER: Are there?

BAL: Reasons because I chose not to shake one more time, or one less time. Reasons why I threw hard or not so hard. Reasons for my hands being sweaty—or dry. Reasons. I may be tense. I might be preoccupied. I may be uncomfortable in this shirt—the sleeve might be too tight. Luck's got shit to do with anything. There are reasons.

CRAP-PLAYER: If you say so, Bal. *(He starts to leave, stops again at the window. They both look out now. Pause.)*

BAL: Women seem more prone to suicide than men. Maybe it has something to do with hormones.

Scene Four (a)

(River bank. Park bench. JOHNNY *sits on the bench,* MAN WITH A FISHING POLE *fishes.)*

MAN WITH A FISHING POLE: *(To the fish)* Come on fishies. Come on now. You're trying my patience. Yum-yum fishies. Yum-yum.... *(Pause. He fishes. Then to* JOHNNY:*)* I've never seen it like this. Two hours and not a bite. You don't happen to have a match, do you? *(*JOHNNY *gives him a match. Man lights it.)* This is a trick I thought up myself. Burn half of the worm. They like that. Fish are getting more sophisticated every day. Well-done, medium rare. They have their tastes like you or I. Just got to find out what it is, and you got them. *(Fishes)* I give 'em a few more years before they start asking for ketchup and English muffins. Come on now, don't we have any well-done worm lovers in this crowd? *(Pauses; fishes)* Come on fishies. It's chow-time. Soup's on, fishies. I said, soup's on. *(Fishes)* Nothing. Well, I guess I can't blame 'em, I mean I wouldn't bite on no worm, if it is cooked to taste, when I had a whole young girl down there to chew on.

VOICE OFF: They've found her!!!

*(*MAN WITH A FISHING POLE *quickly collects his things and starts to hurry off.)*

MAN WITH A FISHING POLE: *(To* JOHNNY*)* You better hurry, fella, if you want to see. They'll be covering her up once they get her on dry ground. *(He runs out.)*

(Pause. JOHNNY *starts to get up, stops. Pause. Suddenly and violently he turns against the bench and begins kicking and hitting it. Boards are broken. He smashes these boards, too, against the bench until finally the bench is a pile of rubble.* JOHNNY *pants. Pause.)*

JOHNNY: *(To himself)* I had to get that out.

Scene Four (b)

(A confessional. Church bells ring. BAL *kneels before a closed curtain. He is sobbing.)*

BAL: *(After a pause)* See, now that's just my point, Father. Do you see? Here I am sobbing. I can't help myself. But the point is not that I can't help myself, but it's the phrase itself—"I am sobbing." Or rather, it's the idea that I am sobbing, not the phrase. After all I don't want to make this a linguistic problem. It's the idea that is so terrifyingly inappropriate, or, better, so horrendously untrue. Take my feet, Father. Are *they* sobbing? Can they sob? Or my hair. Or my elbow. What have *they* got to do with sobbing? Have you ever heard the expression— "The sum of all parts"? I am the sum of my parts, Father, so then how can I sob? My eyes, they tear. My throat, it dries. So then who or what is doing all this sobbing? *(Short pause)* Not me. It's definitely not me. Each part's too goddamn busy touching the next—like cogs, you see. Like electrical wires. They're much too busy to sob. Oh, I know what you're going to say—I know your argument. You're going to say—if I were to whack a finger off, would that finger still be me? Would that bloody finger over there in the garbage be me? And you'd say, of course it wouldn't. It's not the finger, you'd say, it is the pain. It is what you are feeling which is you. Which is me. But Father, the pain would only be in here. In here. *(Points to his head)* Just here. Not in my foot. Not in the back of my neck. Only here. So it always comes back to what's in here, does it? *(Pause)* But Father, I am more than a brain. There's more. There is! I am not just a goddamn brain!!! *(He sobs. Pause. He relaxes.)*

*(*PRIEST *enters from the side, holding a small paper bag.)*

PRIEST: Can I help, son?

BAL: *(Standing)* Done. I got it out.

PRIEST: But...?

BAL: I said, I got it out.

*(*BAL *leaves.* PRIEST *opens the curtain, there is no one there. He takes a cup of coffee out of the bag, opens the lid, sips.)*

PRIEST: Next! *(Closes the curtain)*

Scene Five (a)

*(*BAL*'s attic.* JOHNNY, *alone, sits in a chair, waiting. He hears steps and hides.* BAL *enters with* SOPHIE, *who is in her twenties.)*

SOPHIE: Hey, let go! Let go of my arm! *(*BAL *lets go.)* I don't even know who you are. *(Looks around)* Jesus, is this where you live? What are you, a criminal or something? *(Turns back to* BAL*)* Hey, what makes you think you can just snatch a girl off the street and drag her off to your filthy room?

BAL: You weren't dragged. You walked.

SOPHIE: So I walked. What's that supposed to mean? I was afraid you'd hit me.

BAL: Oh. *(He opens the door so she can leave.)*

SOPHIE: What are you doing? You telling me to leave? What are you, sick? You drag me off the street and up God knows how many steps to this rat's nest just to tell me to leave? I'll leave when I'm ready to leave. I have to catch my breath.

BAL: Oh. *(He closes the door again.)*

SOPHIE: If I'm not home by nine they'll lock me out.

BAL: There's your incentive to hurry.

SOPHIE: If my mother found out she'd throw me out. My own mother would. I hate her. What's your name?

BAL: Bal.

SOPHIE: That's a stupid name. Mine's Sophie and that's a stupid name too. My grandmother was Sophie too and she was even stupider than her name. What do you do?

BAL: Eat.

SOPHIE: Oh that's clever. A man who not only lives in a hole in the wall but is clever besides. Boy, this is my lucky day. You want to know what I do?

BAL: No.

SOPHIE: Hey, you've got a great line, you know that? You're a real charmer. *(*BAL *tries to kiss her.)* Stop that! Haven't you ever heard about conversation? It's when two people talk. One after the other. See, first you talk, then I talk. Or first I talk, then you talk. I'm flexible. *(*BAL *tries to kiss her again.)* Hold it, will you? *(*BAL *backs away.)* Brother, how long you been in this closet, a million years?... Now, so you want to know what I do, do you, well, I'll tell you....

BAL: *(Screams)* Look!!! *(Calm)* Try for a minute to understand my side of this, okay? I am trying very hard to forget someone. As you may know there are many ways one can go about accomplishing this. Alcohol is but one. Drugs another. And a third and possibly the best way to forget someone you have had sex with is to find someone else to have sex with. To get that someone else's smell on my body. That sort of thing. I could be more poetic if you want, but I am tired. So that is what I am trying to accomplish, and if it's not going to be you, then I would like to know now while there's still enough time tonight to dig up someone else. *(*JOHNNY *comes out of hiding.* SOPHIE *reacts in shock and surprise.)*

BAL: Johnny. *(Pause)*

JOHNNY: Bal. *(Short pause)* Bal, don't you ever make your bed? Or... change your sheets? I'm not a fanatic or anything, but that's just the kind of thing that would drive me mad. If it were my bed, I mean.... You want me to get some clean sheets? Be no trouble. God, you must have had them on since... for weeks. *(Pause)* It's really a shame about—you know. I mean if I've said it once I've said it a thousand times, someday someone's going to fall into that river. That bank's pretty damn steep.... Not all that steep, but steep. And the current... I've said it a thousand times. *(Pause)* But who knows, you know. A lot of possible things could have happened to.... Anything could have happened. Right? There are a thousand possibilities. *(Pause)* Aren't there? *(Pause)*

BAL: Uh. *(Thinks)* No, I don't think so. *(*JOHNNY *makes a slight groan. Long pause.)* You know, I've been thinking about you. I know at the moment it may not look like it, but I have. I've been thinking a whole lot about you, Johnny. I've been thinking... *(Begins to count out his thoughts)* how very sorry I am—not only for Johanna, but also for you. I've been thinking what a jerk you were for letting your girl get to know me. I've been thinking, that because you never got the chance yourself, that I've wanted to tell you that Johanna, she was, Johnny, quite a spirited lover. Very lively and instinctual. *(Short pause)* I've been thinking a lot of things, Johnny, but some of those thoughts have been about *you*. *(Pause)* I wanted you to know that. It might help to know that you've been on my mind. *(Pause)*

JOHNNY: I'm peeing. *(Short pause. To* SOPHIE.*)* Excuse me, I can't help it. *(His pants are wet.)*

Scene Five (b)

(The attic. BAL *and* SOPHIE *in bed.* JOHNNY *sits at a distance with his head down. In the dark,* BAL *screams.)*

SOPHIE: You scared me half to death.

BAL: *(Turning on a light)* I had a nightmare. *(He sits up.)* Hand me that notepad. *(She does and goes back to sleep. To* JOHNNY.*)* I have to write down my nightmare before I forget it. *(Writes)* Whenever I have a dream such as I just did, I find I am compelled to get as much as I can down on paper. I take it as almost an obligation. As if my brain were sending signals and clues about me, Bal. *(Writes)* The real trick is to try not to structure the dream. Just get it all down as I remember it. But, of course, some structuring is bound to happen; but that itself can be significant, because what one remembers can tell you as much about yourself as the dream itself can. Maybe more. *(Writes)* There are days when I do nothing but read through years of my dreams. It's after one of those days that I feel that my two feet are firmly planted on the ground. *(Finishes. To* SOPHIE.*)* Roll over. Your breath smells. *(She rolls over. To* JOHNNY.*)* What are you doing, Johnny?

JOHNNY: Praying.

BAL: Mankind is so resilient. And that warms my heart. *(Short pause)* But not my feet. *(To* SOPHIE*)* Quit stealing the covers, will you? *(He pulls covers over him and continues to read through his dreams.)*

Scene Six (a)

(A garage. BAL *fiddles with a generator;* JOHNNY *sits and watches;* BOSS *is screaming at an unseen customer.)*

BOSS: So take your lousy generator and shove it!!! You think I care?! You think you're breaking my heart?!! Oh, it's breaking. My heart is breaking. Ouch! Ouch! I said get the hell out of my garage! I don't need any business from an asshole! *(Turns to* BAL *and* JOHNNY*)* Did you hear me? I don't need business from any asshole. Who the hell does that man think I am? What am I, his lackey? Just because he's in a shitty mood, just because he's got a hag for a wife—oh I've seen her. Thank God I was wearing my sunglasses! *(Turns back)* Don't dump on me fella!! *(Back to* BAL *and* JOHNNY*)* Tell me something, do I look like a shrink? Do I look like I work in a hospital? Then why are so many of my customers mentally sick?!! Tell me that, will you? Will somebody please explain that to me?!! Oh Christ. *(Calms down. Points at* BAL*'s generator.)* So what's wrong with that one?

BAL: It's broken.

BOSS: Oh that's clever, that's very informative. Maybe I should restate my question—what is broken, Mr. Bal?

BAL: The casing is cracked. Cracked casing, no vacuum, no vacuum, no pressure, no pressure, no movement, no movement, it's broken.

BOSS: Cute. Very cute. Can you fix it? *(*BAL *looks over the generator.)* I said, can you fix it? Is it fixable?! Watch my lips!

BAL: Have to seal the casing.

BOSS: Good, then do it. *(*BAL *stands, staring at the* BOSS.*)* What are you doing? I said, do it. *(*BAL *stares.)* Oh Christ, I said fix it! *(*BAL *doesn't move.)* Look, I'm not in the mood to take any shit from a punk. I don't need shit from a punk. Do you understand me, punk? *(Pushes him)* Do you, punk? Punk. Punk. Get the hell out of here and don't come back. You make me sick to my stomach. *(Starts to leave, turns to* JOHNNY*)* I don't need any shit from an asshole! *(He leaves.* JOHNNY *looks at* BAL. *Pause.* BAL *sits down with the generator. Throughout the beginning of the next speech,* BAL *repairs the generator, sealing the casing with tape, etc.)*

BAL: So I'm fired. I'm out of work. If I'm out of work I'll go on the dole. I'll become part of the idle poor. My dole will come out of the pockets of the middle class who will then grow to resent me. I will have no incentive to work, because I'll be paid not to work. I'll wear tennis shoes and carry radios and stand on streetcorners. Programs will be set up to help me which the rest of society will pay for and resent. Then they will lose *their* incentive. More people on the dole, less work. Prices will rise. Governments will get bigger. Maybe I'll get into trouble with the law. Money will be spent to keep me in jail, then to keep me out of jail. I will eat other people's money. I will be an open wound, a gaping hole that devours money.... *(*BAL *has fixed the generator. He now turns it on—it works. He turns it off. Throughout the rest of the speech, he takes the generator apart, piece by piece.)* On the other hand, maybe I'm the type who will pull himself up by his bootstraps. I will forge ahead. Maybe I'll bounce into a new position and turn this once bad break to my advantage. Maybe something great and wonderful will come along and I will learn to feel superior to all the shmucks I've surpassed. And I will grow to resent every lazy bugger who has his hand in my pocket or stuck in my face. And I will learn to project my face into theirs and refrain: "I did it, why can't they?" And I will breathe disgust but appear to give handouts gladly, because gladly I will want to keep them in their place. While at the same time voting against all social programs—not out of spite, but as an act of education, because I will want it shown just whose hand has been feeding whom.

Or maybe I will become a liberal thinker and drop phrases like "fairness" and "equal protection" as if I were a pigeon dropping my shit, while at the same time I send my kids off to private school and while at the same time I keep an eye on their Puerto Rican mammy making sure she does not get the rickets. Or the silver.

Or maybe I'll be a good old boy and simply flail frustrated and angry and call a nigger a nigger, a spade a spade, and a bottle of beer mother's milk. Or maybe I'll become a communist. Or a socialist. Or a socialist with communist leanings, or a social democrat, or a populist conservative Democrat, or a conservative populist Democrat with Republican sympathies, or a Fascist, or a neo-Fascist conservative, or simply a Fascist communist.

Whatever. There are many possibilities, aren't there? And we'll just have to wait and see what kind of man I am. I don't know about you, Johnny, but the future intrigues me—and I can't wait to watch. *(The generator is in pieces.* BAL *stands, kicks over the generator.)* See, I know how these things work.

Scene Six (b)

(A road on the way out of town. BAL *and* JOHNNY *sit on the edge of the road. Evening.* BAL *now has a very large radio which is playing very loud dance music. He wears tennis shoes which are unlaced.* BAL *is eating a sandwich. He looks at* JOHNNY, *offers him half of the sandwich,* JOHNNY *shakes his head.* BAL *turns down the radio.)*

BAL: Eat. Then digest. Then shit. Then fertilize. Then grow. Then pick. Then eat. We have to eat, Johnny. We have an obligation to eat. *(Turns up the radio, then turns it down again)* Johnny, have you ever had that urge to startle yourself? You know, to do something, then after you've done it, you're surprised that you did it. It's not easy, is it? *(Short pause. He belches.)* Nope, I knew that was coming. *(Pause. Suddenly slaps himself in the face.)* Nah, I wasn't surprised. But I'm sort of surprised how much that hurt. I wonder if that counts. No. *(Short pause)* Wait, I have an idea. *(He stands.)* First I have to think of something else—so my mind's preoccupied. What should I think about, Johnny? Wait, I got it. *(Recites)* "Shall I compare thee to a summer's day...?" *(He suddenly throws his feet out from under himself and falls.)* No. I caught myself with my shoulder, so I must have known that was coming. I'll try it again. *(Stands)* Where was I? *(Recites)* "Shall I compare thee to a summer's day? Thou art more lovely and more temperate. Rough winds do... something to the something buds of May. And something something something." I can't remember it. That sort of surprises me. *(He suddenly throws his feet out from under himself again and falls.)* Nope. The shoulder again. God damnit. This is difficult, Johnny.

JOHNNY: Bal...?

BAL: *(Getting up)* Johnny, do me a favor, will you, and divert me for a moment. Come on, divert me. Maybe if my mind's occupied with something you do, I'll be able to startle me.

JOHNNY: Bal, I know what you've done.

BAL: So do I. *(Suddenly turns to his side and yells)* There's Johanna! Look!!! (JOHNNY *looks.)* God damnit!!! That startled you, but not me. Well, anyway, thanks for trying. Thanks for trying to divert me. *(He sits and takes out the sandwich again.)* You know, I really don't know if maybe I'm just a complete jerk. I haven't decided yet. *(Pause)* Johnny, have you ever thought ahead? I mean, have you ever thought not about what you were doing, but what you were about to do? And if what you were about to do, you did, have you ever thought about what you would do then? And then? Have you ever thought so far ahead that you forgot that you were breathing? Have you? I'm asking you, Johnny. I'm very interested in what other people have to say—it gives me time to catch my breath, before we get back to talking about me.

JOHNNY: Bal....

BAL: *(Interrupting)* On my more confident days, I feel like I am the most fascinating person alive. On my more lethargic days, I am the laziest man there ever was. When I'm thirsty I'm as parched as a desert. When I piss, it terrifies me to think that there are other toilets flushing clear across the Earth.

JOHNNY: Bal, I want to talk.

BAL: I thought we were. (JOHNNY *looks away.)* Ah! I see. When you say "talk," I'll bet what you really mean is "argue." I understand. What you in fact mean, Johnny, is that you wish me to commit myself to some phrase or some line of thought, so you can cut me off in mid-stride and twist and distort what may have only been meant to be an off-hand remark into something I must now defend with my life, for my self-respect. I see.

You want to take the aggressor's role and leave me the defender's. You want to jab away and pick at my words as if they were the last pieces of flesh on a white bone.

And all you'll need is that one phrase out of my mouth and you'll think you've got me pegged and cornered, and me, like a trapped mouse, I'll be too afraid to breathe, too afraid to utter shit because I'll see you there set to pounce and criticize and humiliate and abuse, set to make me feel not only less than you—less witty or less eloquent— but also make me feel less a man than I think I am. Fine.

Well, let's try it. Try me. I'm game. Go ahead and answer me. Answer me!!!

JOHNNY: Bal...!

BAL: *(Screaming)* Answer me! Debate! Debate! Debate! *(Suddenly jumping up and down)* I win! I win! I win! *(*JOHNNY *turns away.* BAL *shrugs, turns the radio back up.)*

BAL: *(Moving to the music)* I'd love to be dancing right now. *(Short pause)* Actually, it's not so much the dancing that I want, as it is the sweating. I'd love to be sweating right now.

Scene Seven (a)

(The edge of the woods. BAL *and* JOHNNY *have stopped walking.* SOPHIE *is a short distance from them.)*

JOHNNY: She must have gone out of her mind trying to find us.

SOPHIE: So?

BAL: She's desperate.

SOPHIE: It wasn't so hard. Really.

JOHNNY: She looks exhausted, doesn't she?

SOPHIE: I'll be all right. Don't worry.

BAL: *(To* JOHNNY*)* And whenever I see someone who is desperate, I immediately think—fair game." I wonder why that is. *(Pause)*

SOPHIE: You know, you can just tell me to go. You can. *(Pause)* I don't care.... I mean, who cares? *(Silence. To* BAL.*)* My mother locked me out.

JOHNNY: I'm sorry.

SOPHIE: *(To* JOHNNY*)* Fuck off! *(Pause. To* BAL.*)* She wouldn't even come to the door.... Yeh, and I'm pounding 'til my knuckles start bleeding. And then, see, she sticks her stupid head out the window and starts screaming—"Slut! Slut!"

JOHNNY: Bal...?

SOPHIE: *(Screams)* Leave him alone, he's listening to me!!! *(Pause. She tries to smile but is close to tears. To* BAL.*)* My legs were shaking. *(He looks at her.)* I was out there all alone on the street, see, and then like these other heads, you know, they're popping out of other windows. And they're shouting. Some of 'em are even spitting down at me. My mother's yelling to everyone how I hadn't come home that night and how she, you know, didn't have a daughter. It was kind of like being a kid again. Looking up at everybody. You know that feeling? So I start running off and then I fall and cut myself and they're laughing and me, wouldn't you know it, me I'm just trying to be dignified. *(Crying now, but trying not to show it. Pause.)* Bal, I really love you. I do love you, Bal.

BAL: I heard you the first time. *(To* JOHNNY*)* Whenever I hear someone repeating themselves, I immediately think—"desperate." *(Pause)*

SOPHIE: *(Very awkward and self-conscious now)* You want me to go, I'll go. I'll understand. I must look a mess. *(Pause)* Look, who's begging? I'm not begging. *(Silence)*

JOHNNY: *(Quietly)* How long ago was this?

SOPHIE: *(Shaking)* Do you know what today is?

JOHNNY: *(Shrugs)* Saturday?

SOPHIE: *(Shrugs)* Maybe a week ago. Maybe.

JOHNNY: And since then?

SOPHIE: Bal, I want to be with you!

BAL: If you stay, I'll hurt you. I'll mistreat you. You'll end up despising me.

SOPHIE: I don't believe that.

BAL: *(Yells)* It's true!!! *(Pause. Calmly.)* Look, I know me.

Scene Seven (b)

(The woods. Grey. Nearly winter. JOHNNY *and* SOPHIE *stand together watching the sky.* BAL, *at a distance, stands over what we learn is a corpse. Pause.)*

JOHNNY: Grey. Going to snow.

SOPHIE: *(Nods)* You can feel it.

JOHNNY: You can. In your bones.

SOPHIE: No. *(Pause)* For me it's the shoulders. I always feel it first in my shoulders. I have sensitive shoulders.

JOHNNY: Huh. For me, it's my bones. *(Pause. They watch the sky.)*

SOPHIE: Makes me feel like I'm on a ship.

JOHNNY: What does?

SOPHIE: The snow coming. Like I'm standing on a ship and way over there on the horizon, across the sea, it's coming. And I'm bobbing up and down—watching, leaning on a rail. Of course I've never been on a ship, but it makes me feel like I'm on one. *(Pause)* It's coming. *(Long pause)*

JOHNNY:
"When all aloud the wind doth blow,
And coughing drowns the parson's saw,
And birds sit brooding in the snow,

And Marion's nose looks red and raw;
When roasted crabs hiss in the bowl,
Then nightly sings the staring owl,
'Tu-whit, tu-who!'—
A merry note."

SOPHIE: What's that? Something you made up?

JOHNNY: *(Shakes his head)* Something I know. *(They move toward* BAL.*)*

BAL: *(Over the corpse)* Dust to dust. Rotten flesh to rotten flesh. His eyes are closed. He must have known what was happening to him. Starvation, I would guess.

JOHNNY: *(Retches)* Jesus!

SOPHIE: Bal, can we go?

BAL: Once I asked a doctor what exactly takes place when a body dies. He told me that dead bodies were none of his business. I've been meaning to ask an undertaker ever since. But what I've been able to surmise or what I remember of what I once surmised, from the light reading I had done on the subject, is that more often than not, the heart goes first, then the blood stops flowing, the brain fails once it has used the blood that remained in the brain, then the veins become quickly limp then just as quickly tight, and they stretch and then they crack. The flesh then soaks up what remains of the body's fluids; so the product then is not unlike a marsh, that is where on the surface there are solids, but underneath there is only soft mud.

SOPHIE: Bal, really, it makes me sick.

BAL: That, Sophie, is due totally to your upbringing. Death has been hidden from us, so it frightens us and makes us ill. Actually, a body like this cannot harm you, Sophie. Your fear is all in your head.... Go ahead and touch it.

JOHNNY: Bal!

BAL: Go ahead, Sophie, it won't bite.

SOPHIE: *(Hesitating)* But I....

BAL: Forget it. *(Starts to leave)*

SOPHIE: No, Bal, wait! *(She touches it.)* It's spongy.

JOHNNY: Why do you listen to him?

BAL: See, it didn't jump up and eat you.... Now kiss it. Come on, on the mouth.

JOHNNY: Bal, how can you ask her to do that? *(*BAL *shrugs.)*

SOPHIE: Kiss it? Oh, I can't, Bal. Really I...

BAL: *(Moves to leave)* Suit yourself.

SOPHIE: Wait, Bal! *(*BAL *stops. She bends down and kisses the corpse.)* Worms! *(She chokes. Pause. They start to leave.)*

JOHNNY: Bal, aren't you going to touch it?

BAL: Me? *(Pause)* No. No, corpses give me the willies.

Scene Seven (c)

(A hut. BAL *and* JOHNNY *sit at a table drinking.* SOPHIE *sits on a bed sobbing. She is slowly taking off her clothes, getting ready for bed. Pause.)*

BAL: *(To* JOHNNY*)* Excuse me. *(He walks over to* SOPHIE.*)* You're crying. You're upset. You're feeling terrible. Eyes bloodshot. Hands pale. You're trembling. You have regrets. Regret after regret. You have a tear that has crawled all the way to your chin. *(He moves away, turns back.)* It helps to know how you are. *(Returns to the table.* SOPHIE *continues to sob, though very quietly now. Long pause.)*

JOHNNY: Why don't I leave? Was that the question?

BAL: Yes. *(Silence)*

JOHNNY: The way you abuse that woman makes me sick to my stomach.

BAL: Is that just a way of speaking or is your reaction really so physical? *(*JOHNNY *looks away.)* Just curious. *(Silence)* Johanna. *(*JOHNNY *looks back at him.)* Did I say something wrong? Can I help it if when I look at you I think of her? If I see your eyes and remember hers? That's how my mind works. Can I help that? *(*BAL *puts his head on the table and cries.)* The problem with tears is that they are difficult to read. Even from the inside. Once I thought I was very sad, but I only had a speck of dust on my pupil. I've had a similar experience with a lump in my throat. Whenever I now feel a lump in my throat, I immediately think—"chicken bone." *(Pours drinks for himself and* JOHNNY.*)*

(Silence)

JOHNNY: *(A little drunk)* What you said about the lump in your throat and the chicken bone made me think about a certain park bench. I shattered this bench with my own hands. When I was through I felt a lot better. I felt better because my hand hurt now. The pain was there. I could see it. *(Suddenly he takes out a notepad and writes furiously; finishes.)*

BAL: *(Takes what* JOHNNY *has just written and reads)* "Sunday in January. Bal cries. He talks of sadness. All I want to do is slit his throat. I want to take a broken bottle—a green broken bottle, or a red one with two jagged edges, and I want to hold it right next to his throat and I want to watch his eyes. I want that. I want to slit that throat. The throat. His...." *(To* JOHNNY*)* What's this word?

JOHNNY: *(Looks at the notepad)* "Throat."

BAL: "His throat. His throat. Please." *(Pause.* BAL *hands back the notepad.)* It helps to get upset every once in a while. *(*SOPHIE *cries.* JOHNNY *is almost frozen.* BAL *stands, looks at one and then the other, and puts out one hand for each of them.)*

BAL: *(Proud)* We're a very emotional group. We are. *(Smiles)*

Scene Seven (d)

(The hut. BAL *and* JOHNNY *at the table, as before.* SOPHIE *is asleep in bed. Pause.* JOHNNY *stands and begins to strip down to his shorts. He sits back down.)*

JOHNNY: Hot. *(*BAL *nods. Pause.)*

BAL: *(Points to the bed)* You want to get in?

JOHNNY: What are you, a pimp?

BAL: You don't want to fuck her?

JOHNNY: You're disgusting. She's in love with you.

BAL: Her mother wouldn't let her back in, she had nowhere to go, she felt like the world had closed in on her, she'd run out of options, she ran into us, "an option," she told herself, so she fell in love.

JOHNNY: Is that what you think?

BAL: That's what I think, whether it's true or not. But it is what I think and that is what matters, doesn't it? *(Pause.* BAL *goes to the bed, picks up the covers and shows* SOPHIE*, who is naked, to* JOHNNY*.)*

JOHNNY: Bal, what do you want?

BAL: I want to entice you into bed with her. I've got it into my head that the sight of you two in a good healthy clinch would be pleasing to me. Though at the same time, I am feeling rather guilty at the thought. I'm wondering—is that a sick thought? Does this show me up as having certain perverse inclinations? And then I'm thinking—but it's society that dictates what is and is not perverse. And then I'm thinking—but I am part of society. And then I'm thinking—I am what I am.

JOHNNY: Go to hell. *(*JOHNNY *turns away.* BAL *shrugs and goes back to the table. Pause.)*

BAL: Isn't there anything I can do for you? Something? There must be. You just have to let me know, Johnny. You just have to let me help. I want to offer my help.

JOHNNY: Why?

BAL: I enjoy the feeling.

JOHNNY: Ah. *(Short pause)*

BAL: Once I saw a child screaming in the street. He came up to me and asked me to take him home, to his mother. I said, sure, kid. I said— sure.

JOHNNY: And?

BAL: And then I left him. I felt terrific. What more could I do? I offered. Isn't that enough? I'm offering, Johnny, isn't that enough? *(*SOPHIE *wakes up, gets out of bed—naked.)*

SOPHIE: I'm going to get myself a beer. Anyone want one? *(They don't respond; she shrugs and exits.)*

BAL: *(To* JOHNNY*)* Hot?

Scene Seven (e)

(The hut. Night. SOPHIE *and* JOHNNY *in bed, asleep in each other's arms.* BAL *enters. He suddenly rips the covers off them. They shriek.)*

BAL: Peek-a-boo! *(He laughs and giggles with childish pleasure.* SOPHIE *and* JOHNNY *just stare at him.)*

SOPHIE: *(Coldly, to* JOHNNY*)* He's drunk. *(They cover themselves up. Pause.)*

BAL: *(Quietly)* Yes. *(Short pause)* Everything is chemical.

Scene Seven (f)

(A clearing near a pond. SOPHIE *and* JOHNNY *have just run in, out of breath, though smiling. They have been swimming and are naked.* BAL *sits at a distance.)*

JOHNNY: *(Towelling himself)* One more dip?

SOPHIE: Hand me my blouse.

JOHNNY: It's not cold. It's rather refreshing. I feel refreshed. *(She takes her blouse.)* Don't you? *(*SOPHIE *giggles.)* No? *(She giggles again.)* Might be the last pond for days.

SOPHIE: Might.

JOHNNY: Best make the best of it. You look refreshed. *(Giggles again)* You do. I'll go myself then. *(Smiling, he slaps her fanny with the towel.)* I will. *(He does it again.)*

SOPHIE: *(Laughing, slaps him back—all very playful)* No you won't. Nope.

JOHNNY: *(Continuing)* Here I go! I'm going! *(They stop and just stand and laugh.* SOPHIE *suddenly becomes quiet.)*

SOPHIE: *(With a faint smile)* One more dip. *(She begins to take her blouse off.)*

BAL: *(Calmly)* You two are disgusting. *(*SOPHIE *and* JOHNNY *stop and turn to him.)* You are. They way you act. You take off your clothes right in front of me. Paw each other. Prance around. You're shameless. You're disgusting.... I don't mean that as a criticism. I'm not saying that's either good or bad. All I'm saying is that that is what is generally meant by the word "disgusting." Isn't it? *(Slowly they begin to put their clothes on.)* I mean, you two fit the definition. I'm not saying this against you. I don't mean that. Don't misunderstand me.... What's wrong? What did I do? *(*SOPHIE *and* JOHNNY *are very somber.)* Hey, doesn't anyone want to talk ideas anymore???

Scene Eight (a)

(Plain. Wind. BAL *enters. He holds his hair back and sticks his face into the wind.)*

BAL: Ahhh. Listen to that wind. *(Makes wind noise)* Mmmmmmm. Feel it. Ahhh. *(Makes wind noise. Softly.)* Blow. Blow. Blow. Yes. Ahhhhh. *(Laughs with great pleasure)* *(*JOHNNY *enters. He is cold.)*

JOHNNY: *(Shivering)* Shit.

BAL: Have we lost her?

JOHNNY: You'd like that, wouldn't you?

BAL: I don't know what I'd like. At the moment my mind's pretty much blank. If anything, I guess you could say I'm concentrating on walking, though there is a little tune that keeps running through my mind. *(Starts to leave, stops; to* JOHNNY*)* Do you hear it? *(He exits.)*

JOHNNY: *(Calls)* Sophie! Sophie! *(He runs out. Pause.* JOHNNY *reenters with* SOPHIE, *who is pregnant now.)*

SOPHIE: *(Entering)* That's a hard question for me to answer, Johnny. I'm not sure why I won't go off with you. You'd make a hell of a better father than Bal ever would. You'd be reliable. I could trust you. But I just have this fixed idea in my head that Bal is the man for me. And I can't let go of the thought. I just can't help myself. *(*SOPHIE *starts to leave.)*

JOHNNY: *(Quietly)* Sophie? *(She stops; they stare at each other.)*

SOPHIE: Johnny, *you* see someone in trouble and you just have to help. You're one of those kind. You are. *(She turns to leave.)*

JOHNNY: Sophie!! *(She stops.)* Sophie, I just want you to know—Jesus Christ I can't believe I'm going to say this—

SOPHIE: Say what, Johnny?

JOHNNY: If it matters so much to you, Sophie, I just want to tell you that I can be pretty damn cruel myself. I can be disgusting. I could abuse you. Whatever you want.

SOPHIE: Oh. *(Pause)* What do you know. I was wrong about you. You're not one of those good people like I thought you were, Johnny. You're one of those who will do whatever they can to get what they want. An opportunist. I understand. Oh that's what you are. *(Turns to leave, sees* BAL, *who has reentered. She turns back to* JOHNNY.*)* Johnny, I just remembered, Bal has asked me to ask you something. *(*JOHNNY *nods, waits to be told.)* He wants you to start calling me Johanna. I have no idea why. *(She leaves.* JOHNNY *turns to* BAL. *Silence.)*

BAL: *(Shrugs; quietly)* You know me, Johnny—I can't help myself.

Scene Eight (b)

(A field. JOHNNY *and* SOPHIE *with the* BABY. BAL, *at a great distance, lies on his back, staring at the sky.)*

JOHNNY: *(To* BABY*)* Goo. Goo. Goo-goo. Cute.

SOPHIE: It's not crying. When it's not crying, I start to worry. I start waiting for it to cry. Then I try to shut it up. Then it shuts up and I worry.... It needs me.

JOHNNY: *(Playing with the* BABY*)* Tell me something, do you think I'm the type of person who would kill himself? Am I that type of person? *(Smiles at the* BABY*)* Am I?

SOPHIE: I wouldn't know.

JOHNNY: *(Without looking up)* But you do know. You know all about suicide.

SOPHIE: Do I? Mmmmmm. *(Picks up the* BABY*)* If I were to let it go, it would die. What a strange thought.

JOHNNY: *(Watching the* BABY*)* Well I think I am the type. That's what I think. Gaga. Goo-goo. Pinky toes.... How do you think you'd react to my death, Johanna?

SOPHIE: Mmmmmm.

JOHNNY: *(To* BABY*)* Boo.

SOPHIE: I guess I'd be sad. Though my sadness would soon pass. Then I'd worry that my sadness passed too quickly, because I was brought up to feel sad for a long time. Or maybe I was brought up to feel bad that my sadness passes too quickly.

JOHNNY: Maybe. It's watching me.

SOPHIE: Yes.

JOHNNY: *(Playing with the* BABY*)* I love you, Johanna.

SOPHIE: I doubt it.

JOHNNY: *(Thinking seriously about it)* Maybe you're right now that you mention it. Maybe I just want to take you away from him. Maybe all I'm really thinking is: "beat him" and you're just the stakes. Maybe I'm thinking all I want is to see his face when you go away with me. I don't know. But that's what I'm thinking. And then I'm thinking—is that so bad? I'm thinking is that abnormal?

SOPHIE: You know who you sound like?

JOHNNY: Who? I'm always interested in how other people see me. *(The* BABY *make a noise.)*

SOPHIE: Goo. Goo. *(Cradling the* BABY*)* No doubt I'll slap it silly when it gets old enough to answer back.

JOHNNY: No doubt, Johanna. Goo. Goo.

Scene Eight (c)

(A plain. Cold. BAL, JOHNNY, *and* SOPHIE, *who carries the* BABY *in a sling across her front, enter.)*

BAL: It's getting dark, let's camp here.

JOHNNY: Bal, there's a village just up the way. Look, you can see the lights.

BAL: So?

JOHNNY: There'll be decent food in that village. And beds. Warm beds.

BAL: So?

JOHNNY: So then how can you make them sleep in the dirt another night when all we have to do is walk another ten, maybe fifteen minutes to make them and ourselves comfortable?

SOPHIE: Bal, we really wouldn't mind a bed now. And a bath. We'd kill for a hot bath.

BAL: Uh-huh.

JOHNNY: Then it's settled, let's go before it gets any darker.

BAL: No. I don't want to.

JOHNNY: For Christ's sake, why?

BAL: *(Quietly)* Two men and a woman with a baby. It'd look funny. People would talk. They'd stare. Innuendos would be made. I'd feel embarrassed. I might blush. I try to avoid situations like that.

JOHNNY: And that's your reason? *(*BAL *nods.)* And what about her? *(*BAL *shrugs.)* And the baby?

BAL: Okay, you've succeeded.

JOHNNY: Then we'll go into the village?

BAL: No. You succeeded in getting me to dislike myself. *(*BAL *rubs his hands together, blows on them.* JOHNNY *turns away.)* Cold. *(He stops rubbing, looks at* SOPHIE, *walks up behind her, puts his arms around her and hugs. She presses her head against his shoulder.)* Warm. *(*JOHNNY *turns back, he is crying now.* BAL *looks at him, lets go of* SOPHIE, *and moves to* JOHNNY, *almost runs to him with arms outstretched and hugs him.* JOHNNY *cries on his shoulder.)* Warm. *(*SOPHIE *joins them and snuggles against them. The three hug.* BAL *moves away, feels his hands.)* Better. *(*BAL *takes out a bottle, starts to drink, stops.)* Don't even bother to ask, there's only enough booze left for me. *(*JOHNNY *and* SOPHIE *nod,* BAL *drinks.)*

JOHNNY: *(Touching his tears)* It's raining.

SOPHIE: *(Hugs the baby)* Warm.

BAL: *(Finishing the booze)* Better.

Scene Nine

(A tree. JOHNNY, *alone, sits on the ground with a long piece of rope. Throughout the beginning of the speech, he ties the rope into a noose.)*

JOHNNY: *(To the audience)* Honestly, I never dreamed I would find myself in a situation like this, and even if I had *imagined* the possibility, no doubt I would have imagined the experience of the situation to be quite different. I would have thought my head would be filled with images of my life. That is—I would have thought I'd be "seeing my life pass before me." Or another possibility—I would have thought I'd find some humor in my situation. I've read about certain individuals who have survived such experiences as this and who claim at the very last moment they found themselves funny. And they laughed. I can understand that. *(He finishes the knot, tries it on, takes it off, looks up at the tree.)* Or yet a third imaginable possibility would have been to be consumed by thoughts of my own funeral. Who would come? What would they say? Will I be missed? So—if someone would have come up to me a year or so ago and asked me what I would be thinking at the moment of my death, I no doubt would have said one of *these* possibilities—or perhaps some grouping of these possibilities. And I would have felt quite confident that I was correct. *(He throws the rope over the branch of the tree.)* However, I know now—from experience—how wrong I really would have been. Because my one urge now, in fact my only urge—is to talk. *(He puts the noose around his neck, climbs up on a stump.)* It's as if my mouth was the only chunk of me that is not yet ready to be nailed shut. It's like I'm just not talked out yet. So here—at the point of suicide—I find that my greatest concern is in finding something interesting to say. *(Pause, he tests the rope.)* So—what do I end up saying? What have I found to talk about? POSSIBILITIES—that's what. The possibility of imagining my life pass before me. The possibility of finding humor in my death. Possibilities. *(Pause)* You know, Johanna was wrong. She said I was one of those who will do whatever they can to get what they want. That's not me. I'm no opportunist. A man who thinks only about possibilities at the moment of his death is but one thing—an optimist. And that's just what I am. I am a hopeless optimist. That's me all right. *(He jumps. Blackout. Suddenly we hear a* FEMALE SINGER *singing a sad song.)*

Scene Ten

(A nightclub. In the black we hear the final refrain of the sad song, then wild applause. BAL *and* CRONY *sit at a table.* CRONY *reads a newspaper.* FEMALE SINGER *stands next to* BAL. WAITER *stands at a distance.)*

FEMALE SINGER: I'm told you want to buy me a drink.

BAL: I do.

FEMALE SINGER: *(Sitting)* I haven't seen you around here before.

BAL: No. *(*CRONY *turns a page.)*

FEMALE SINGER: Well, did you enjoy the show?

BAL: *(Perking up)* Your first song moved me. I was all yours. I followed every lyric.

FEMALE SINGER: *(Relaxes)* How wonderful.

BAL: *(Smiles)* Then with the second my mind began to wander. It did. I began to watch your throat. I began to watch how you breathed.

FEMALE SINGER: *(Uncomfortable)* Uh-huh.

BAL: Yes. And then I watched the lights. Then the people at other tables. By the third song I was lost in my own thoughts. I wondered whether I should leave. I wanted to be somewhere else.

FEMALE SINGER: What?!

BAL: *(Continuing)* I played with my ice.

FEMALE SINGER: You...?

BAL:... played with my ice. By the fourth song I'd forgotten you. You were like traffic in the background.

FEMALE SINGER: *(Standing up, to* WAITER*)* Is this somebody's idea of a joke?!! *(She leaves.)*

BAL: *(Calling after her)* By the fifth song, you were a slight irritation. Like something in my eye. Like a pebble in my boot! *(He shrugs. Drinks.)*

CRONY: *(Pointing to a picture in the paper)* Did you catch this? Poor boy—found hanging in the forest.

BAL: *(Looks. He is surprised.)* Johnny.

CRONY: You knew him?

BAL: I knew his girlfriend. *(Short pause)* So that's the kind of person he was.

CRONY: What kind of person is that?

BAL: The kind who can only take so much. *(Short pause)* I feel terrible. He shouldn't have killed himself. I wouldn't feel like this if he hadn't. *(Pause. He shakes his head, obviously upset. Then he suddenly notices his position.)* I remember seeing a movie once where a man sat in just such a position as this, holding just such a glass out in front of him. He talked to himself too. *(Pause)* Ever since then, this position has become for me—the drowning one's sorrows position. *(Breaks the position, nods)* We never stop learning how to behave. *(Works himself back into the "drowning one's sorrows position")*

END OF PLAY

ON THE VERGE

Eric Overmyer

ABOUT THE AUTHOR

Eric Overmyer is an associate artist of Center Stage, Baltimore. His other plays include NATIVE SPEECH (*Broadway Play Publishing, 1984*), IN PERPETUITY THROUGHOUT THE UNIVERSE (*Broadway Play Publishing, 1989*), IN A PIG'S VALISE (*published in the Broadway Play anthology* 7 DIFFERENT PLAYS, 1988), MI FAMILIA TROPICANA, and HAWKER. Additionally, Mr. Overmyer has written for television's *St. Elsewhere, The Days and Nights of Molly Dodd,* and *The 'Slap' Maxwell Story.*

Mr. Overmyer is the recipient of grants and fellowships from the McKnight Foundation, the Le Comte Du Nouy Foundation, the New York Foundation for the Arts, the National Endowment for the Arts, and the Rockefeller Foundation.

On The Verge (or *The Geography Of Yearning*) received its professional premiere on January 5, 1985 at Center Stage, Baltimore, Stan Wojewodski, Artistic Director, Peter Culman, Managing Director. The production was directed by Jackson Phippin, with the following cast:

MARY	Mary Layne
FANNY	Brenda Wehle
ALEX	Marek Johnson
GROVER et al.	James McDonnell

The sets were by Tony Straiges, lights by James F. Ingalls, costumes by Del Risberg, sound and music by Paul Sullivan and Janet Kalas, and props by Susan Andrews and Barbara Robinson.

On the Verge
Is dedicated to
Arnold Cooper
On the occasion of his sixtieth birthday

The play begins in 1888.
In Terra Incognita.

Perhaps the imagination is on the verge
of recovering its rights.

André Breton
(paraphrased by E.O.)

FANNY
MARY
ALEXANDRA
GROVER, ALPHONSE, THE GORGE TROLL, THE YETI, GUS, MADAME NHU, MR. COFFEE, and NICKY PARADISE

All three ladies are *adventurers.*

ALPHONSE, GROVER, et al., are played by a single actor.

The ladies are American, and speak a good 19th-century American speech—not British, nor mid-Atlantic.

The ladies are in full Victorian trekking dress, plus practical accessories—pith helmets, etc.

The titles and journal entries separate each scene. The titles of each scene should be conveyed visually, or aurally, by slide, sign, or recording. The titles are essential, and *must* be used.

The Journal Entries are done to the audience as direct address. They are not being written in the moment, but have been composed previously, and are now being shared.

ACT ONE

(1) On the Verge

(The ladies are in a hot, white light.)

MARY: Day One. Landfall.

FANNY: Beach.

MARY: Island or continent?

ALEX: Isthmus or archipelago?

FANNY: Beach. Narrow ribbon. Cliff face. Sheer. Beyond—?

ALEX: Up and over—?

FANNY: Unbearable anticipation.

MARY: Mysterious interior.

(They sigh.)

MARY: We have reached our embarcadero.

ALEX: Into thc unknown.

MARY: 1888. The last undiscovered, unexplored—bit.

ALEX: Of globe.

FANNY: The sudden force of circumstance.

ALEX: An inheritance.

MARY: Money and time. Time and money.

FANNY: Grover said—

MARY: A mandate from the Boston Geo—

FANNY: "Go!"

ALEX: We find ourselves—

FANNY: Up against it—in the Antipodes—

MARY: Latitude 15 degrees south—

FANNY: Of the Equator.

MARY: Longitude 125 degrees west—

FANNY: Of Greenwich.

ALEX: Somewhere east of Australia, and west of Peru.

MARY: Tropics.

FANNY: Should be good anchovy fishing.

MARY: Poised.

FANNY: On the brink.

ALEX: On the beach.

MARY: On the verge.

ALEX: Set to trek.

MARY: Trekking in *Terra Incognita*!

(*They clasp hands.*)

MARY, ALEX, AND FANNY: Terra Incognita!

(MARY *comes down to do her journal entry.*)

> MARY: Before I began my travels in the uncharted reaches of the world, an avuncular colleague took me aside. "I have heard your peregrinations are impelled, in part, by scientific curiosity," he said. "Allow me to offer you some sage counsel. Always take measurements, young lady. And always take them from the adult male." (*Beat*) Sound advice.

(2) Taking Stock—or—on Sartorial Custom, Civil and Savage

MARY: I have always traveled solo hitherto.

FANNY: As have I.

ALEX: As have I.

MARY: Occasionally encountering a sister sojourner on a trek—

FANNY: Pausing briefly for the pro forma cuppa—

ALEX: And then going our separate ways, alone.

MARY: By "alone" you mean of course in the company of dozens of native bearers, beaters, porters, sherpas, and guides.

FANNY: We agreed. No porters.

ALEX: (*Sighs*) No sherpas.

FANNY: You carry what you collect.

(*They begin to do inventory.*)

MARY: Machetes. Three.

FANNY: Umbrellas. A brace.

ALEX: Rope. Some yards.

FANNY: A gross of hand-tinted picture postcards.

MARY: By your own hand, Fanny?

FANNY: I had them fabricated. I anticipate they will not be readily available en route.

ALEX: Imaginative preconceptions of Terra Incognita, Fanny?

FANNY: Preconceptions? Precisely.

ALEX: Are you clairvoyant, Fanny?

FANNY: Look. Generic scenes of general interest. Generic fauna. Generic jungle. Generic bush.

MARY: They will complement our cartography, which is highly speculative and totally fanciful. Ink pens. Journals, hand-sewn and leather-bound.

FANNY: Hand me my toothbrush, won't you?

MARY: Peacock feathers. Beads. Colored glass. Patent medicines. Specimen bags. Lanterns. Butterfly nets. Cello. Ocarina. Mandolin. Rock-climbing apparatus. *Sherry*. A Persian carpet of modest dimension. Parasols. Mosquito netting. Mineral water. Canteens. Water colors. Sketching canvas. Canopy clips. Bamboo staves. Quartz knives. Iodine. Shepherd's pie. Barley sugar. Lemon drops.

FANNY: Pith helmets.

(*She distributes them. They don them ceremoniously, and in unison.*)

MARY: We're not short of pith—that's sure.

(FANNY *pulls out a rhinestoned tiara and blonde wig.*)

FANNY: Whenever I must palaver with pasha or poobah, I don this tonsorial getup. And lay out a formal tea. It never fails to impress.

MARY: I don't wonder.

FANNY: It stands to reason. Savages are naked. For the most part.

ALEX: I for one am impressed. I've a Kodak! (*She rummages.*)

MARY: No, really?

FANNY: Where did you get it?

ALEX: Friends in high places.

FANNY: Show.

(ALEX *shows.*)

FANNY: Is that it? That little box?

ALEX: The film, it's called, captures the image.

FANNY: Oh?

ALEX: Like honey. Insects in amber. Silver nitrate. I have no way of printing the images. That requires a laboratory. Which would have meant porters.

FANNY: We agreed.

ALEX: We did. Fanny—

(FANNY *models tiara and wig.* ALEX *Kodaks her.*)

FANNY: You won't see what you've Kodaked?

ALEX: Not until we return home.

FANNY: How do you know that it works?

ALEX: You just trust. You "click". You store. You protect. You wait.

FANNY: You hope and pray.

ALEX: You trust. Transport. Guard with your very life. Years of deserts, mountains, pagan tribesmen, and inclement weather. Back in civilization, you hand over your nascent images. Have they survived the travails of the trek? Breathless, you await the results of the chemical revelation. With a little luck—voilà! Kodaks! Lovely mementos. And, best of all, incontrovertible proof for posterity. Documentation.

MARY: I wouldn't trust 'em. Misleading. The natives say they steal your spirit.

ALEX: Funny word, native.

MARY: A Kodak is no more the thing itself than an etching. Flat. A shadow. Physical specimens are what count. Hides, horns, and bobtails.

FANNY: We agreed. No porters.

ALEX: Your natives are mistaken. An unseen moment that would have vanished without a trace is brought to light. The spirit is not stolen. It is illuminated.

MARY: Mysticism.

ALEX: Science.

MARY: That's not science, dear. That's engineering. No, Alexandra, we must have something the Boston Geo can lay hands on.

FANNY: You carry what you collect.

MARY: Physical evidence. Not impressions. Not imagery. Not emotion. Objectivity. Not poetry, m'dears. Not romance. You know what I'm saying.

ALEX AND FANNY: Mmmmmmmmmmmmmmm.

MARY: Shall we saddle up?

(*Something in the sand catches* ALEX's *eye. She uncovers it.*)

ALEX: A glint in the sand.

FANNY: Hooper do!

MARY: An artifact! So soon! This is lucky!

ALEX: Qu'est ce que c'est?

(*She picks up a metal button and hands it to* MARY.)

ALEX: Gloss this.

MARY: Metallic button. Writing. Oh, this is lucky. Latin letters. What a surprise. I'd have thought runes.

FANNY: I'd have thought glyphs. Can you make it out?

MARY: Not English.

FANNY: Phonetically.

MARY: (*Puzzles it out.*) "Hec—kwhod—ont".

FANNY: There's a question mark after it. It's a question.

(*They try various pronunciations and inquisitive inflections.*)

ALL: "Hec—kwhod—ont"? "Hec—kwhod—ont"? "Hec—kwhod—ont"?

FANNY: Pity it's not English.

ALEX: You didn't expect English, did you, Fanny?

MARY: It would not have surprised me. English is everywhere.

FANNY: A good thing, too.

MARY: Is it? English is the vehicle, and its engine is Empire.

FANNY: Stuff.

ALEX: Perhaps we'll find a translator.

MARY: The first of many mysteries!

(ALEX *does her journal entry.*)

ALEX: I have seen wonders in the Himalayas. Magic. Mystery. In Ladakh, it was a quotidian trick for the lamas to raise their body temperatures by mere mental exertion. Sheer dint of will. They would sleep all night in snowbanks. At dawn, they would douse themselves in freezing streams. Then, ice-blue and on the verge of extinction, they would sit lotus and meditate ferociously. Instantly, steam would sizzle off them in clouds, rising past their furrowed brows. In an hour, their robes would be dry as toast—and neatly pressed. (*Beat*)

In the blue shadow of Crystal Mountain, I watched a Bon shaman wrap himself in his black cape, fold himself thrice, become a giant origami crow, flap flap flap his wings, rise into the sky, and fly across the saffron moon. (*Beat*)

In Lhasa, on the bone-white hill of the Potala, before the lunar congregation of Buddhist alchemists, I saw the Dalai Lama himself transmute great buckets of gold coins. (*Beat*)
Into yak butter.

(3) Up and Over

(*The ladies saddle up.*)

MARY: Let us trek.

FANNY: Mary! Alexandra!

ALEX: Ladies! To the wall!

(*They trek.*)

FANNY: Look behind us.

MARY: Is something gaining?

FANNY: In the sand.

ALEX: Ooooo!

MARY: Our footprints.

FANNY: Making our mark.

(*They continue trekking.*)

MARY: (*A deep inhalation*) Salt air always brings out the metaphysician in me.

FANNY: I always leave Grover in Terre Haute. The Antipodes are not the sort of place one should bring a man.

(*They reach the cliff face.* FANNY *eyeballs it.*)

FANNY: Steep.

MARY: Daunting.

FANNY: Truculent.

MARY: Vertiginous.

ALEX: Child's cake.

(*They prepare their ropes.*)

ALEX: Surely you will both agree trousers would be far more practical for scaling this promontory.

MARY: Alexandra, the civilizing mission of Woman is to reduce the amount of masculinity in the world. Not add to it by wearing trousers.

The wearing of trousers—by women—leads inexorably to riding astride a horse. Instead of the modest sidesaddle.

FANNY: And encourages the use of the bicycle. Which for women can never be proper.

ALEX: I happen to be a "wheel enthusiast". And I have often worn trousers—out of sight of civilized settlement, to be sure—whilst wheeling. Or riding horseback. *Astride*. Far more comfortable and sensible than sidesaddle.

FANNY: What can one say?

ALEX: Out of sight of sedentary eyes, I whip off my skirt, under which I have worn sturdy trousers, and am set for practical traveling.

FANNY: Alexandra, are you wearing trousers at this moment?

ALEX: Trousers, ladies, are the future!

MARY: Yes, I am constantly told by armchair travelers that I must wear trousers in the jungle, and leave my skirt at home.

FANNY: Men can be soooo trying.

MARY: I pay no heed, and have often had cause to celebrate my independence. One evening in Malaya near dusk, I fell ten feet into a man-eating tiger trap. Found myself nestled on a cathedral of punji sticks. If I had been wearing trousers, I would have been pierced to the core, and done for. Instead, I found myself sitting on a dozen razor-sharp spikes, in comparative comfort.

FANNY: A petticoat is the only thing for punji sticks. A good stiff petticoat is worth its weight in gold. (*Snorts*) Trousers in the tropics!

ALEX: Oh, jungles. In the Himalayas, trousers are de rigueur. Allons!

(ALEX *leads the way. They scale the cliff. Jungle light. Jungle sounds. Dazzled, they survey the surround.*)

ALEX: A jeweled jungle!

(FANNY *comes down to do her journal entry.*)

> FANNY: I introduced croquet to the headhunters of the headwaters of the Putamayo. The sport of kings. They loved it. Simply adored the game. Of course, I insisted they use only regulation wooden balls. I would accept no substitutes. The rascals were always batting their latest trophies about. I was strict. They respected me for that.

(4) The Mysterious Interior

ALEX: Terra Incognita!

FANNY: Ooooo. Hooper Do!

MARY: The mysterious interior.

ALEX: Fantastic! A jeweled jungle! I am extruded! I mean ecstatic. Not extruded.

MARY: Ladies, shall we bushwhack?

(*They step forward and bushwack.*)

FANNY: Some years back, while on assignment in the Amazon River Basin, for my favorite tabloid, *True Trek*, my arch nemesis on *The Globetrotteress* reported I had got myself up in male haberdashery.

MARY: Did you sue?

FANNY: Grover sued. I would have had the wretch horsewhipped.

MARY: I would sooner saunter across the Sahara sans sandals than don trousers.

ALEX: Ladies, I am not advocating trousers for general usage. Or polite society. But there are times one simply must—bite the bullet!

MARY: An umbrella comes in handy. In the jungle.

ALEX: Jungle is not my metier.

MARY: We know. Fanny, what thousand and one uses do you find for your umbrella?

FANNY: Prodding the suddenly faint of heart. Marine soundings. Poking hippopotamii. And whacking the recalcitrant croc. Thwack! The Mighty Silurian!

ALEX: What is a Mighty Silurian?

MARY: So Fanny's lurid tabloids call the crocodile.

ALEX: (*Working out a lyric*) Umbrella. Hmmm. Chum. Fella. Drum. Fun. Swa—swa—swa—swa—Swoon! Ta—ta—ta—Typhoon! La la—tropical fever has got me in its mighty thrall.

(*A sudden downpour. The ladies blossom their umbrellas.*)

FANNY: No, dear. There's no protection from a tropical downpour.

ALEX: None?

FANNY: It must be endured.

ALEX: Jungle jungle, what a foreboding—

(*The rain stops.*)

ALEX: —what a mystery. A jeweled jungle!

FANNY: It'll do. Puts one in mind of the great cloud forest of the Orinoco.

MARY: Not annoying! Not annoying at all! (*With great resolve*) Ladies—shall we whack the bush?

(*They start forward, whacking the bush.*)

FANNY: Ah, the familiar chop chop swack swack. Takes me back. The cloud forest of the Orinoco. Now there is a jungle, ladies. Spiders the size of flapjacks! They flop on you out of the trees! You have to get 'em on the fly! Cut 'em in half in mid-air! Thwack! Spider blood splatters!—hello, what's this? Mysteries underfoot.

(FANNY *finds something: An old-fashioned egg beater, slightly rusty. She holds it various ways, rotors it, giggles.*)

FANNY: What do you think it could be?

MARY: A fan. For this glaze of tropical heat.

FANNY: (*Rotors*) Does not generate the slightest breeze.

MARY: A talisman.

FANNY: Totem.

MARY: Amulet.

FANNY: Taboo. Alexandra?

(*She hands it to* ALEX, *who turns it beaters-down, and rotors it with resolve.*)

ALEX: Marsupial's unicycle.

(*Hands it to* FANNY, *who puts it in her belt, like a six-shooter.*)

JOURNAL ENTRY:

> MARY: The bane of my many travels in the tropics is a bland, mucilagenous paste called manioc, made from the forlorn and despicable cassava, a tuber of dubious provenance. A vile concoction, manioc tastes, in the best of recipes, like the bottom of a budgie's cage—and is more suited for masonry than human consumption. Manioc is the quintessential native chop, occurring circumglobularly in the tropics. For those with a taste for prussic acid, manioc may be just your cup of tea.

(5) Native Chop

(The ladies are bushwhacking. Jungle noises all about.)

ALEX: I am delicious! I mean delirious. Not delicious.

MARY: Ladies! Shall we whack the bush?

(*They start off.* ALEX *pricks herself on a thorn.*)

ALEX: Ow! Ligament, juicy Nordic, quiz!

FANNY: Marvelous strange oaths, Alexandra.

ALEX: These spikey stickers are a bother. Itch! Lasso pork liquor!

MARY: The bush has its logic.

ALEX: Fine. The glacier is my milieu. Give me an ice face, a mountain of howling wind and stone, or an impassable crevasse. Below zero, I'm in my element. Why can't a jungle be more like a park?

FANNY: Regulated undergrowth?

ALEX: Why not? A little order.

MARY: A jungle has its order, of course.

ALEX: Tips for lady travelers? Or just brushing up on your next address to the Boston Geo?

MARY: Don't snip, or snipe. Dear.

FANNY: When I was last at the Explorer's Club, I had the most extraordinary meal. It was written up in *True Trek.*

ALEX: Please, Fanny, not one of those stories.

MARY: This jungle is not so awful. As jungles go, this jungle is not annoying.

ALEX: It is nothing but. It is one annoyance after another.

MARY: It is dry. A dry jungle is a mercy.

ALEX: Mary, it is soggy. It is saturated. I have fungi growing on my corset stays.

MARY: Comparatively dry. As jungles go, this one is almost arid. Oh, I have waded through swamps for hours on end, emerging at last with a frill of leeches around my neck like an astrakhan collar.

ALEX: There are no astrakhan leeches in the Himalayas. No spikey swamp stickers, no mighty silurians—

MARY: But there are abominable snowmen. I've read Fanny's tabloids.

FANNY: Abominable snowman was on the menu when I was last at the Explorers' Club. But I suspect it was yak. They pride themselves on their Native Chop. I always have something outlandish. Thinking about the Explorers' Club whets my appetite. We must stop for refreshment. (*She puts down her pack and rummages, preparing a snack.*) On my last visit, we had bear chops, buffalo hump, glacé bees' knees, and armadillo knuckles. Which I for one never suspected armadillos had. Followed by muckleshoots, sweet and sour zebra, wolverine surprise, porcupine quills à la Louis quatorze, locust liqueur, and the celebrated moose mousse. I hear not a good year for gnu, I said. I'd skip the snake salad, if I were you, my companion replied, and the candied cats' eyes aren't worth a penny postcard home. We both agreed to eschew the jellied viscera.

ALEX: Fanny, you make the gorge rise.

FANNY: The Explorers are famous for their grubs. Their motto: Grubs from around the globe! And there are always the usual boyish sallies about mighty good grub. Ho ho. Sheer bravado. The Explorers are always throwing up in their top hats at the end of an evening.

MARY: I regret I have never had the pleasure.

FANNY: The grand art of Native Chop is quite impossible to recreate in the effete precincts of civilization.

MARY: Native Chop, in my experience, is inevitably manioc.

FANNY: Always and forever, world without end. Have you ever had manioc fritters?

MARY: No.

FANNY: Not bad. Not good—but not bad.

ALEX: I am famous.

FANNY: Date bread?

MARY: Please.

ALEX: I mean famished. Not famous.

MARY: (*Takes date bread.*) Thank you. This is scrumptious, Fanny.

FANNY: Alex—

ALEX: Thank you. Mmmm, lovely.

MARY: Super, Fanny. Puts manioc to shame.

FANNY: High praise.

MARY: Ubiquitous manioc. We won't escape it. Mark my words. (*Shudders*) Native Chop.

FANNY: This is not Africa, Mary. This is Terra Incognita. Cream cheese?

ALEX: I don't believe I've ever. What is it?

FANNY: Not cream and not cheese, but it's thick and rich and comes in tins.

ALEX: Thick and rich? Like Mrs. Butterworth!

MARY: Who is Mrs. Butterworth?

(*Pause*)

ALEX: Oh. (*Beat*) I don't know.

MARY: I'll hazard some. Looks harmless. Spread it on my date bread. Thank you. Has the same consistency as manioc.

FANNY: Mary!

ALEX: What a treat! Is it new?

FANNY: Invented in Chicago, I believe. Well, everything is. Take the ice cream sandwich.

ALEX: I've never had one. This is rather nice. Where did you get it? Friends in high places? Will it keep?

FANNY: We must devour it immediately. You know, I don't remember packing it. Or buying it for that matter. I didn't make it. I made the date bread.

(*Pause*)

MARY: Another slice, Fanny.

FANNY: You know, only a few days on, and I am desperate for a bath.

MARY: I concur. What is life without a loofah? Look!

(*They peer ahead.*)

ALEX: He's wearing a uniform.

FANNY: What power? Whose sphere of influence is this plateau?

MARY: This is Terra Incognita! A New World. Sans spheres.

FANNY: Manifest Destiny and the American Way are not spheres.

ALEX: (*To herself*) Rhomboids of influence, trapezoids of destiny.

FANNY: We are emissaries, Alexandra, of the good will and benignity of President McKinley. Cleveland. Taft. Whoever is president now. You know. One of those Ohio politicians. Muttonchops.

ALEX: Can you name the vice-president?

FANNY: Not if my life depended on it.

ALEX: Nor I.

MARY: Perhaps he traded for it.

FANNY: The vice-presidency? Of course he traded for it. He's a Democrat. Well? Isn't he?

MARY: No, the native. Perhaps he traded for the uniform.

ALEX: Shall we palaver? He sees us. (*She waves.*)

MARY: I once traded twelve calico blouses to the Masai. Empress sleeves.

ALEX: What did you trade them for?

MARY: My life. White knuckles and chewed nails, dear.

ALEX: (*Dreamily*) The Masai. Sigh.

MARY: When worn by a brawny warrior with nothing—but red paint—and a necklace of leopard tails—(*Beat*) a calico blouse—(*Beat*) is really quite—(*Beat*) fetching.

ALEX: I should think so.

FANNY: I once encountered the Masai. I said: Wow! Wow! Wow!

ALEX: And how did they reply?

MARY: He's approaching.

FANNY: They seemed to like that. Let's set tea. I'll change.

(FANNY *goes off to change.* MARY *and* ALEX *watch the native's approach, as they prepare for tea.*)

ALEX: Funny word, native. Assuming he is a native. Everyone is a native of somewhere, when you think about it. So I guess he must be a native at that. Where are you a native, Mary?

MARY: I haven't a thing to wear. I wish I could wash. Oh, what is life without a loofah!

JOURNAL ENTRY:

> MARY: In Kuala Lumpur, the seraglio of the Sultan was—a honeycomb. It was as many-chambered as the heart of a tribe. I recall the cavernous steam rooms on cold evenings, full of echoing voices and escarpments of mist. The inlaid geometric gold-leaf calligraphy. The rattan sofas. The acres of tile the color of sky. And a sponge conjured from the exoskeleton of an indigenous fruit. The loofah. Loofah—

(6) High Tea—or, Many Parts Are Edible

(*The ladies have set tea.* FANNY *has donned not only her wig and tiara, but an elaborate rhinestoned gown. Their guest,* ALPHONSE, *wears an impeccable German airman's uniform, and speaks with an extravagant German accent.*)

ALEX: Loofah. Loofah. Now there's a word to conjure with! Powerful juju.

FANNY: More date bread?

ALPHONSE: Oh zank you zo much.

FANNY: Another cup of tea?

ALPHONSE: No, zank you. Mein kidneys are floatingk. Heh heh.

ALEX: Are you a native?

ALPHONSE: Zorry?

ALEX: You don't mind my asking.

ALPHONSE: Nein.

MARY: If you don't mind my saying so, Mr. Bismark—

ALPHONSE: Please. Call me Alphonse.

MARY: Alphonse. If you don't mind my saying so, you sound a trifle German.

ALPHONSE: Alsace-Lorraine.

ALEX: Fascinating.

FANNY: How do you happen to find yourself here?

MARY: Is Alsace-Lorraine French or German these days?

ALPHONSE: Gut qvestion. Geography iz deztiny, ladies!

ALEX: Oh, that's good! I'll make a note of it.

MARY: Alphonse, sprechen sie Deutsch, s'il vous plait?

ALPHONSE: Nein. I never haf been dere.

FANNY: How do you happen to find yourself in this country, did you say?

ALPHONSE: I am a native.

ALEX: This is not Alsace-Lorraine—am I wrong?

ALPHONSE: I never haf been dere. I haf not der foggiest notion vich vay Alsace-Lorraine iz. Schtraight up in der air, vy not, eh?

MARY: Forgive me, but I don't follow.

ALPHONSE: He vas! Him. Not me. No! No! No! No eat! No eat! No eat Alphonse! No eat Alphonse! I am varningk you! I am schtringy! No eat Alphonse! Aaaaaiiiieeeeeeeeeeee!

(*A stricken pause*)

FANNY: I no savvy, as they say out west in Indian Territory. What is this fellow's problem?

MARY: He is not Alphonse from Alsace-Lorraine.

ALPHONSE: No vay, José. I'm from right here at home. Dat vas him. Alphonse. Der von I ate. His uniform, his accent. His syntax. Zide effects. Occupational hazard. Hoppens everytime I eat schomevon.

FANNY: Oh, goodness.

ALPHONSE: I should schtick to date bread. Delicious. (*He has another slice.*)

ALEX: He's a cannibal.

FANNY: Now that's really native chop.

MARY: Nothing to be alarmed about. Cannibals are perfectly rational human beings.

FANNY: You are a liberal, Mary.

MARY: I am an anthropologist. I traveled extensively amongst the Indigos. Cannibals—but lively. Anthropophagii tend to be sluggish, you know. I found them no bother to me at all. Of course, you had to keep them from eating your porters. Frequent head counts were the order of the day. There are two sorts of folks in the world. The sort you drink with, and the sort you eat with. Cannibals you drink with.

ALPHONSE: Ja! I am a Free Mason! (*Pause*) Or, radder, that little rascal Alphonse vas a Free Mason. Egxcuze me, ladies, I am, at der moment, a little confuzed. Too zoon after zupper.

MARY: A Free Mason. What else do you know about your—about Alphonse.

ALPHONSE: He vas a pilot.

FANNY: A riverboat?

ALPHONSE: Nein, nein, nein. He flew. May I have some more of zis date bread, pliz? Und creamcheese? Good schtuff, zis creamcheese.

MARY: You were saying, Alphonse?

ALPHONSE: I vas sayingk, I vas sayingk, ja, um, I vas, he vas, ve vas, whoever ve vas now, ve vere a pilot. Of a flyingk machine.

FANNY: Nonsense.

ALPHONSE: Ja, you betcha. Heavier dan der air. A dirigible.

MARY: A dirigible.

ALPHONSE: Ja. Dirigible.

FANNY: A dirigible.

ALEX: Dirigible.

ALPHONSE: Dirigible, ja, dirigible.

MARY: What is a dirigible? Alphonse?

ALEX: What a succulent word! Dirigible, dirigible, dirigible. Dirigible. Dirigible.

MARY: Alex!

ALEX: Up your old dirigible. Give us your huddled dirigibles, yearning to breathe free. Have a dirigible on me, big fella. One mint dirigible to go.

(*A pause.* ALPHONSE *regards* ALEX *askance.*)

ALPHONSE: Vell, it's a balloon.

MARY: Hot air?

ALPHONSE: Inert gazz.

ALEX: Inelegible dirigible. Illegible dirigible. Incorrigible dirigible. Gerbil in a dirigible! I'll wager it's one of those words which has no true rhyme in English. Of course, it's not an English word, is it?

FANNY: You must explain your obsession with rhyme. It borders on the unhealthy. I've read that preoccupation with rhyme is one of the symptoms of incipient hysteria.

ALEX: Knackwurst!

MARY: What happened to the dirigible, Alphonse?

ALPHONSE: Schtill dere, as far as I know. You vant a look, cuties?

FANNY: You, sir, are growing impertinent.

ALPHONSE: Zay, dat's a nice vig you got dere. Mein zizter haz a vig like dat.

FANNY: Does she enjoy it?

ALPHONSE: She lofs it! A lot!

MARY: How do we locate your dirigible?

ALPHONSE: Follow der yellow brick road, shveeties.

MARY: Sorry?

ALPHONSE: Take der segund egxit. Vatch for der Burma Shave signs. Oh, buoy. I should never had taken dat exxtra schlice of date bread. Never eat on a full schtomach.

MARY: Alphonse—

ALPHONSE: Egxcuze me, ladies. Zank you for der chow. You must come to eat viz me shomeday. I make a mean manioc strudel.

ALEX: Manioc, my favorite.

FANNY: Have you ever had manioc fritters?

ALPHONSE: Ve vill haf to trade recipes.

MARY: Alphonse, couldn't you see your way clear to guide us to the dirigible? We'll pay wages.

ALPHONSE: Zorry. I am not vell. I haf to get zis Alphonse out of mein zyztem. Perhops ve meet again, mein blue angels. Vaya con Dios!

MARY: Auf wiedersehn.

ALPHONSE: (*He hands* FANNY *a bundle.*) A token of mein steam. Big juju. Lof dat vig. (*He exits.*)

FANNY: His steam, indeed.

(*She unwraps it. It's another egg beater, a rather different model.* FANNY *hands it to* ALEX.)

FANNY: I've already got one.

ALEX: Thank you so much. I'll keep it with me always.

(*They rotor at one another and laugh.*)

MARY: A cannibal from Alsace-Lorraine. Will wonders never cease?

FANNY: Yes, Mary, there are two sorts of people in the world. There are cannibals—and there are lunch.

MARY: Fanny, you are a Social Darwinist.

ALEX: What do you suppose he meant by Burma Shave?

FANNY: I've been to Burma.

MARY: As have I.

ALEX: (*With sudden fierce conviction*) There are no cannibals in Tibet! No matter what the Red Chinese claim!

(*Pause*)

MARY AND FANNY: What on Earth is a Red Chinese?

JOURNAL ENTRY:

> MARY: By and large the company has been charming. As a confirmed-since-childhood solo sojourner, I am astonished. Perhaps I have overvalued the pleasures of solitude heretofore. (*Takes a deep breath.*) I feel the rare air of Terra Incognita working its way upon me like acid on an old coin, the tarnish of the past dissolving in a solvent of iridescent light. I tingle. Objects shimmer on the horizon. At sunset, a tantalizing mist, a web, a membrane envelopes us.

(7) Ember Tales

(*Twilight descends. A campfire. The ladies are telling tales.*)

MARY: There is nothing so fascinating as fire.

FANNY: When I was sleeping in a rice paddy under a blood moon, near the Irriwaddy River Delta, I awoke to find myself surrounded. By a band of cut-throat dacoits. Thuggees. Brigands. Buccaneers. They wore turbans with rubies set in the brow, and bejeweled daggers. And they were led by a woman—a Bandit Queen! She was a devotee of Kali, the Goddess of Death!

ALEX: I am often asked about Tibetan cuisine. In Lamdo, I apprenticed myself to a sorcerer. My mentor had quarrelled with a rival shaman. A blood feud. One morning, Master Dzo baked two great cakes of ground millet. He baked them flat as platters and hard as wheels. When the cakes were cool, he spun them into the sky. Hurled them, as though they were discuses. They spun and spun, rising in the sky, sailing over the city until they searched out the stone hut of the second sorcerer. The cakes whirled like saw blades, swooped down, and sliced the hut in half. Battered it to crumbs. (*Beat*) I think that sums up Tibetan cuisine. It is not haute.

FANNY: While travelling in the Rocky Mountains some years back, I repelled a rabid drooling grizzly bear with a series of piercing yodels. (*She demonstrates: three bloodcurdling yodels.*)

MARY: That reminds me of my father, who was a famous pharmacist.

ALEX: Did your father yodel, Mary?

MARY: No. He invented a tonic for catarrh.

ALEX: After an hour, their robes would be dry as toast. And neatly pressed. Extraordinary visages. They would *concentrate.*

FANNY: I once encountered the Masai. I said—"Wow"!

MARY: Talking drums always bring out the Neolithic Man in me.

(*Pause*)

(FANNY, *reflecting on the Masai, silently mouthes a "Wow!" The ladies settle in for the night.*)

(FANNY *does her journal entry.*)

FANNY: Dear Grover. We had lunch today—or was it yesterday—with the most amicable cannibal. He admired my wig. The tabloids will feast. I can hear *The Globetrotteress* licking her chops now. "Fanny's Cannibal—Discovers Maneating Balloonist in Darkest Antipodes—Boston Geo Views Claim Warily." The jaundice of yellow journalism. One more card in the catalogue my critics are fond of calling Fanny's Follies. (*Beat*) Terra Incognita exhilarates. Intoxicates. There is an hallucinatory spiciness to the air. We are in the grip of a communal fever dream. Alex mutters continually about the "Red Chinese", and Mary makes reference to an anthropological penny-dreadful entitled *The Naked and the Dead.* Myself, I dream about mysterious machinery, discover strange objects in my baggage, and strange phrases in my mouth: "Air-mail." "Blue-sky ventures." "So long."

(8) An Apparition

(*The ladies are sleeping around the fire.* FANNY *snores, a ferocious sound. A figure appears on the edge of the light:* GROVER, FANNY'S *husband, a prosperous Mid-West broker. He is wearing a large black oval carved African mask. He listens to* FANNY *snore. Scratches his eyebrow. Growls softly.* FANNY *awakes with a start.*)

FANNY: What? Who? (*Looks closer. Mouthes a silent "Wow!" She gets up and approaches him.*) I have no calico blouses, but I will trade you cream cheese. It is not bad. Not manioc, but not bad.

(GROVER *chuckles.* FANNY *examines* GROVER'*s suit and shoes.*)

FANNY: Are you or are you not Masai?

GROVER: I'm just your grizz-a-ly bear, Fanny. (*Taking off mask.*) What a snore, Fanny. You'll keep the leopards away.

FANNY: Grover!

GROVER: Don't be cross.

FANNY: Why shouldn't I be? Bother a body in the middle of the night. In the middle of the jungle.

GROVER: I came to give you a message.

FANNY: I'm all ears.

GROVER: Don't speculate on the future.

(*Pause*)

FANNY: Your mother warned me you were hermetic.

GROVER: I also wanted to say goodbye.

FANNY: Grover, we said goodbye. In Terre Haute. Some months ago. Are you staying dry?

GROVER: Dry as toast. Well, Fanny. I had something up my sleeve for Arbor Day next. It was—sorta special. Yikes. Well, Fanny. Goodnight.

FANNY: Goodnight, Grover. Are those new shoes?

GROVER: Don't forget to write.

FANNY: Do I ever?

GROVER: You are a faithful correspondent, Fanny. Goodbye.

(*He disappears.* FANNY *stares after him. Shivers a little.* ALEX *wakes, gets up, goes to* FANNY, *and taps her on the shoulder. She starts.*)

FANNY: Oh!

ALEX: Fanny—are you a somnambulist?

FANNY: What? Oh, I must be. Fancy that.

ALEX: Come back to the fire.

(ALEX *returns to the fire.*)

FANNY: I have had the most vivid dream.

(MARY *arises and does her journal entry.*)

MARY: At dawn and dusk, the essence of the jungle increases a hundredfold. The air becomes heavy with perfume. It throbs with unseen presence. A savage tapestry of squawks, cries, and caws presses upon one with an almost palpable pressure. A cacophonous echolalia—snarling, sinister menace—as though the sound of the jungle itself could tear one limb from limb.

(9) Fort Apache

(*Dawn breaks. Jungle noises. The ladies break camp. The ladies travel. Jungle noises all about. The ladies are alert, cautious.*

Suspenseful.

The jungle noises increase in ferocity. They become menacing.

The ladies draw and open their umbrellas. They form a defensive triangle, shoulder to shoulder.

The jungle noises attack, snarl, and snap.

The ladies fend off the jungle noises with their umbrellas, fencing and jabbing sharply.

The umbrellas blossom.

The ladies rotate across the stage, a vanquishing star, scattering the jungle noises, which howl and flee.

The ladies lower their umbrellas. They celebrate quietly.)

JOURNAL ENTRY:

ALEX: Funny word, native. Native. Native. (*She Kodaks an imaginary native.*) Image. Native. Image-native. Imaginative. I am a native of the image. An indigine of the imagination. Gone native. Renegade. Commanchero.

(10) In the Jungle—The Mighty Jungle

(*The ladies bushwhack through a swamp.*)

ALEX: Ooo, ow, natter blast! Savage sour lichtenstein! Lactating minuet! This jungle exhausts me! Surely you must agree trousers would be far and away more practical for this primeval muck.

MARY: On the contrary, Alexandra. One evening near dusk, as we were negotiating the treacherous Black Quicksands of Baluchistan, I slipped off solid ground, and found myself sinking into infinite bog. Fortunately, my sturdy skirt ballooned around me, held its shape, and kept me buoyant until assistance arrived. A few moments later, I lost half a dozen porters in the blink of an eye. Sucked under the sands, like that! Fooop! Poor men weren't wearing skirts.

ALEX: Ah! Look!

(*Sound of a croc.* FANNY *vanquishes it.*)

FANNY: The mighty Silurian! Thwack!

(The ladies reach solid ground.)

MARY: Time for a nose powder.

FANNY: I could do with a bit of a primp.

ALEX: I'll follow suit.

(They pull beaded handbags from their packs, move some distance through the jungle, and freshen up.)

MARY: In the Congo, I was known as Only Me.

ALEX: Only Me?

MARY: I would enter a village or burst into a clearing or emerge from the bush shouting, "It's only me, it's only me!"

FANNY: Immediately disarming the hostile natives, who naturally enough spoke English.

MARY: Dear Fanny. Tone of voice is everything.

FANNY: I was known as Bébé Bwana.

ALEX: Bébé?

FANNY: It's difficult to explain. Out of context.

MARY: I never got over being called "Sir."

ALEX: Nor I.

FANNY: Nor I.

MARY: Human once more.

FANNY: I am revivified.

ALEX: I am refurbished. I mean refreshed. Not refurbished. Ah! Feel that breeze, ladies!

(The wind comes up. The ladies prepare for cold weather, donning scarves, goggles, etc.)

JOURNAL ENTRY:

FANNY: I felt as though I were a prisoner in a kaleidescope.

(11) A Prisoner in a Kaleidescope

(The wind comes up. They move across the stage. The wind whistles. They stop.)

FANNY: Alexandra. Here's your howling ice field.

ALEXANDRA: My forte. Allons!

(They cross the ice field in slow motion. The invisible rope between them breaks, and they begin twirling slowly over the ice, in different directions, away from one

another, toward the edges, in silence. At the brink, they stop. Teeter. Freeze. Relax. They catch their breath.)

MARY: A narrow one—

ALEX: Whoo whistle lug—

FANNY: A scrape—

(*Relieved laughter. They make their way carefully to the center and one another.*)

MARY: What happened, did the rope—

ALEX: The rope—

FANNY: It snapped, I felt it go—

ALEX: Broke—

MARY: Spinning like a gyro—

ALEX: Spinning—

MARY: Graceful, I was so—

FANNY: So—

MARY: Calm—

FANNY: Calm, yes—

FANNY AND MARY: Calm—

FANNY: Eeerily calm—

ALEX: Spinning toward the lip of the void—

MARY: My mind clear—

ALEX: Into the infinite cerulean—

MARY: I thought of my father, the famous pharmacist—

ALEX: Did your life, you know, flash before you?

MARY: Too dizzy, my dear—

ALEX: They say drowning sailors—

MARY: No, just him.

FANNY: I felt as though I were a prisoner in a kaleidescope.

ALEX: Oh, Fanny, that's good.

MARY: A book title. I'd make a note of it.

(FANNY *does. They sigh.*)

ALEX: Whew, lacerated fingerbowl!

MARY: Fingerbowl, indeed! Well said, Alex.

FANNY: A scrape. A palpable scrape.

MARY: Sheer luck, running into that ice wall.

FANNY: Fortuitous.

ALEX: I'm all over bruises in the morning.

(FANNY *is hit by a snowball.*)

FANNY: Alexandra!

ALEX: Yes?

FANNY: High spirits need not always be accompanied by hi-jinks.

ALEX: You always cast your eye upon me because I'm the youngest. But that missile came from over there.

(*They all look. A barrage of snowballs. They dodge.*)

MARY: Oh, dear!

FANNY: Watch yourselves! Oh, Alexandra!

(*Dodging,* ALEX *slips and pratfalls. The breath flies out of her.*)

ALEX: Whomp!

MARY: Are you all right?

(*A yeti appears at the stage edge—a silky mane from head-to-foot.*)

YETI: (*Growls beast language*) ARRGGGGRRRACKAAACK!

MARY: A silkie.

ALEX: (*Picking herself up.*) Silkies are seals, silly. That's a yeti.

YETI: (*Growls beast language*) LLLLLLLUUUUUUUURRRRRAAAAAAA-EEECCCCCKOOO!

ALEX: Oh, yes you are!

YETI: (*Growls beast language*) RASSRASSRASS!

ALEX: Tibet teems with 'em, m'dears. Yes, Fanny's tabloids call them abominable snowmen.

FANNY: He's not so abominable.

MARY: He's rather adorable.

ALEX: He's smallish, for a yeti.

MARY: He's a baby yeti.

FANNY AND MARY: He's sweet.

(*The ladies chick and coo and gush, luring the yeti closer. He retreats, terrified.*)

YETI: (*Growls beast language*) WHHHUUUWHHHAAAASNARP! (*He vanishes.*)

MARY: Oh, dear. Frightened him off.

ALEX: The yeti is shy and elusive. Although his cry is often human, and tuneful.

(*From offstage:*)

YETI: (*Growls beast language*) AIIIIIYIIIIIIIYAIIIAIWHA!

FANNY: The little sasquatch has gone for more snowballs, no doubt. (*She is hit by a snowball.*) AHHHH!

MARY: Baby yeti may have yeti cronies. I think prudence dictates we move on.

(*They hike downstage. Peer into a deep gorge.*)

ALEX: Ooo!

FANNY: Precipice.

MARY: Chilling.

ALEX: This gorge is so like the Himalayas!

MARY: There's a bridge. Vines and planks. Shall we risk it?

FANNY: By all means.

(ALEX *takes three Andean breaths.*)

ALEX: Now—this (*Breath*) is (*Breath*) air (*Breath*) ladies!

JOURNAL ENTRY:

FANNY: An awful yawning chasm. An antediluvian suspension.

(12) Not Quite Robert Lowell

(*The ladies are crossing a high gorge on a swaying, single-plank, vine-rope bridge.*)

MARY: "Mysticism and Mesmerism in Madagascar" was a paper I delivered to the Ladies Fetish and Taboo Society of Annapolis. It was a sensation. I followed that with "Tribadism in the Tropics"—which caused quite a stir. Rubbed several spectators the wrong way.

ALEX: What is "tribadism"?

FANNY: (*Knowing exactly what it is*) I'm sure I haven't the least notion.

ALEX: This gorge is so like the Himalayas.

FANNY: I am convinced that the modern craze for anthropology is actually a subterranean sexual inflammation, flimsily got up as scientific curiosity.

ALEX: I am hypnotized.

FANNY: An unhealthy obsession with rites—

ALEX: I mean homesick. Not hypnotized.

FANNY: Mating rites, puberty rites, rites of sacrifice, rites of passage, poly this and poly that and poly the other—

ALEX: Nacho frazzle asterisk! It is so delicious to be out of that leech-infested swelter. Look! (*They turn in the direction* ALEX *points.*) Oh! Dirigible!

MARY: Pilotless. Caroming off the canyon walls.

FANNY: The Flying Dutchman dirigible! What a story for *True Trek*!

(*They have nearly completed their crossing. Their way is blocked by the* GORGE TROLL, *a young man in a leather jacket, blue jeans, t-shirt, and sideburns and greased-back hair.*)

TROLL:

What have we here but travelers three
Comin' cross the bridge to rap with me
In Xanadu said Ka-u-ba-la Khan
Hey there sweet things what's goin' on?

(*Pause*)

FANNY: Alex, I believe verse is your province.

ALEX: You speak English!

TROLL:

This ain't Swahili, I gotta confess
You hearin' more if you talkin' less

FANNY: Swahili seems mathematically more probable than English, my good man. Although I welcome its appearance in this obscure corner of the globe—even in your ghastly patois.

TROLL:

Castigate the way I talk—
I'll agitate the way you walk!

(*He sways the bridge.*)

ALL: Whoooooooo!

MARY: English is the language of Empire, Fanny.

FANNY: I do not wish to embroil us in a political discussion on *the lip of the void*, Mary. Don't you think we ought to seek Terra Firma?

TROLL:

You may not dig my lingo but I'll settle your hash
You wanna get by me gotta have some cash

FANNY: I don't believe I savvy.

TROLL:

This is my bridge, baby, and I'm the Troll
To step on over you gotta pay the toll.

ALEX: A troll's toll. How droll. He's good. But not quite Robert Lowell.

FANNY: Alex.

ALEX: Whoever he is. Robert Lowell, I mean.

FANNY: This is extortion!

TROLL:

You want sun sometimes you get rain instead
If you can't hack it you shoulda stood in bed

MARY: When in Rome.

(*She pays. They cross off.*)

MARY: Baksheesh! In Terra Incognita!

TROLL: Baksheesh-kabob, baby.

ALEX: What's it like, being a troll?

TROLL: Like?

ALEX: How do you find it?

TROLL: This is just my day job.

FANNY: You're not a born-to-the-bridge troll?

TROLL: I'm an actor. I study.

FANNY: Where do you study?

TROLL: At the Studio.

FANNY: That seems reasonable. Have you done Congreve?

TROLL: I don't think so.

FANNY: What have you done?

TROLL: C'mon, I've done it all. "Sense memory," "emotional recall," "private moment"—

MARY: These must be new plays from Terra Incognita. Indigenous drama. How would you characterize "Private Moment"?

TROLL: Intense.

FANNY: You aren't, by any chance, Mr. Coffee?

TROLL: Not the last time I looked. Hey, ladies. Costume drama—get over it. (*To* ALEX) You I like. What about a spin on my chopper?

ALEX: Some other time.

TROLL:

Your loss, angel food.
Ladies, take it light
And everything will be all right.

(*He exits.*)

ALEX: Vaya con díos!

(*Sound of an enormous unmufflered motorcycle roaring off into the sunset.*)

MARY: I think we must presume English to be the Lingua Franca of Terra Incognita.

FANNY: (*Snorts*) None dare call it English.

MARY: Did you fancy his lyrics, Alexandra?

ALEX: No. But I admired his dedication to his art.

MARY: Irony is not one of your strong suits, is it?

ALEX: What do you mean? I understand that troll! Despite outward appearances, I am an artist, not an intrepid polytopian.

FANNY: Oh, Alex, for goodness sakes, yes you are. You're one of the original polytopians, don't dissemble.

ALEX: Well, yes, I am. High adventure and stupefying risk are my metier. But, ladies—all this rigor and unimaginable hardship, all this uninsurable danger, all this adrenal giddiness, all this oxygen debt and spartan discipline and rude hygiene—all this is mere prelude. A prologue to my brilliant career. I'm not making a life out of all this tramping about, you know. I shall shed my wanderlust like a damp poncho. And become a lyricist. Of popular songs.

FANNY: Victor Herbert quakes.

MARY: I wonder what that conveyance was?

ALEX: He called it a chopper.

FANNY: Loud.

ALEX: (*With sudden conviction*) The future is loud!

JOURNAL ENTRY:

> MARY: I feel a sea change coming over me. A disturbance of my very molecules. As though the chemical composition of my blood has been altered by breathing the rare air of Terra Incognita. I have begun to dream in a new language. My imagination seems to sculpt the landscape. Images flow between the inner and outer worlds, and I can no longer determine their point of origin. I have a growing premonition we are about to pierce the membrane.

(13) Plot Thickener

(*The ladies have moved some distance from the bridge.*)

FANNY: I rather think that Troll is one of the elusive Mole People. The speculative literature on the Antipodes postulates the existence of a subterranean race. Oh, look— (*She has spied a bit of paper caught in a branch. She plucks it.*)

ALEX: Share, Fanny.

FANNY: A clipping. Folded thrice. From *The New York Times.*

MARY: Reputable. Trustworthy.

FANNY: The *Herald-Tribune,* pour moi. This sheds new light. Terra Incognita cannot be utterly benighted if one can get *The New York Times.* (*Studies clipping*) A Kodak of a man. Never heard of this fellow. Behind him an impressive array of snow mountains. His arms are spread—so: (*Imitates a man gesturing about the size of a large fish.*) The caption reads: President Nixon. Grand Tetons. June, 1972. Quote: "I had trout from the lake for dinner last night. They were so good I had them again for breakfast. I haven't had anything but cereal for breakfast since 1953." Endquote.

(*Pause*)

MARY: 1953? 1972?

ALEX: Printer's errors?

MARY: Two such errors in one tiny *Times'* item? Not credible.

FANNY: Dickensian character. Looks like something off the bottom of the sea bed. (*Pause*) President. President Nixon. President of what?

ALEX: Some eating club or other. Where men have breakfast, and compare their trophies.

MARY: No. The United States.

FANNY: How do you know?

MARY: I just know. Don't ask me how.

FANNY: I thought McKinley was President.

MARY: Garfield.

ALEX: Taft, you daft duo.

FANNY: Alexandra, the interjection of song lyrics into otherwise civilized conversation is strictly prohibited.

ALEX: Surely not president of the United States. How could a man who hasn't had an egg for breakfast in twenty years be president of the United States?

FANNY: You know, he rather resembles an orangutan in a dinner jacket.

MARY: I could do with some trout.

ALEX: The Grand Tetons are a lovely little range.

FANNY: Someday they will be preserved as a national park by Teddy Roosevelt.

MARY: Teddy Roosevelt?

ALEX: I've never heard of him.

FANNY: Oh, yes you have. Bully bear and San Juan Hill, and all that.

ALEX: No.

FANNY: His statue is in front of the Museum of Natural History.

MARY: In New York? No. It is not. Not when I was there last.

FANNY: Certainly not. That statue will not be erected until 1936.

(*Pause*)

ALEX: Do you know why there is evil in the world?

FANNY: Metaphysical speculation, Alexandra?

MARY: I don't think so. Do you?

ALEX: Yes, I do.

FANNY: You are so young.

MARY: Why is there evil in the world, Alexandra?

ALEX: To thicken the plot.

(*Pause*)

FANNY: I believe you are exactly right.

(ALEX *seizes the clipping.*)

ALEX: (*Happily*) This is plot thickener!

MARY: Yes!

FANNY: Yes! Ladies, we are in a strange new world.

MARY: Terra Incognita, by definition, could not be otherwise. I have a theory. One that explains the unknown objects. The strange words in our mouths. The references to persons unknown that spring to mind. Spring to mind. It is spring in our minds, ladies. A New World. Blossoming! Within and without! I believe, with each step, each chop of the machete, we are advancing through the wilderness of time as well as space. Chronology as well as geography. Not—as we usually do in savage lands, moving backward into the past, into pre-history—but forward, into the future! A New World, within and without! Beckoning!

(*Pause*)

FANNY: A new world! Within and without!

ALEX: It would explain the dirigible.

FANNY: The clipping from 1972.

ALEX: The Nixon.

MARY: Mrs. Butterworth. Burma Shave. Cream cheese.

ALEX: Robert Lowell. The troll.

FANNY: It would explain why, now, burning in my forebrain like a Mosaic tablet, is the copyright date for a novel entitled *Herzog*.

MARY: Something else is happening, obviously. Something even more astonishing. Not only are we advancing in time, not only are we encountering the future with every step—(*Beat*) Ladies, we are beginning to know the future! (*Beat*) It is entering into our consciousness. Like mustard gas. Whatever that is. Wait a moment. I'll tell you. (*She osmoses.*) Oh. Oh. Oh. Unfortunate simile. I withdraw it.

ALEX: We are absorbing the future! Through osmosis!

FANNY: As long as you're at it, osmos Red Chinese for us.

ALEX: Let me try. (*She osmoses.*) Something's coming in, yes, like a radio transmission. (*She holds up a hand.*) Don't ask. (*She osmoses.*) Hmmmm.

FANNY: Yes?

ALEX: Little Red Book. Great Leap Forward. Swimming the Yang-tze River. Tractor Operas.

FANNY: Operas about tractors?

ALEX: Running dogs. And— (*Osmoses.*) They're friends of Nixon!

(*The ladies leap about excitedly.*)

MARY: Ladies, this is fantastic. I presume you are feeling—with me—slightly tremulous—a bit fluttery around the gills. Ladies, I don't know about you, but I am experiencing a definite, a palpable—yearning for the future!

ALEX: Oh, Mary! Yes! (*Osmoses a moment.*) Radio. Radio is. Oh. I can't believe that! Voices on the air, ladies! Sounds voodoo. You'll just have to osmose your own description.

(*Pause*)

MARY: We are imbued with the future.

(*Pause*)

FANNY: One doesn't have to like it.

(*Pause*)

MARY: Nostalgia for the future.

(*Pause*)

ALEX: I shall make my fortune in radio.

(*Pause*)

MARY: We shall go from year to year, as if we were going from tribe to tribe.

ALEX: Big fun!

(MARY *finds a button in the grass.*)

MARY: Look. Another button. Similar to the one we found our first day on the beach.

FANNY: "Hec—kwhod—ont"?

MARY: Once could be a fluke. Twice is a trend.

ALEX: What what what does the button read, Mary?

MARY: "I—Like—Ike".

(*Pause. Simultaneously:*)

MARY, ALEX, AND FANNY: Who's Ike?

(*They laugh. Pause.*)

FANNY: I don't know about all of you, but I do have a sudden craving. A burning desire. Intense, painful longing. (*Beat*) For "Cool Whip."

(*Pause*)

ALEX AND MARY: Hmmmmmmm.

(*The ladies come downstage, grasp hands, and survey their prospects.*)

MARY: Ladies! Let us segue!

(*They disappear in a blaze of light.*)

Act Break

ACT TWO

(14) Fanmail from the Future

(*The ladies are fording a stream, their skirts hiked up.*)

FANNY: Ladies, we are in a strange new world. Where life as we know it is, well, not as we know it.

MARY: Treacherous underfoot. Careful on the bank.

ALEX: You will agree that trousers are eminently more sensible for situations like these.

MARY: Not at all.

FANNY: They'd be drenched. Damp for days at this altitude.

ALEX: You roll them up! You roll them up! You roll them up! You roll them up!

FANNY: Alexandra, collect yourself!

MARY: For all our sakes.

(*They have reached the other side and unhike their skirts.*)

ALEX: You cannot resist the future! It is futile! You must embrace it with all your heart!

FANNY: Alexandra. One has to accept the future. One doesn't have to embrace it.

ALEX: Pendejo!

MARY: Ladies, we are on the frontier of the future.

FANNY: I have always been a pioneer.

MARY: We have been encountering residue from the future. Flotsam from many different moments.

FANNY: "Fanmail" from the future.

MARY: What is "fanmail", Fanny?

FANNY: (*Osmosing*) Mash notes. Autographed glossies. Secret decoder rings.

MARY: Multiple mysteries!

(*A pathway of light. Objects appear in the air before them: a dazzling array of toys and junk and gadgets and souvenirs and appliances and electronic wonders, everything from an acid-pink hula hoop to a silver laser video disc.*)

(*The ladies gasp, delighted.*)

FANNY: "Fallout" from the future!

(*They begin to examine the objects, oooing and murmuring and clucking.*)

(FANNY *tries to osmose an odd toy.*)

FANNY: "Tweezer"! No. "Yo-yo"! No. "Mr. Coffee"! No. My osmos is not quite right.

(ALEX *follows suit.*)

ALEX: "Slot machine." "Juke box." "Squirt gun." "Brass knuckles."

(FANNY *finds a magazine.*)

FANNY: A tabloid *"The National Review"*. (*She puts it in her pack.*)

ALEX: "Ovaltine." "Bosco." "Double Bubble." "Velvee-eeta."

MARY: A rain forest of fossils from the future.

ALEX: Oh, look! A mini-dirigible! (*She reads the fine print on an inflatable banana.*) "Not to be used as a life preserver." Hmmmm.

(FANNY *peers into a side-view mirror from an automobile.*)

FANNY: "Objects in mirror may be closer than they appear"? Hmmmm. Well, Mary, here is your physical evidence. What do you make of it?

MARY: Ladies. We have the artifacts—

(*They hold up their artifacts, including egg beaters and buttons.* FANNY *and* ALEX *have been wearing their egg beaters like pistols.*)

MARY:—we must find their historical moment. Let us camp tonight in this—orchard of the future. Tomorrow we shall enter fully the era that awaits us.

FANNY: I hope with all my heart I shall be able to have a bath. And find a post office.

(ALEX *points at* MARY'*s Ike button.*)

ALEX: Ladies, let us not forget. "Ike" is waiting.

(FANNY *and* ALEX *rotor at one another.*)

JOURNAL ENTRY:

MARY: We spent the night in the future. Around us swirled a silent storm of images, a star shower of light from a new world.

(15) The Starry Deep

(*A starry night falls. The ladies pitch a gossamer canopy. They light lanterns. They write in their journals, each by her own light.*)

ALEX: Under a calliope of stars. Below the firmament. The glittering empyrean. The night above the dingle starry. (*Beat*) That's not mine. Damn this interference. (*Beat*) The vasty deep. The starry deep. (*Beat*) Under welkin.

MARY: Difficult to hack one's way through this thicket of voices from the future.

FANNY: Grover, my tender parsnip—shall I ever see you again?

MARY: Notes for a paper for the Boston Geo. I have tentatively dubbed this phenomenon we are experiencing—chronokinesis. (*Beat*) Fanny's tabloids will call it "time travel."

FANNY: Time travel is a tricky business, dear Grover. Beyond our ken.

MARY: Chronokinesis! Life membership in the Boston Geo. The Academy of Arts and Sciences. Honorary membership in the Royal Geo and Academie Française. Director of the Smithsonian. The first woman. The Nobel Prize in physics—

ALEX: My fellow polytopians are splendid and intrepid. Mary is excessively anecdotal, and Fanny scorns my lyrics.

FANNY: Mary and Alexandra are quite sweet, really. Appalling politics. Appalling. If we are detained in this country, I shall order them both a subscription to *The National Review*. I am quite certain you would adore *The National Review,* Grover. I do. It is the sole thing I've so far discovered in the future which reminds me of the nineteenth century.

ALEX: I foresee the day—it is exceedingly easy to foresee the day here—I foresee the day Fanny will eat her words. I shall secure an exclusive recording contract with a multinational conglomerate, and make consecutive gold records. (*Beat*) Note: meditate and osmose what those things are, exactly.

FANNY: The possibility exists that we shall not return, dear Grover. Certainly—in the northern hemisphere—one cannot simply go back and forth in time as one pleases. Time is not a revolving door. We have access to the future here. Do we have egress as well?

ALEX: We are beseiged by a barrage of fact. From here the future looks—

MARY: The future looks—

ALEX: The future looks positively—AMERICAN.

FANNY: Loud—

MARY:—invigorating. Quite promising, except, perhaps, for the theatre—

which threatens to degenerate into imitations of anthropological kinship studies.

FANNY: We ought to be approaching a post office. Of course, it is a verity that the tropical post will forever be a sink of inefficiency, world without end.

ALEX: I expect to publish these memoirs with an insert of Kodak reproductions. I adore Kodaking.

FANNY: Can the post office deliver to you, in 1889, a letter from me—some decades later? I know they can do it the other way round. That's commonplace.

MARY: I for one am looking forward to meeting this "Ike." "Ike" "Ike" "Ike." "Iko Iko." "Willy and the Hand Jive."

FANNY: Beyond our ken, dear Grover. Trust you are staying dry. All my love. From Terra Incognita to Terra Haute. Fanny.

(*As* MARY *and* FANNY *sleep,* ALEX *comes down and does her journal entry.*)

> ALEX: (*Taking a deep breath*) The rare air of the future. Breathe. Aspirate. Aspire. A—spire. (*She takes another deep breath.*) One of the ecstacies of hiking in the Himalayas was to crest a ridge, and suddenly confront the infinite surround. Mountains and rivers without end. Untouched. Glistening with possibility. We are climbing a spire of time. The topography of the future is coming into view. Unmapped and unnamed. Distant vistas shining. You must not shrink. You must embrace it with all your heart.

(16) Manna from Heaven—or, Among the Jesuits

(*Dawn. The ladies stir, take down the gossamer canopy.*)

FANNY: I slept not a wink.

MARY: Nor I.

ALEX: Nor I.

MARY: Fascinating as fire imagery. I long to learn more about "Willy and the Hand Jive."

FANNY: From what little I could fathom, the future seems a dubious prospect.

ALEX: (*A sudden transmission*) Beep!

FANNY: I beg your pardon.

ALEX: Wrong!

FANNY: Are you contradicting me, young lady?

ALEX: College bowl! State for twenty! The future is not a dubious prospect! The future is—just a bowl of cherries!

FANNY: Mary, we must locate a translator. Alexandra will soon be totally incomprehensible.

ALEX: Fanny, the future is now!

FANNY: Alexandra. (*Sighs*) I would elude the future, if I could.

ALEX: Fanny, you must embrace it with all your heart.

FANNY: Why? Why why why why why?

ALEX: Fanny, you sound like a broken record, a busy signal, a car alarm—

FANNY: Alexandra! (*Beat*) I must accept the future, Alexandra, as I accept the existence of cyclones and pit vipers and bad grammar. But you would have me embrace them?

ALEX: Yes!

FANNY: You would. Cyclones? Pit vipers? Bad grammar?

ALEX: In a way. Yes.

FANNY: You are a feckless child.

ALEX: And you, Fanny, you—are—so—so—so—SQUARE!

(*Pause*)

FANNY: I have seen the future. And it is slang.

(*Pause*)

MARY: It is uncommonly close this morning. I must put on a new face.

ALEX: I'll follow suit.

(MARY *and* ALEX *exit.*)

(FANNY *takes out her letter to* GROVER, *which has grown into a small volume. She calms herself by writing.*)

FANNY: Dearest Grover. Another addendum. As we home in on the future, I begin to feel curiously at ease, and happy. Content. We have been cantering along at a terrific clip. The future looms. (*Pause. She opens a music box. It plays.*) The future looms as steady and stable as a table top. I anticipate we shall find a year which suits me perfectly, and settle in for a long refreshment. I shall have a bath. There will be a post office. Oh, dear Grover—I feel we are on the verge of something grand.

(*An elegant gentleman in a beautiful white suit—*MR. COFFEE*—appears at the end of the path.* FANNY *is quite taken with him.*)

MR. COFFEE: Good afternoon, Madame.

FANNY: Sir.

(*He moves to her. He takes two cigarettes from a silver case, lights them, and gives one to her.*)

FANNY: Thank you. (*A little giddy*) And I don't even smoke. (*A sultry dual inhalation*) Oooo. In my day, sir, a lady did not smoke tobacco.

MR. COFFEE: Modern times, Fanny, modern times.

FANNY: Too true.

MR. COFFEE: How are you finding your travels?

FANNY: Trying.

MR. COFFEE: Worth the candle?

FANNY: Without question. (*Beat*) Are you Mr. Coffee?

MR. COFFEE: I've been called worse.

FANNY: I've had a premonition about meeting you.

MR. COFFEE: I'm sure you have.

FANNY: You are not of this era.

MR. COFFEE: No. Not exclusively.

FANNY: Much too well spoken. Let me tell you, Mr. Coffee—language takes a beating in the future.

MR. COFFEE: And that goes double for diction. These things are cyclical, my dear. Do not despair. What goes around, comes around.

FANNY: Is that a local proverb?

MR. COFFEE: One of my favorites. An airmail letter?

FANNY: "Air-mail"? How funny. If you say so.

MR. COFFEE: (*Without looking*) Terre Haute, 1889. Airmail part of the way. Then Pony Express.

FANNY: (*Laughs*) Terre Haute is not Indian Territory, Mr. Coffee. This letter is a long-running serialization by now. I must mail it before the cost of postage becomes absolutely prohibitive.

MR. COFFEE: Preserve it for posterity. A fascinating memoir. You wouldn't want people to forget.

FANNY: Oh, no, it's much too long to copy. I suppose I could edit out the personal parts.

MR. COFFEE: If you venture on into the future, you'll eventually come across something called a Xerox.

FANNY: Oh, zeeroxen, I've seen those in Greenland.

(*Pause*)

MR. COFFEE: There is no hope of Grover ever receiving your letter, Fanny.

FANNY: The postal system is worrisome, Mr. Coffee, but not yet hopeless.

(*Pause*)

(FANNY *understands.*)

FANNY: Do you know Grover?

MR. COFFEE: We've met.

FANNY: Recently?

MR. COFFEE: Seems like only yesterday. But I have no sense of time.

FANNY: How was he? Was he dry?

MR. COFFEE: Dry as toast. Frankly, he's been better. Bit of a cough. His wife was not unduly concerned.

FANNY: I'm his wife.

MR. COFFEE: His second wife. He had you declared legally dead, dear. Terre Haute Superior Court, 1910.

FANNY: That man.

MR. COFFEE: Remarried a few years later.

FANNY: He never minded being alone when we were married.

MR. COFFEE: The Great War made him anxious. And wealthy.

FANNY: I thought those were new shoes. He came to me, Mr. Coffee. In a dream. (*Beat*) He told me not to speculate on the future.

MR. COFFEE: In his own brokerish fashion, Grover was trying to say—so long.

FANNY: So long. So long. (*Beat*) When did you last see Grover, Mr. Coffee?

MR. COFFEE: Our one and only meeting. October, 1929.

(*Pause*)

FANNY: How—?

MR. COFFEE: He hurled himself off the top of a grain silo.

FANNY: Oh, dear.

MR. COFFEE: Part of a gentle rain of brokers who fell from heaven that autumn all over the country.

FANNY: I've been out of touch.

MR. COFFEE: Grover was speculating on the commodities market. Blue sky ventures. You know. Futures.

FANNY: Blue sky ventures. Did he miss me?

MR. COFFEE: Very much, once he realized you were never coming home from Terra Incognita. Less and less, over the years. He'd get a little misty on the seminal holidays. Christmas. Easter. Arbor Day. Each and every Arbor Day he'd have three or four peppermint schnapps, in your memory, and plant a bush in the back yard. (*Beat*) At heart, he wasn't surprised you never returned from Terra Incognita. He'd always suspected you'd disappear one day. Vanish without a trace.

FANNY: Yes. He was always rather taken aback whenever I walked through the front door. Well. Thank you, Mr. Coffee.

MR. COFFEE: My pleasure.

FANNY: Tell me, Mr. Coffee. Do you find it easy to foresee the future?

MR. COFFEE: I've never had any trouble.

FANNY: No. I don't suppose you would.

MR. COFFEE: But I confine myself to the basics.

FANNY: We will meet again, I trust.

MR. COFFEE: I feel certain of it.

FANNY: But not for many years.

MR. COFFEE: You never know. (*He takes her hand.*)

FANNY: I have been wanting to speak to you.

MR. COFFEE: Yes. Here I am, after all. (*Kisses her hand.*) A bien tot.

FANNY: Vaya con diós, Mr. Coffee.

MR. COFFEE: Charming. See you later. Alligator.

(*He exits. Passing* MARY *and* ALEX:)

MR. COFFEE: Ladies. (*He disappears.*)

MARY: Who on earth was that?

ALEX: (*Osmosing*) That was "Bebe Rebozo"!

FANNY: That was Mr. Coffee.

ALEX: Oh. Really. Sometimes this osmosing is wildly inaccurate.

MARY: The multiple possibilities of the future, dear. A man might be Mr. Coffee, or he might be Bebe Rebozo. What's his line?

FANNY: Prognostication. He had news. We're on the right track.

MARY: Splendid. Saddle up.

(ALEX *and* MARY *pick up their stuff and start off.*)

JOURNAL ENTRY:

FANNY: (FANNY, *after a moment, silently folds the letter, tucks it away, and closes the music box.*)

(17) Vintage Crystal

(*Moonlight. A beautiful unearthly snow begins to fall.*)

ALEX: What is that?

FANNY: Snow. Unless I miss my guess.

ALEX: Cold and wet on the tongue. Melts right off.

FANNY: Snow it is.

ALEX: Like no snow I've known before.

FANNY: A new snow. A strange snow. An unknown snow.

MARY: Lambent. Luminous.

ALEX: Snow from the moon, ladies!

FANNY: Yes!

MARY: Yes! Lunar snow is not annoying!

(ALEX *catches snow and tastes.*)

JOURNAL ENTRY:

ALEX: Lunar snow is, despite its apparent immaturity, a vintage precipitate. Coarser and sweeter than Himalayan, it stands up to all but the most robust Karakoram. Fruitier than Rocky Mountain powder, and a touch more acidic than Vermont sludge, it is altogether full-bodied and elusive. This is a young snow but not a callow snow, and should be confronted early—like the finest Hindu Kush—before the blush is off the slush, and the bloom is gone.

(18) Woody's Esso

(*Music:* "Rock Around the Clock" *playing on a radio. A gas pump and an Esso sign appear. Music fades out.*)

ALEX: Civilization.

MARY: The outskirts.

FANNY: How far our standards have fallen.

ALEX: If I were wearing trousers at this moment, I would change.

FANNY: (*An outburst*) You needn't suck up to me, Alexandra!

MARY: Fanny! Is that a vulgarity?

(*A pause*)

FANNY: I am sorry, Alexandra. I plead the future.

ALEX: I understand.

FANNY: You needn't mollify me, is what I meant. It seems to me that you were right.

ALEX: How nice. About what, dear Fanny?

FANNY: Trousers. Trousers trousers trousers. It seems clear to me that everyone in the future wears 'em. I am so glad I shan't live to see it. Of course, I am seeing it. I am so flummoxed. I wonder if we will remember all this when we return home.

MARY: If we return home.

(*A palanquin, with its shades drawn, rolls on. On it, a sign: The Dragon Lady, Fortunes Told, Palms Read, Charts, Crystal Ball, Tarot Cards, Etc.*)

MARY: I know what that is—

ALEX: A "hot rod."

MARY: A palanquin.

FANNY: Honestly, Alexandra, how quickly you've forgotten our own era.

MARY: Do you realize that palanquin is now an antique?

FANNY: So are we, my dear, so are we.

MARY: But what is it doing here? (*Indicates gas pump*) And what is that? And who is The Dragon Lady?

FANNY: Warrants investigation.

(*They start forward. A hand with long painted fingernails pulls back the shade suddenly, startling the ladies. It is* MADAME NHU, *who is wearing a beautiful if slightly ferocious half-mask. The eyes of the mask are Asian, the cheekbones high, and she wears a wig of long, jet-black hair. The effect is at once feminine and frightening. She looks them over. Her voice is low* (*not falsetto*), *and she speaks with a slight accent, both French and Asian.*)

MME. NHU: Come closer. Let me scrutinize you.

(*They approach cautiously.* MME. NHU *holds up a hand. They stop. After a moment, she begins to speak.*)

MME. NHU: Serious trouble will pass you by. Your mind is filled with new ideas—make use of them. He who does not accept cash when offered is no businessman. You are worrying about something that will never happen. Your talents will be recognized and suitably rewarded. You will never need to worry about a steady income. Soon you will be sitting on top of the world. The night life is for you. Praise your wife, even if it frightens her. You have an unusual equipment for success, be sure to use it properly. Be as soft as you can be and as hard as you have to be. Someone is speaking well of you. A new diet or exercise program can be unusually beneficial for you now. An unpleasant situation will soon be cleared to your satisfaction. Read more fine books and better magazines. Avoid fried foods, which angry up the blood. Let them eat barbecue!

(*A pause*)

(*The ladies look at one another.*)

(MME. NHU *thrusts out a plate with three fortune cookies on it. They each take a cookie.*)

MME. NHU: Let me tell you secret. The future is now. (*She pulls the shade and disappears.*)

ALEX: That was an image.

MARY: An oracle.

FANNY: An inscrutable pancake.

ALEX: What are these? (*Osmoses*) "Fortune cookies"!

MARY: No smell.

FANNY: No taste.

ALEX: Edible?

FANNY: Definitely not.

MARY: (*Breaks hers open.*) Inside—a scrap of paper.

ALEX: (*Likewise*) A message.

FANNY: (*Likewise*) Fanmail from some flounder.

(*They read their messages.*)

ALEX: You will become rich and famous.

FANNY: You will meet a tall dark stranger.

MARY: You will go on a long journey.

ALEX: This is exhilarating!

(*She approaches the palanquin, steps on an invisible rubber-tube gas station bell. It chimes: ding-dong, ding-dong.*)

(*A sign flies in: Woody's Esso.*)

(GUS, *a fresh-faced American teenager, appears, wearing a baseball cap and chewing gum. Boundless energy.*)

GUS: Hi! What'll it be? Hey! Wow! Gosh! Hello!

FANNY: Greetings, young man, from President McTaft.

GUS: Swell feathers and fancy duds! You ladies look kinda like Kitty! Golly! You goin' to the prom or what! Gosh!

ALEX: Kitty?

GUS: Didja watch *Gunsmoke* last night? Or *Cimarron City*?

ALEX: Kitty?

GUS: Kitty see she runs the saloon and she's in love with Marshal Dillon who's the sheriff but he'll never marry her 'cause he's a bachelor—see *Bachelor Father*?

FANNY: My dear boy, a bachelor father is a paradox. An oxymoron. A contradiction in terms.

ALEX: Ladies—the future.

FANNY: (*Snorts*) Bachelor father. Mary, you have found your niche. Your prurient interest in anthropological smut should stand you in good stead. Bachelor father.

MARY: Oh, Fanny. Let us introduce ourselves.

ALEX: I'm Alexandra. This is Mary—

MARY: Hello, young man.

ALEX: And this is Fanny.

GUS: Hi! Hi! Hi! I'm Gus!

ALEX: Good afternoon, Gus.

GUS: Great! Wow, you ladies are kooky, no offense.

ALEX: How nice of you to say so.

FANNY: Gus, we are so very pleased to meet you. You are the first person we have encountered in our travels with a reasonable accent and an acceptable demeanor.

GUS: Lucky for me, huh? You ladies broke down somewhere? I don't see your eggbeater. Say, who do you like in the Series? The Dodgers or the Yanks?

(*Pause. Finally,* ALEX *smiles sweetly and says judiciously:*)

ALEX: Whom do you like?

GUS: I like the Dodgers.

ALEX: Then so do I.

GUS: Great!

MARY: Gus, dear, tell us about the palanquin.

ALEX: About the Dragon Lady.

MARY: A lady of ferocious aspect.

GUS: Madame Nhu.

ALEX: Madame Who?

ALEX: Madame Who?

GUS: Madame Nhu. She rents a parking space from Woody.

GUS: Just showed up one day. Out of the blue.

FANNY: Gus, dear, what year is it?

GUS: You don't know?! Come off it.

ALEX: We do not know. Honestly. It's hard to explain.

GUS: 1955. Everybody knows that.

ALEX: We don't.

GUS: Gee, I'm sorry. I'd give you a calendar—(*Blushes*) but they're not for girls. (*Beat*) Hey, you guys are kidding me. Huh? Huh? Come on, lay off. Just 'cause I'm a teenager.

MARY: What's a teenager?

FANNY: What's an Esso?

GUS: Esso is service, parts and dependability. So you're tourists, huh? I thought you had to be, I woulda remembered *you*.

MARY: Travelers, not tourists.

ALEX: Polytopians. Travelers to many lands.

FANNY: Charting the unknown.

MARY: Geography, cartography, ethnology, and the natural sciences.

GUS: Great. I could use a vacation myself. You need anything? Soda, gum, roadmaps, oil? Chiclets?

ALEX: I would like a "Chiclet", please.

GUS: Take two, they're small.

(GUS *gives* ALEX *some Chiclets. She examines them, pops them into her mouth, and chews.*)

GUS: Where you ladies from?

MARY: We are traveling through time, Gus.

GUS: You dames are some kidders. No? You mean it? You're on the level? Wow! Like you're from another time?! Another dimension?! PARALLEL UNIVERSE?! Wait'll I tell my Dad! I saw this show—(*Beat as he looks them over.*) Wow, so this is how they dress in history! Gee! Do you wanna come to my social studies class? So, do you believe in UFOs?

ALEX: Chiclets are sweet and tough, like dried manioc.

FANNY: Ah, Gus. We are looking for someone. Perhaps you know him.

ALEX: Ike.

MARY: Perhaps you've heard of him.

GUS: Ike who?

ALEX: We do not know his surname.

MARY: We found his name on this button.

GUS: Nicky might know. He knows everybody.

(MARY *hands* GUS *the button.*)

GUS: Ho ho.

FANNY: You know this Ike.

GUS: Yeah, sure I know this Ike. Hangs out at the station. Wants to be a grease monkey in his spare time. I'm showing him the ropes. You guys. Whatta buncha kidders.

ALEX: You don't know him?

GUS: My dad voted for him. Come on. What are ya, gonna vote for that other clown, the Chicago egghead? "I Like Ike." Great.

ALEX: Do you like Ike, Gus?

GUS: My dad likes him! I betcha Nicky knows this Ike. 'Sides, you wanna stay there while you're in Peligrosa, doncha? Hold on, let me draw you a map. (*He disappears.*)

ALEX: Mary! Fanny! Facts!

FANNY: Chronological and geographical. We are in Peligrosa!

MARY: In the vicinity of 1955!

ALEX: Perhaps 1955 is the apotheosis of the future!

FANNY: This Ike must be a local Poobah!

ALEX: We shall palaver.

(GUS *reappears, with a map.*)

GUS: Okay, dokey, here's directions to Nicky's.

MARY: Is it far?

GUS: Just a hop skip and a jump. We're giving these away with a full tank. But for you guys—it's on the house.

(GUS *hands* MARY *an egg beater of yet a third design.*)

MARY: Marvelous! A matched set!

ALEX: Ladies! Whip them out!

(Fanny *and* Alex *whip out their egg beaters. They all rotor and laugh. From this point on, the* Ladies *always wear their eggbeaters.*)

Gus: You collect 'em?!? I'd give you green stamps, but Woody'd kill me if—

Fanny: Gus, dear, does this Nicky fellow have a bath?

Gus: Nicky's—are you kidding? Does he have a bath? Are you kidding? He's got everything! He'll probably put you up. Wait'll you see the set-up at Nicky's. You are gonna flip!

Fanny: Hooper Do! (*She grabs the map.*) Gus, my undying devotion. Ladies—dog my heels.

Alex: Adieu, Gus.

Gus: See you later, alligator.

Mary: Thank you, Gus. Perhaps we'll pass this way again.

Gus: After awhile, crocodile.

Mary: Ah, Gus! The Mighty Silurian!

Gus: Whatever you say, lady. Give Nicky some skin for me.

Mary: Whatever you say, Gus.

(Gus *exits.*)

(*Traveling music throbs: The theme from* Peter Gunn. *The ladies travel. They reach a spot, and huddle around a map.*)

Mary: X marks the spot.

(Peter Gunn *fades away.*)

Alex: Have we misread it?

Fanny: Impossible. But perhaps we've passed it.

Alex: My eyes were peeled.

Fanny: In time. Perhaps we've passed it in time. Perhaps it was here once. But now it's gone.

Mary: I think not. I have an unshakable conviction we have come to the center of 1955.

Alex: Smack dab in the middle.

Mary: Well said, Alex.

Fanny: If the map's right, and the time's right, where the devil is this Nicky fellow? I'll horsewhip anyone who stands between me and a hot bath.

Alex: I broke up a knife fight with a whip once. Oh, yes I did. Two sherpas were vying for a place by the fire.

(*Strains of Big Band music.*)

MARY: Do you hear that music?

FANNY: A mynah bird escaped from a cocktail lounge.

ALEX: Fanny, you redefine pessimism. What is a "cocktail lounge"?

FANNY: Osmose it yourself.

ALEX: (*Osmosing*) "Happy Hour"!

(*A loud burst of Big Band music.*)

MARY: Ladies—I believe we're on the verge!

(*All three ladies do journal entry in unison.*)

ALEX, MARY, AND FANNY: We arrive in '55!

(19) Paradise '55

(*Lights! A flashy sign, neon:* NICKY'S. *Some palm trees and streamers: A gaudy, prerevolutionary Havana-style nightclub.*)

(NICKY *rolls on with a piano and live mike. Does a splashy finish.*)

NICKY: Vaya! Vaya! Vaya! Con! Diós! Wo Wo Wo Wo Wo—yeaaaaaah! Pow!

(*The ladies applaud.*)

NICKY: You're too kind.

(*Checks them out.*)

NICKY: My my my my my my my. Holy cow. What have we here. Our humble joint. Nicky's Peligrosa Paradise Bar and Grill. Graced by style, beauty, pulchritude and wit. Hi, I'm Nicky Paradise. Welcome to paradise—where hospitality still means something.

ALEX: (*Instantly smitten*) O brave new world, that has such creatures in it!

FANNY: Alex, you are a terrible plagiarist.

MARY: Instantly smitten.

NICKY: Make yourselves at home. (*His best smile*) Mi casa es su casa! (*Reprise—best smile*) My house is your house. Toss back a coupla stiff ones, grab a bite, cool out in the casino, catch a show, let your hair down, loosen your corsets—

MARY, FANNY, AND ALEX: Mr. Nicky!

NICKY: Please. Nicky.

ALEXANDRA: Alexandra Cafuffle.

FANNY: Mrs. Cranberry. You may call me Fanny.

NICKY: It would break my heart if I couldn't.

MARY: Mary Baltimore. From Boston.

NICKY: Such tropicana, such feminality. Overwhelmed, truly.

(He dashes to the piano and plays and sings a phrase of "Bad Boy.")

NICKY: "I'm just a bad boy-oy-oy-oy-oy-oy-oy-oy-oy-oy-oy—
All dressed up in fancy clothes
I am takin' the trouble
To blow all my bubbles away."

ALEX: Mr. Paradise!

NICKY: Nicky.

FANNY: Mr. Paradise—

NICKY: Nicky, Nicky, Nicky!

FANNY: Nicky, Nicky, Nicky. I hope you won't think me indelicate—

NICKY: Never.

FANNY: —but I simply must have a scrub immediately. Post haste. It's been eons. Can you arrange for me to have a bath?

NICKY: For you, Fanny—a whirlpool. (*He snaps his fingers and plays the piano. A light appears.*) Follow that light, Fanny. Don't be stingy with the bubbles. That's what they're there for.

FANNY: Bubbles. I won't ask. I'll just hold my nose and dive in. Ladies.

(*She exits.*)

(NICKY *sings and plays after her:* "Vaya Con Diós My Darling/Vaya Con Diós My Love.")

MARY: Nicky's Peligrosa Paradise Bar and Grill?

NICKY: Be there or—(*Smiles his best smile*) be square.

(MARY *holds out her button.*)

MARY: Perhaps you can shed some light.

NICKY: Oh yeah. I like Ike. Who doesn't?

MARY: Who don't?

NICKY: Have it your way, Mary. I'm easy.

MARY: I like Ike. Heck, who don't?

NICKY: Hardly anybody.

(MARY *pulls out the original button she found on the beach.*)

MARY: Indeed. "Heckwhodon't?" Heck—who—don't. It's a companion button. I like Ike. Heck, who don't?

NICKY: You're sharp. Need a job?

ALEX: Brava, Mary! I love a good mystery, don't you?

(MARY *pins the buttons on* ALEX.)

MARY: Do you know him? Gus said you might.

ALEX: We would very much like to meet him.

MARY: He has become a point of some interest with us.

ALEX: Do you know this Ike?

NICKY: We're like this. Never vacations anywhere but Nicky's. He and Mamie are nuts about the joint. He's gonna make Nicky's a national monument.

ALEX: Is he in residence at present?

NICKY: Yeah, he's in back, smoking a cigar. I'll take you around.

ALEX: Oh, goody. I'll Kodak him for posterity!

NICKY: You'll like Ike. Everybody does. He's a likeable guy. Plays a fair round of golf. No duffer, Ike. You play?

MARY: The Scottish game? No. Speaking of games, am I correct in understanding that there is a gambling emporium on the premises?

NICKY: The casino. First rate. Slap a little blackjack, shoot some craps, spin the wheel, pull some slots, float a check. Whatever.

MARY: Gambling provides a fascinating study in cross-cultural comparisons. For instance, did you know that the Ute Indians of the American West are avid gamblers, and will wager their life's possessions on a single throw of the dice?

NICKY: No, I did not know that. Did you know that the Nevada looney bins are full of catatonic blue-haired ladies going like this? (*He demonstrates: catatonic slot-machine addicts plus sound effects.*)

MARY: No, I did not. Fascinating. I do not indulge, personally, of course, but with your permission, I should like to take notes.

(NICKY *hands her some chips.*)

NICKY: Have a ball, Mar'—knock yourself out.

(*He snaps his fingers, plays the piano. A light appears.*)

MARY: Not annoying! (*She follows the light. As she is about to exit, she turns;*) Ah, Nicky. Gus said to give you some of his skin.

NICKY: Thanks, doll.

(*She exits.* NICKY *plays, sings after her:* "There Goes My Baby/Movin' On Down the Line.")

(*He turns his attentions to* ALEX)

NICKY: Great kid, Gus.

ALEX: He drew us a map. That is how we located you.

NICKY: No, it's not.

ALEX: I beg your pardon.

NICKY: I said, that's not how you came to Nicky's, Al.

ALEX: Are you contradicting me?

NICKY: It wasn't a map that brought you to me, Al. It was—(*Best smile*) Kismet.

ALEX: I don't understand.

NICKY: You were destined to come to Nicky's.

ALEX: Perhaps you're right. I do have a positive feeling about 1955. It's—it's—it's—*keen*!

NICKY: I'm having a great year. So you stopped at Woody's. See the Dragon Lady?

ALEX: Madame Nhu?

NICKY: Madame Nhu. She's usually parked out front, filing her foot-long nails.

ALEX: Lovely palanquin.

NICKY: Isat what it is? I thought it was a chopped Chevy. Ike should be done with his cigar now. Want to meet him?

ALEX: Desperately.

(NICKY *snaps his fingers plays the piano. A light.*)

NICKY: Second door on the right. Knock three times. If Mamie answers, come back. We'll do it later.

ALEX: At long last, Ike! I'm off to meet the Ike! Ta! Ike get a kick out of you! Ike, can't get you out of my mind!

NICKY: Hold your hula hoops! Al, you aren't, by any chance, a lyricist?

ALEX: How did you guess?

NICKY: I can spot talent! I could use a good word jockey. Meet me in the lounge later. We'll pen some tunes. I have a lucrative new contract to script some billboards for Burma Shave.

ALEX: Fantastic! I've been dying to know what Burma Shave is.

NICKY: Al, I told you. Kismet.

ALEX: Ike can't get no satisfaction!

(*She exits. As* NICKY *styles on the piano* FANNY *enters, resplendent and transformed in 50's cocktail dress and blonde wig, still wearing eggbeater.*)

NICKY: Holy smokes! I have not seen duds like that since High-School Confidential.

(*He sweeps* FANNY *off her feet.*)

NICKY: What do you say we trip the light fantastic?

(*They do a slow romantic dance to Duke Ellington's* Dual Highway, NICKY *showing* FANNY *some sharp moves.* FANNY *grows more confident with every step. By the end of the dance, they are falling in love. They finish the dance and go to the table.*)

NICKY: Fred and Ginger have nothing on us—nothing! (*Gets intimate.*) Say, do you remember those little Danny Boone hats with the wacky raccoon tails?

FANNY: I'm afraid not.

NICKY: They were a gas. How was the whirlpool?

(*After a sensuous pause,* FANNY *says:*)

FANNY: Wow—wow—wow! Captivating. All those little jets of water were—quite—mesmerizing. I feel light-headed. Swoozy all over. (*Beat*) Jacuzzi all over.

NICKY: I don't follow you.

FANNY: Your whirlpool is called a jacuzzi. Or will be.

NICKY: I like the sound of that. Jacuzz'.

FANNY: Your establishment is uncanny. A veritable pleasure dome.

NICKY: I like to think of it that way.

(*She pulls out one of her postcards.*)

FANNY: It's just like my postcard.

NICKY: Hey! Where did you get this? These are sharp!

FANNY: I brought it with me. It's a postcard from the future. Of Nicky's. The view come true! Generic nightspot.

NICKY: Like I always say, Fanny—the future is now. I'm gonna put 'em in all the rooms with the Gideon Bibles.

FANNY: Mister Paradise—

NICKY: Hey, I'm gonna get cross wit' you—

FANNY: Nicky. Since we've been in the vicinity of 1955, there's something I've had a craving for—

NICKY: Please. Say no more.

(*He prestidigitates a huge glass goblet and two spoons. As* FANNY *closes her eyes—*)

FANNY: I am agog with anticipation.

(He holds the goblet under her nose. She inhales deeply, with ecstasy, and slowly opens her eyes.)

FANNY: Cool Whip!

NICKY: The Real McCoy.

(He hands her a spoon. They each dish out a spoonful of Cool Whip. They lock eyes. They lock arms, as though drinking champagne. They raise the spoons to their lips.)

NICKY: Here's to you—Fanny.

(They clink spoons. They take a bite. A dazzled pause.)

FANNY: Oh! good!

(Freeze. Music swells. NICKY *and* FANNY *exit.)*

*(*ALEX *enters and does journal entry.)*

ALEX: *(Formally, still, a bit out of rhythm, and trying to snap her fingers, perhaps using* NICKY*'s mike.)*
On the go or at the beach
After hours or safe at home
For a cheek as smooth as a Georgia peach
You need the shave that's like a poem—
Burma Shave!

(20) Later That Same Evening

*(*ALEX *moves to the table and examines Cool Whip.)*

ALEX: *(Osmoses)* "Mo hair". No. "Jello mold". No. *(Tastes)* Noxema! Yes! Heaven!

*(*MARY *enters, to a swirl of music, tipsy and exhilarated.)*

MARY: I have experienced an epiphany in the casino. I beat the one-armed bandit, kid! As they say here in 1955. Look!

(She pours a cascade of nickles out of her helmet onto the table.)

ALEX: Fantastic! I love the future!

MARY: And how did you do, Alexandra? Did you run the elusive Ike to ground? Tree him? Beard him in his lair?

ALEX: Mamie answered.

MARY: You'll collar him tomorrow. Quite a card, Ike. Una tarjeta, en español. Not many people know that.

ALEX: And how do you know that?

MARY: A bulletin from the future.

ALEX: What else does your bulletin tell you about Ike?

(MARY *osmoses.*)

MARY: He is a poobah of the first water. Golf clubs. Cardigan sweaters. (*Rubs her head.*) Cue ball.

ALEX: Cue ball?

MARY: (*With great dignity*)
"He has got a cue ball head that is hard as lead—
But he is all right with me.
Wo wo."

ALEX: Mary.

MARY: It is extraordinary what blossoms in one's brain in this country. That is from something called—(*Osmoses*) "Rock and roll."

ALEX: "Rock and roll." . . . Whomp bop a lula a wombat too!

(*She then scats the guitar part to the Surfari's* WIPEOUT!, *doing 50's rock moves, and ending with a big finish.*)

ALEX: Wombat!

MARY: My. Osmosing the future is far more strenuous than navigating the upper reaches of the Congo.

ALEX: The January 1955 *Variety* magazine says rock and roll will be gone by June. Oh! What month are we?

MARY: I've no idea.

ALEX: I hope it's not June. I am dieting to rock and roll. I mean determined. Not dieting.

MARY: Hello, what's this? Manioc? (*She takes a spoonful of Cool Whip.*)

ALEX: Noxema.

MARY: Have you tried it? (*She smears some on her face.*)

ALEX: Mmm. The texture is indescribable.

MARY: (*Takes a big bite—savors*) Why, this is sheer heaven, Alexandra.

(FANNY *floats on, now in a tight evening dress, looking blowzy and wonderful, still wearing her eggbeater.*)

FANNY: More than sheer heaven, Mary. Paradise.

ALEX: You look the cat that swallowed the canary.

FANNY: We were dancing!

ALEX: Really.

FANNY: Nicky is a divine dancer.

ALEX: Have some Noxema.

FANNY: Cool Whip!

ALEX: Oh!

MARY: So this is Fanny's Cool Whip!

FANNY: Luscious, isn't it? I had the most extraordinary experience earlier this evening in a celestial contraption called a jacuzzi.

MARY: You should have seen the ecdysiastical "floor show" in the casino. The natives call it *Girls A Poppin'!* As fascinating as fire. From an anthropological point of view. Reminiscent of the vernal fertility rites in Sumatra, which always culminated in a riot of gymnastic—

FANNY: Mary, spare us your salacious anthropological details.

MARY: Remarkably supple. A cornucopia of concupiscence.

ALEX: Ladies—get a load of this! I am osmosing jingles like crazy! (*She licks a finger, presses it to her hip, makes a sizzling sound, and uses* NICKY's *mike.*)
Okay, tiger, striped and brave
A close clean scrape is what you crave
To fashion's whim you are no slave
You take it off—with Burma Shave!

FANNY: Wow! Wow! Wow!

ALEX: Jingles are the art form of the future!

FANNY: Why do they call it Burma Shave? What's it got to do with Burma?

MARY: I've been to Burma.

FANNY: As have I.

ALEX: The future is not dull!

FANNY: This is not the future, Alexandra. This is 1955.

MARY: Not annoying!

FANNY: Not bad! And that jacuzzi is really something.

(ALEX *dishes out a spoonful of Cool Whip. The others follow suit.*)

ALEX: To the future!

MARY: To us!

ALEX: To yetis and dirigibles—

FANNY: Jacuzzis—

MARY: To our adventures, many more!

ALEX: And here's to the elusive Ike!

(*They all clink spoons.*)

ALL: Cheers! Ike!

(*They all take a bite. A dazzled pause.*)

ALL: Oh, good!

(*Lights change.* FANNY *and* ALEX *exit.* MARY *comes downstage and does her journal entry.*)

MARY: The pleasures of Nicky's Peligrosa Paradise Bar and Grill were—philharmonic. I blossomed into—I almost blush to recall it—a bonafide voluptuary, sampling an assortment of what were called, in the native parlance, 'leisure-time activities'. Re-creation. The casino was an anthropologist's field day, an anthology of human mis-demeanor. It's fascinating as fire floorshow, *Girls-A-Poppin'!*, held, I felt, the key to the culture, and was worth years of intense scrutiny. Television proved an addictive, if ultimately incomprehensible, hypnotic. And I thought the jacuzzi the greatest piece of engineering since the wheel. In short, I went, as the topical lingo had it, on a "bender." (*Beat*)

The Byzantine pleasures of Nicky's intoxicate—but do not satiate. I flash and yearn for adventures beyond the jacuzzi.

(21) Go-Go Boots—or, Rock and Roll Is Here To Stay

(FANNY *and* ALEX *enter. It is some months later:* FANNY *is wearing a sensible 50's sun dress and* ALEX *is dressed in pedal pushers, carrying a surfboard.* FANNY *has a picnic basket and cooler. Both wear eggbeaters.*)

ALEX: (*To* FANNY) I've yet to catch a glimpse of him. That Mamie guards him like a gryphon.

FANNY: Perhaps Ike is a yeti.

ALEX: Mary—look what I found! Surfboard!

MARY: What is the cultural application of a surfboard, Alexandra?

ALEX: Hang ten. Shoot the pipeline. Curl the Big Kahuna.

MARY: Whatever you say, Alex.

(FANNY *pulls out a pair of white boots.*)

FANNY: Alexandra may have her surfboard, but I have my "go-go boots". A white ceremonial shoe. Worn while mashing potatoes, riding ponies, and palavering with the Watusi.

MARY: I've found a tile. (*She holds up a green tile.*)

FANNY: Terra cotta?

MARY: Congoleum.

FANNY: Congoleum. What's it got to do with the Congo?

MARY: I know not.

FANNY: I've been to the Congo.

MARY: As have I.

ALEX: Mary, you are the ginchiest. Hang in there.

MARY: I shall. I shall hang in there. I owe you a great debt, Alexandra.

ALEX: No prob, Mar'. No sweat. No skin off my nose.

FANNY: Alexandra. Only a moment in 1955, and already your language is beyond redemption.

ALEX: Loosen your living girdle, Fanny.

MARY: Ah, Alexandra, how are your jingles?

ALEX: I've given them up for rock and roll.

FANNY: A fleeting fad.

ALEX: Fanny, rock 'n roll is here to stay. So, when's the shindig?

MARY: Shindig?

FANNY: I believe she means the authentic suburban charred meat festival you promised us.

MARY: Ah, yes. The bar-be-cue.

ALEX: Yes, what are we having—barbecued manioc?

FANNY: I am so excited. I haven't set foot outside the Paradise since our arrival.

(MARY *picks up her pack, which is fully rigged out for trekking.*)

FANNY: Mary! Where on Earth is this picnic? You have enough gear for a trek.

MARY: I have discovered within myself a new world. A voluptuousness which astounds me with its magenta sunsets, its incarnadine passions, its indigo fevers, tropical storms, and throbbing scarlet heart. Having discovered my voluptuous inclination, I have no intention of leaving it unexplored. Ladies—the future beckons! Don't you see? What we all need is further adventures!

ALEX: Oh, Mary, yes!

FANNY: Might be nice. A few days trek. See something of the hinterlands.

MARY: I had in mind going on.

ALEX: Oh, I don't want to go back.

MARY: Not back. On.

FANNY: I adore 1955. It would break my heart to leave. (*Beat*) I love this. The occasional barbecue. (*Beat*) Entre nous—we're engaged!

MARY AND ALEX: Oh, Fanny!

FANNY: Thank you. We are very happy. The night Nicky popped the question, I was agog with anticipation. Yes I said yes yes oh yes I will my mountain flower as well you as another my flower of Andalusia and the pink and blue and yellow houses—(*Stops herself*) Goodness.

ALEX: What will Grover say?

FANNY: Ah, Grover, dear Grover, my tender parsnip. Grover will have apoplexy. You know, I can scarcely recall what Grover looks like. His face is fading from my memory like a hand-tinted picture postcard. I never told you. Grover passed on in 1929. Did away with himself, poor dear. Despondent over pork belly futures.

MARY: Poor Fanny. How do you know?

FANNY: Mr. Coffee told me. That man. Did you know he had me declared legally dead?

ALEX: No!

MARY: Well, three cheers for you, Fanny. (*Turns to* ALEX) Alex? There are new worlds out there. Where the air is rare.

ALEX: I have a date. I'm writing tunes with the Gorge Troll. We've got an offer from the House O' Hits. They want to buy our new number, *Mind Your Own Beeswax*. Then we're going for a spin on his chopper. Now that I know what a chopper is.

(*Pause*)

MARY: It seems a shame to break up the team.

ALEX: You don't have to.

(*Pause*)

MARY: Perhaps we are meant to be solo sojourners after all.

(*Pause*)

FANNY: I'll go scout out a spot to fire up the briquets.

ALEX: I'll follow suit.

(*As they leave:*)

FANNY: Are you reading your subscription to *The National Review*?

ALEX: Troll and I are writing tunes. I haven't time for arcane political journals.

FANNY: Not arcane. Germane.

ALEX: That's not a true rhyme. But it's not bad.

FANNY: High praise.

(*They're gone.*)

(*Nicky's Peligrosa disappears as* MARY *comes downstage and does her journal entry.*)

MARY: My brain is full of exhilirating bulletins. On the horizon, a transcendent light flashes off the spires of the future. This New World is a garden. Splendors and wonders, marvels and mysteries. Miracles which top even Cool Whip.

(22) The Geography of Yearning

(ALEX *enters, in motorcycle leathers.*)

ALEX: Nothing shall ever replace Cool Whip in my affections. So. You're really going?

MARY: Yes.

ALEX: Seems a shame.

MARY: I'm restless. Wanderlust. You know.

ALEX: I have a faint recollection. (*Beat*) I do feel a tug. But I belong here.

MARY: This is what you wanted. The Show Business.

ALEX: It's Kismet. Here in 1955 is my brilliant career. I am part of the entertainment industry.

MARY: Good for you.

ALEX: I am wanton.

MARY: Alex.

ALEX: I mean weepy. Not wanton.

(*They embrace.* FANNY *enters, dressed for bowling.*)

FANNY: You're still here. Thank goodness. Alexandra, what a get up.

(ALEX *shoots a look at* FANNY'S *own get-up.*)

MARY: Dear Fanny.

FANNY: I do have a bit of a hankering to hit the trail with you, old friend. But 1955 suits me. To a T-Bird. Nicky is such a—dancer.

MARY: Will you invite Ike to the wedding?

FANNY: Entre nous, he's Nicky's best man.

ALEX: Goody! I'll Polaroid him for posterity.

(NICKY *enters, also ready to bowl a few frames.*)

NICKY: Fan, you look sensational, doll. Al, I ran your latest lyric up the flagpole, and I saluted, sweetheart, Mar'.

MARY: Nick'.

NICKY: And I used to think you had no sense of humor.

MARY: Live and learn.

NICKY: I sure will. So, what's the word, thunderbird?

MARY: Mr. Nicky, your emporium is most enticing. The sirens seduce.

NICKY: They really wail, don't they?

MARY: But I have strapped myself to the mast, and must sail on.

NICKY: When you gotta go, you gotta go. (*He hands her a container of Cool Whip.*) A little pick-me-up for the open road. You're not gonna find a lot of St. Bernards with Cool Whip in their kegs. Happy trails.

MARY: Oh, Nicky. Congratulations.

NICKY: Fanny spilled the beans, huh?

MARY: I think so.

NICKY: Sorry you won't be here for the big day.

MARY: I shall be here in spirit.

NICKY: So long. Just remember the immortal words of Satchel Paige. Don't look back—something might be gaining on you.

MARY: Ah, the sage Satchel Paige. He also said, to keep the juices flowing, jangle around gently as you move.

NICKY: I'll keep it in mind.

MARY: Sound advice. I intend to follow it to the letter.

ALEX: Mary. Before you go. You must give us the lowdown on the future.

MARY: I've only had glimpses, mind you. Flashes. Bits of light.

(*She osmoses, uttering each new word as if it were being spoken for the very first time. Coining place names for a map of the New World:*)

MARY: Electric eyes. Automatic tellers. TV dinners. And that's just the beginning.

Trailer parks. Mobile homes. Home economics.

O! Revolving credit! Spinoffs. Tax shelters, Subsidiary rights. Offshore banking. Venture capital. Residuals.

Non-dairy creamer. Non-profit foundations. No-fault insurance.

Pot stickers. Nehru jackets. Lava lamps. Day glo. Black light. The Peace Corps. Soul music. The Fab Four. Fern bars. Fondue. Free love. Romanian Cabernet Sauvignon.

Disposable income. Significant others. Mood elevators.

Mood rings. Mud wrestling. Super stars. Floating anchors. Guest hosts. Low riders.

Slam dancing. Soft ware. Prime time. Time sharing. Word processors. Double speak. Hyper space. Holograms.

Aura cleansing. Angelic intervention. Pace makers. Walk mans. Synthesizers. Ghetto blasters. 45's. Saturday Night Specials.

Pulsars. Fiber optics. Remote control. Double think. Think tanks. The Domino Theory. The Third World. Boat people. Heavy water. Enhanced radiation. Silly Putty. Patty melts. Melt down. Ground zero.

Fellow travelers.

Windows of vulnerability.

(*Pause*)

FANNY: Fellow travelers, yes, yes, yes, yes, yes we are, yes!

ALEX: And vulnerable windows! Marvelous!

MARY: Ladies, what do you say we have one last rotor? Just—one for the road, as it were?

FANNY: Splendid idea.

(*Egg beaters appear.*)

FANNY: Ready?

ALEX: Set?

MARY: Rotor!

(*They rotor vigorously. A good long rotor and a good long laugh.*)

(*Finished,* MARY *steps downstage, whips off her long Victorian skirt—*)

ALEX: Mary!

FANNY: Nicky, don't look!

(*—With a flourish. Underneath, she is wearing trousers.*)

ALEX: Brava, Mary!

MARY: I told you, Alexandra, I owe you a great debt.

ALEX: Intrepid trekking. Perhaps our paths will cross again, at some caravanserai of the future.

MARY: I feel certain of it. Our parabolas will intersect once more.

(*Sound of an enormous unmufflered motorcycle pulling up outside.*)

ALEX: That's Troll. Gotta go. Ciao.

FANNY: Dig you on the flip side.

(*She exits. Motorcycle roars off.*)

MARY: Mr. Nicky, thank you for everything.

(*She shakes his hand, and turns it into a hip handshake.*)

NICKY: Hey, hey, hey—

MARY: (*Gives him a wink*) Willy and the Hand Jive.

NICKY: You're hip, Mar'.

MARY: You, Nick', are impertinent. Give Gus some skin for me.

NICKY: So long.

FANNY: See you later, alligator. Au revoir, bon voyage. Stay dry. Try to write. And look out for zeeroxen.

MARY: Goodbye, Fanny.

FANNY: Vaya con diós.

(NICKY *and* FANNY *exit.*)

(MARY *saddles up and comes downstage.*)

MARY: The splash of galaxies across the night sky always brings out the phenomenologist in me.

(*The stars come out.*)

MARY: Billions of new worlds, waiting to be discovered. Explored and illuminated. Within and without. The nautilus shell mimics the shape of the Milky Way. Quarks and quasars. My face is bathed in light from a vanished star. (*Beat*) I stand on the precipice. The air is rare. Bracing. Before me stretch dark distances. Clusters of light. What next? I have no idea. Many mysteries to come. I am on the verge.

(*She surveys the horizon and her prospects.*)

MARY: I have such a yearning for the future! It is boundless! (*She takes a deep breath.*) Not annoying. Not annoying at all!

(*She disappears in a blaze of light—*)

End of play

PRODUCTION NOTES

The author wishes to thank Peter Culman and Stan Wojewodski, Managing Director and Artistic Director of Center Stage, respectively, for their continuing support.

The language of the play, since it is, at least in part, a play *about* language, cannot, must not, should not be naturalized or paraphrased. Rhythm and sound are sense. "One tiny *Times'* item" is very different from "One tiny *Times'* article."

Simple, plain, unaffected American speech, please. If the words are decorated, oversung, or have English lacquered over them, they become arch, unbearable, precious.

This is a play about the imagination, and about theatricality. It should be conveyed imaginatively and theatrically, not literally—in other words, with light, movement, and sound.

The titles and journal entries separate the scenes. The actress speaks the journal entry directly to the audience while the others prepare for the next scene.

MARY is the oldest, the leader, a passionate scientist, ebullient, joyful, not dry or academic. She is from Boston, but does not affect a pronounced Boston accent.

FANNY is from the Midwest. She is conservative, and has a wry wit.

ALEX is the youngest. An apostle of the future, she is most modern, most out of place in the Victorian world. She has boundless energy.

Disclaimer

On The Verge is not a docu-drama. I first encountered the historical Victorian lady travelers in Evan S. Connell's *A Long Desire,* Luree Miller's *On Top of the World,* Alexandra Allen's *Traveling Ladies,* and Dorothy Middleton's *Victorian Lady Travelers,* beautiful books all, and there is currently a plethora of books about and by the lady travelers. Research about them should be done for insight into their spirit, and for the pleasure of it. The characters of the play are NOT modeled upon particular individuals, even though I have raided the historical record for detail, flavoring, and anecdote. The spirit of the lady travelers inspired *On The Verge,* and that spirit is the play's true concern: the quality of yearning, courage, and imagination.

HIGHEST STANDARD OF LIVING

Keith Reddin

ABOUT THE AUTHOR

Keith Reddin's plays include LIFE AND LIMB, RUM AND COKE *(Broadway Play Publishing, 1986)*, BIG TIME *(Broadway Play Publishing, 1988)*, and NEBRASKA. He has received productions at the New York Shakespeare Festival, Playwrights Horizons, The Joyce Theater, American Repertory Theater, Goodman Studio, Trinity Square Repertory, Wisdom Bridge Theater, Remains Theater, Yale Repertory Theater, Coconut Grove Playhouse, La Jolla Playhouse, and the South Coast Repertory Theater. BIG TIME was produced at the Gate Theater in London, and was filmed for presentation on PBS' *American Playhouse.*

HIGHEST STANDARD OF LIVING was produced in New York by Playwrights Horizons on 13 November 1986, André Bishop, Artistic Director; Paul Daniels, the Managing Director. The cast was as follows:

BOB	Steve Culp
VLAD	Tim Carhart
MAN ON FERRY	Kevin Skousen
LUDMILLA	Leslie Lyles
TATIANA	Lola Pashalinski
TOM	Jim Murtaugh
LONNIE	Lola Pashalinski
MOTHER	Sloane Shelton
SERGEI	Clement Fowler
DMITRI	Peter Crombie
YURI	Kevin Skousen
RODGER	Robert Stanton
LARRY	Jim Murtaugh
DON	Clement Fowler
GARY	Kevin Skousen
HELEN	Sloane Shelton
JEAN	Lola Pashalinski
MAN AT BUS STOP	Robert Stanton
JACK	Tim Carhart
DOUG	Peter Crombie
ADELE	Lola Pashalinski
ESKIMO PIE MAN	Robert Stanton

Director	Don Scardino
Set design	John Arnone
Costumes	David Wollard
Lights	Josh Dachs
Sound	Scott Lehrer
Stage manager	Fred Ohrner

ACKNOWLEDGMENTS

Many people were involved in shaping HIGHEST STANDARD OF LIVING into its final form. I wish to thank Doug Hughes, who staged the earliest version of the play in Seattle; Jerry Patch and John Glore of South Coast Repertory Theatre; Larry Sloan of the Remains Theatre, Chicago; Gail Merrifield and Morgan Jeness of the Public Theatre; and, finally, André Bishop, Artistic Director of Playwrights Horizons, and Don Scardino, director of the New York production.

HIGHEST STANDARD OF LIVING was first developed and produced by South Coast Repertory Theatre, Costa Mesa, California. The world premiere was directed by David Emmes. The play opened two weeks later at the Remains Theatre, Chicago. It was directed by Michael Maggio.

Special thanks to the National Endowment for the Arts for their generous grant that enabled me to finish this play.

ACT ONE

Scene One

(Ferry to Leningrad. BOB *at the railing, looking out.* VLAD *approaches him.)*

VLAD: *(In Russian)* That is Leningrad. You live in Leningrad?

BOB: *(In Russian)* No, I don't. Excuse me, do you speak English? My Russian is poor.

VLAD: I speak English not so good, but I try.

BOB: No, your English is very good.

VLAD: You are American, right?

BOB: How can you tell?

VLAD: You can tell American. You are going to Leningrad?

BOB: Just landing there. I'm going to Moscow.

VLAD: Yes.

BOB: Moscow University actually. I'm a graduate student in Russian literature. Actually, Soviet literature from the late twenties to early thirties.

VLAD: Yes.

BOB: Incredible period. Very exciting.

VLAD: So I hear.

BOB: This is my first time to the Soviet Union. I could have flown directly to Moscow, you know, but I thought it would be special to take the ferry from Finland.

VLAD: I come from Finland too.

BOB: Business?

VLAD: No, I was shopping. I go to Finland to buy things.

BOB: You from Leningrad?

VLAD: Yes. Do you study Russian poetry also?

BOB: Oh yeah. Akhmatova. You heard of her?

VLAD: No.

BOB: Uh, Mandlestam? Pasternak? Derzhavin? No, huh?

VLAD: Sorry, I don't know these people.

BOB: Mayakovsky? You never heard of Mayakovsky?

VLAD: Is he Russian?

BOB: Uh, yes, he's a famous Soviet poet. Very famous. I'm surprised you never heard of him.

VLAD: Well you know I am car salesman in Leningrad. I sell cars I do not read poetry a lot. I know some American poems though. When they teach me English I learn famous American poem.

BOB: That's great.

VLAD: You maybe know this famous American poet? I had to memorize it in English.

BOB: That's great....

VLAD: *(Declaiming)* A bunch of boys were whooping it up
in the Malamute saloon
The kid that handles the music box was hitting a jagtime tune
Back of the bar, in a solo game, sat dangerous Dan McGrew,
And watching his luck was his light o' love, the lady that's known as Lou.

BOB: Great, uh.

VLAD: When out of the night, which was fifty below, and into
the din and glare
There stumbled a miner fresh from the creeks, dog-dirty
and loaded for bear....

BOB: Listen, this is a Canadian poet.

VLAD: He looked like a man with a foot in the grave and scarcely the....

BOB: Look, we're about ready to dock. I should get my bags.

VLAD: But I haven't finished the poem.

BOB: I know but....

VLAD: I learn entire poem in English.

BOB: I'm sure you did. You spoke it in perfect English. Excellent. Really wonderful.

VLAD: Thank you. You will like the Soviet Union.

BOB: I think I will.

(MAN enters and stands at the upstage railing of the ferry.)

VLAD: Many Americans have bad idea of Soviet Union, but this is wrong.

BOB: I'm sure you're right. I think very highly of the Soviet Union. We're not so different, really, once you get past the propaganda.

VLAD: There is so much to take in here.

BOB: Yes. I am very interested in Soviet literature and art and the Futurist and Constructivist movements.

VLAD: Yes, we have that and it is very good.

BOB: I'm very excited to do my research. My thesis is on Bulgakov. Mikhail Bulgakov. Soviet satirist and playwright.

VLAD: Yes, we have him too.

BOB: A real genius. I'm told I can look at his manuscripts, some of his journals, his letters. This is... well, I can't tell you how excited I am I'm here, I'm really here in Russia. I'll see the places he saw, hear the language he heard. Maybe even talk to people who knew him. This is a once-in-a-lifetime experience. I'm very lucky.

VLAD: If you spend time in Leningrad you must say hello and we will drink together.

BOB: That's very hospitable of you. See, I've made my first Russian friend.

VLAD: Yes. My name is Vladimir.

BOB: And I'm Robert, Bob.

VLAD: Well, Bob, welcome to Soviet Union.

BOB: This is great. I'm gonna have a great time.

(BOB and VLAD start to exit. MAN upstage climbs the railing and jumps off the boat. Lights fade.)

Scene Two

(A hotel room in Moscow. A bed. A window looks out to a brick wall.)

BOB: Oh Christ. Save me. Save me. *(Gets up. Bent over.)* Where is the toilet? I can't remember where the toilet is. Oh right. Down the hall. I gotta pass that fat old lady in the hall, to get to the bathroom. Fucking Russians. Okay. Okay, you can make it. You can make it to the toilet.

(He takes a step.) Oh no, no. *(He throws up behind the bed.)* Good move, Bob. Beautiful. I need assistance here. I need help. Oh God I am so sick. *(Knock at door)* Okay, somebody is at the door here. *(He scurries back to the bed, throws covers over himself.)* Come in.

(LUDMILLA *and* TATIANA *enter.)*

LUDMILLA: Good morning.

BOB: Strasvitsa, kak dela?

LUDMILLA: We will continue talking in English I think as your Russian is awkward.

BOB: Okay.

LUDMILLA: I am very fluent in English. I am fluent in five languages. I understand you are not feeling well.

BOB: Yeah. I compliment you on your English.

LUDMILLA: I am not here for conversational improvement, I am a physician.

BOB: Great.

LUDMILLA: You are physically ill, yes?

BOB: I am incredibly ill, yes.

LUDMILLA: We first take your temperature.

BOB: Hey wait.

*(*TATIANA *takes his temperature.)*

LUDMILLA: How long have you felt unwell?

BOB: Mmmmmmghrfhjk.

LUDMILLA: I am sorry. You have the thermometer in your mouth.

BOB: Noph prohphlemmm.

LUDMILLA: I will now take your pulse.

BOB: Mmmmmmm?

LUDMILLA: Please do not talk just yet. *(She takes thermometer.)* I see.

BOB: What?

LUDMILLA: How old are you?

BOB: Twenty-eight. What is it? What's my temperature?

LUDMILLA: And you are an American student, yes?

BOB: I'm an American student studying Russian, yes.

LUDMILLA: Yes.

BOB: Look, can I ask a question?

LUDMILLA: Of course.

BOB: How come she doesn't talk?

LUDMILLA: She is my assistant, Tatiana.

BOB: But how come she doesn't say anything?

LUDMILLA: Her English is quite poor. Your temperature is 103.

BOB: Kinda high, huh?

LUDMILLA: We will remove you.

BOB: What?

LUDMILLA: We will remove you to hospital.

BOB: Hold on here.

LUDMILLA: We are taking you out of hotel room to hospital.

BOB: Out of this hotel is fine, but to hospital, no way!

LUDMILLA: I have made my decision.

BOB: Hey, Tatiana, what do you think?

TATIANA: I work for KGB.

BOB: Fuck.

LUDMILLA: She say that to scare you.

*(*TATIANA *and* LUDMILLA *laugh loudly.)*

BOB: Very funny.

LUDMILLA: You were scared.

BOB: Tatiana, I work for CIA. *(Pause)* Didn't work.

*(*TATIANA *and* LUDMILLA *look at each other.)*

LUDMILLA: Now, I feel your chest.

(She puts hands on BOB. BOB *laughs.)*

LUDMILLA: What are you laughing for?

BOB: It tickles. *(He laughs.)*

LUDMILLA: Stop that.

BOB: Well you try it. *(He tries to tickle* LUDMILLA.*)*

LUDMILLA: Stop that. Stop. *(She starts to giggle.)* You must not make me laugh, this is very serious examination. *(She laughs.)*

TATIANA: You should pack and not talk to the doctor any more.

BOB: She is speaking very good English now.

TATIANA: Flirting with doctor is not allowed. Time to leave.

BOB: I'm not under arrest am I?

LUDMILLA: No of course not.

BOB: Can I call the embassy?

TATIANA: That won't be necessary.

BOB: Maybe I should.

TATIANA: They know where you are. If they do not, we will tell them.

BOB: Thank you. What is your name?

LUDMILLA: Ludmilla.

BOB: Okay Ludmilla, I'm putting my trust in you.

TATIANA: Excellent idea. Trust is important. You trust us. Ludmilla will call hospital, I will stay with you. Then you go to Kerenin Hospital.

LUDMILLA: That is too far. I will take you to Gorky Hospital.

TATIANA: Americans go to Kerenin Hospital. That is procedure, Ludmilla.

BOB: No, that's okay....

TATIANA: That is where you go.

BOB: Uh, Ludmilla, is she really your assistant?

TATIANA: You don't believe me?

BOB: Uh....

TATIANA: What do I say about trust?

BOB: I should trust you.

TATIANA: Got it in one, Bob.

(Lights fade.)

Scene Three

*(*BOB *in a hospital bed)*

BOB: A fever of 104. Food poisoning. Every building looks the same. Moscow University looks like Moscow hotel which looks like Moscow department store which looks like Moscow indoor tennis courts. Everything's made out of red brick and red tile and cobblestone. This place looks like my hotel room.

*(*TOM *and a large bear enter.)*

BOB: Uncle Tom, what are you doing here?

TOM: Hey, heard you were sick.

BOB: But last I heard you were living in Atchison, Kansas.

TOM: Still am. This isn't really visiting hours, so we had to sneak in.

BOB: Does this bear belong to you?

TOM: Isn't really a bear, Bob, this is your Aunt Lonnie.

BOB: Aunt Lonnie is a bear now?

TOM: No, she's in a bear suit. Come on out, Lonnie.

(LONNIE takes bear head off costume.)

LONNIE: How you feeling, Bob?

BOB: This is very strange. Aunt Lonnie, why did you come to the hospital in a bear suit?

LONNIE: Think about where you are Bob, think about this.

BOB: I am.

LONNIE: Tom's pretending we're from the Moscow Circus. That's how we got in the door, Bob.

BOB: But I thought you were flying businessmen from Kansas City. Did you fly from Kansas City to Moscow?

TOM: Non-fucking-stop, Bob.

BOB: Make good time?

LONNIE: Not bad. Guess who else is here?

BOB: I've no idea.

LONNIE: Go ahead guess.

BOB: I'm always terrible at this.

TOM: Your mother.

LONNIE: She's here too.

BOB: MY MOTHER'S IN MOSCOW? This is unbelievable.

TOM: She flew with us.

BOB: Is she in a bear costume?

LONNIE: No, I believe she's dressed in a normal fashion.

BOB: Then I should recognize her right away.

(MOTHER enters.)

MOTHER: Hello, Robert, they say you have food poisoning.

BOB: Hello, Mom.

MOTHER: Lonnie, you are a hoot in that bear costume.

*(*TOM *and* LONNIE *laugh heartily.)*

LONNIE: Tom and I pretended we were with the circus.

MOTHER: That's a lot of fun.

BOB: Mom, how long are you here for?

MOTHER: Till you get better.

BOB: I've no idea how long I'll be sick.

MOTHER: I'm in no hurry, Robert. I can walk around, look at all those kooky gold domes, and the streets are so clean.

BOB: It's like "This Is Your Life" here. Everyone here in my hospital room in the middle of the Soviet Union.

MOTHER: Moscow is not like Morristown, Robert, they have lots of flights here, we have current passports, the dollar is doing extremely well now, we can thank Mr. Reagan for that, and why not travel I say. Things won't go to pieces without me standing guard on Bernita Drive, will they?

BOB: I suppose not.

*(*TOM *points to his watch.)*

MOTHER: Oh, only an hour left to catch the Lenin tomb. We don't want to miss that. See you later, Bob.

TOM and LONNIE: Bye!

*(*MOTHER *takes flash picture of* BOB, *then she,* LONNIE *and* TOM *exit.)*

(Beat. Then LUDMILLA *enters with a wheelchair.)*

BOB: Who are you?

LUDMILLA: I am Ludmilla. The doctor who brought you to the hospital. We need to do some tests now. I will wheel you to elevator.

*(*BOB *gets into wheelchair.)*

*(*LUDMILLA *begins to wheel* BOB *out.)*

BOB: Ludmilla, there are all these people in my room.

LUDMILLA: Hello....

BOB: Not now, before.

LUDMILLA: Ssh, you must be quiet. You are very sick and being sick in Soviet Union is no fun. But I am here to take care of you.

BOB: You're the only one I can talk to.

LUDMILLA: I am?

BOB: You're the only one who's really here, you are here?

LUDMILLA: I think so, yes.

BOB: That's good. Ludmilla, don't let me die, okay?

(Lights fade.)

Scene Four

(Hospital room. BOB *in one bed.* SERGEI, *an old man, in another.* BOB *wakes up, looks at* SERGEI.*)*

BOB: Am I dead?

SERGEI: No.

BOB: Where am I?

SERGEI: Here with me.

BOB: Where is that?

SERGEI: What?

BOB: Huh?

SERGEI: I am sorry?

BOB: Are we still in Russia?

SERGEI: Yes.

BOB: Am I speaking Russian?

SERGEI: No.

BOB: You are speaking English?

SERGEI: Yes.

BOB: Okay. You speak English very well.

SERGEI: Thank you.

BOB: How come everybody I meet in Russia speaks English so well?

SERGEI: I don't know.

BOB: If, IF, I was the least bit paranoid, I would think that this was some incredible thing where I was in Russia never speaking Russian, everybody speaking this English to me.

SERGEI: Yes.

BOB: Yes what?

SERGEI: What you said.

BOB: Right.

SERGEI: How many cars you have? In America how many cars do you own?

BOB: You mean personally?

SERGEI: Da.

BOB: None.

SERGEI: You have no cars?

BOB: No, I live in New York. In New York to own a car is insanity.

SERGEI: Every American have lot of cars, right?

BOB: Not in New York. Not enough parking spaces. There are about eight million people in New York.

SERGEI: That's lot of cars.

BOB: Yes. I once.... Well I almost had a car.

SERGEI: What kind?

BOB: You ever hear of a Mustang?

SERGEI: What color?

BOB: Red. Mustang convertible, with a white top.

SERGEI: Holy shit.

BOB: Yeah.

SERGEI: What year?

BOB: Either '65 or '66. Like the second year they came out.

SERGEI: This is classic automobile.

BOB: Now. Now it's considered a classic. Not like a Rolls-Royce but a classic convertible of its type. My father had this car. Every Saturday afternoon I would wash and wax this car. Vacuum the interior. Polish the chrome, turn on the radio as I hosed it down, listen to the Beach Boys or something.

SERGEI: Little Richard?

BOB: No, this is after. My father said Bob, keep this car in great shape, it's gonna be a classic, and it's gonna be yours. You get old enough to drive it, I'm gonna give this car to you. This classic will be yours. A red Mustang convertible, '65 make, white top, interior was black, that was too bad, 'cause black vinyl, shit it gets hot. This car was so fucking hot with this black interior, your behind, you'd have to peel it off the seats, and you'd be sweating.... You following this?

SERGEI: Absolutely, yes.

BOB: My father sold that car a year before I was old enough to drive.

SERGEI: Oh, no!

BOB: I was really upset. He got a good price on it, still I was incredibly disappointed.

SERGEI: I have never owned a car in my life. I am seventy-four and probably dying and I thought all Americans owned more than one car.

BOB: I wish I had that Mustang.

SERGEI: Yes. You know Little Richard?

BOB: Not personally.

SERGEI: Rock-and-roll singer.

BOB: "Good Golly Miss Molly"?

SERGEI: That's the one. I have records of him. He is greatest performer in twentieth century.

BOB: He's pretty good.

SERGEI: I have collected every song he has recorded. That is very difficult especially as here jazz and rock-and-roll is in disfavor. But through lot of people I get these Little Richard records and I listen to them at night. I have to listen to them quietly so many people don't know I have these records because it is bad thing, but really you should play Little Richard loud.

BOB: Very loud.

SERGEI: Very loud yes.

BOB: I like Little Richard.

SERGEI: I have these recordings of songs: LONG TALL SALLY, TUTTI FRUITTI, BABY FACE, GOOD GOLLY MISS MOLLY, SEND ME SOME LOVING, RIP IT UP, READY TEDDY, THE GIRL CAN'T HELP IT, OOH MY SOUL, LET IT ROLL, LET'S ROCK, ROCKS IN MY BED, LEATHER BOYS, LUCILLE, MISS ANN, DIRECTLY FROM MY HEART, TURN OVER AND BURN, I'M BACK BABY DON'T YOU WANT A MAN LIKE ME, SLIPPING AND SLIDING, GROOVY LITTLE SUZY, KEEP A KNOCKING, CHOCOLATE SANDWICH, DO THE JERK LIKE ME, TRUE FINE MAMA, FROG MAN, HIGHWAY 69, THEATRE OF CRUELTY, RUBBER LEGS, CHEATING AND PETTING, WHOLE LOT OF SHAKING, DON'T FENCE ME IN, HOPE TO SEE YOU SOON, TOP DOG, SCRATCH MY ASS,

GARDEN OF LOVE, SNIFFING AROUND MY YARD, HAND JIVE, and MILK MAN BOOGIE.

BOB: You got it all.

SERGEI: Yes.

BOB: He's a born-again Christian now I think.

SERGEI: Excuse me?

BOB: He found God and became a preacher and said the Devil made him sinful and he performed rock-and-roll against his will.

SERGEI: No.

BOB: But now it's okay and he sings gospel and found Jesus and wrote his autobiography.

SERGEI: This is same Little Richard who sings: "Got girl named Sue, she know just what to do?"

BOB: What can I say?

SERGEI: This is terrible news.

BOB: Maybe I'm wrong. But I think it was Little Richard, maybe I'm mixing him up with James Brown.

SERGEI: Godfather of Soul, James Brown.

BOB: Right.

SERGEI: Hardest-working man in show business. How do you feel?

BOB: A lot better, thank you. How do you feel?

SERGEI: I'm dying.

BOB: I'm sorry.

SERGEI: I drink too much for fifty years, I die.

BOB: I bet you didn't drink that much.

SERGEI: Two bottles of vodka a day.

BOB: Wow!

SERGEI: But most people here drink too much.

BOB: People in the hospital?

SERGEI: People in Russia. We all drink too much. Everybody is depressed, unhappy. We drink too much, spend all our money on drink. Can't buy cars, no cars. Wait five years for cars. Can't spend it on houses, no houses. Wait ten years for one-room apartment. Wait all your life to die. Now I'm doing it. I thought if I drink enough, I kill myself. No have to wait for that like everything else. But I have my Little Richard. So Little Richard spread the word of God and good luck. You know drink would be nice now. Actually, bottle would be very nice. When you get out you have drink and think of me, Sergei.

BOB: Okay.

(DMITRI, SERGEI's *son, enters with flowers.)*

DMITRI: *(In Russian)* How are you today?

SERGEI: *(In Russian)* All right.

DMITRI: *(In Russian)* Who is that?

SERGEI: *(In Russian)* He is an American. A student.

DMITRI: *(In Russian)* Here's some flowers for you.

SERGEI: *(In Russian)* Stop staring at him. Say hello if you want.

(Pause)

DMITRI: Hello.

BOB: Hi.

DMITRI: My father says you are American.

BOB: That's right.

DMITRI: What are you doing here?

BOB: Food poisoning.

DMITRI: No, what are you doing in Soviet Union?

BOB: I'm a student. American student, Russian literature. I'm over at Moscow University.

DMITRI: Yes, that is very excellent university.

BOB: It's big.

(Pause)

DMITRI: So, you are American.

BOB: Got it.

DMITRI: Very nice, but how do you defend racism and unemployment in United States?

BOB: I don't defend it.

DMITRI: Yes you are tricky, but we know about your putting blacks in the ghettos and women in their own ghetto.

BOB: Well, personally I think....

DMITRI: There is no racism here.

SERGEI: All right Dmitri....

DMITRI: No racism in Soviet Union. We have many different ethnic origins and we live in harmony here. No riots here. Siberians do not burn cities.

BOB: If you say so.

DMITRI: And there is no censorship here.

BOB: Really?

SERGEI: He's started now, you can't stop him....

DMITRI: No censorship. Anyone can write what he wants here, you are free to complain about government.

SERGEI: My son is a Party member. As you can see he knows what to say.

DMITRI: *(In Russian)* Why are you talking like this in front of an American?

SERGEI: Because we share the same room, Dmitri.

DMITRI: Reagan is reactionary fascist.

BOB: Okay.

(Pause)

DMITRI: Did you hear what I say?

BOB: Yes.

DMITRI: I say your president is fascist.

BOB: Yes.

DMITRI: You are not going to defend him?

BOB: Why should I?

DMITRI: He is leader of United States.

BOB: I didn't vote for him.

DMITRI: Yes, you want me to denounce Soviet government.

BOB: Not really.

DMITRI: You know Reagan is trigger-happy cowboy who thinks he is in Hollywood movie, get rid of Communists by closing his eyes.... You cannot make us disappear by wishing so.

BOB: I agree.

SERGEI: Enough, Dmitri, remember your blood pressure.

DMITRI: Quiet, Father. Reagan is war-crazed madman.

Bob: He is.

Dmitri: No, no he is crazy person who could destroy world. Star Wars in space.

Bob: Absolutely.

Dmitri: No, no, you are not listening to me. He is insane.

Bob: Most Americans think so.

Dmitri: Then why is he president?

Bob: Because we want an insane leader.

(Pause)

Dmitri: No.

Bob: Yes.

Dmitri: No, but wait.... No.... He is bad.

Bob: He is terrible.

Dmitri: A monster.

Bob: Focus of evil.

Dmitri: No... yes, Reagan is evil.

Bob: He is really senile.

Dmitri: He is, he is....

Bob: Stupid.

Dmitri: Yes, and...

Bob: Foolish.

Dmitri: And, and he is...

Bob: Dangerous.

Dmitri: Yes.

Bob: Corrupt.

Dmitri: Yes!

Bob: Defiant.

Dmitri: Yes!

Bob: Ugly.

Dmitri: Yes! A joke, a boring...

Bob: Clumsy.

DMITRI: Rude, uncouth.

BOB: Rustic, noxious.

DMITRI: HE IS AN ASSHOLE.

(DMITRI and BOB start jumping up and down.)

BOB: HE IS THE PRINCE OF DARKNESS.

DMITRI: HE IS DUKE OF EARL.

BOB: HE'S A CRACKPOT WILDMAN.

DMITRI: HE IS SOMETHING. I... I....

BOB: What?

DMITRI: I don't know any more insults in English. My... you know, my vocabulary is not as big. As.... Oh.

BOB: I feel great, how about you?

DMITRI: I feel wonderful. *(He shakes BOB's hand.)* You are great American. We should have a drink. Father, father?

BOB: What's the matter?

DMITRI: Oh no. He's not.... Wait here. I have to get a doctor.

(DMITRI exits. Pause. BOB cautiously moves toward SERGEI's bed.)

BOB: Sergei, uh, are you all right? Hello?

(Noise offstage, BOB scurries back to his bed. A SMALL CHILD opens the door to the room and peeks in.)

BOB: Hello? What room are you looking for? Do you speak English? Can I help you?

(The SMALL CHILD exits. BOB starts to get out of bed, then a group of six or seven CHILDREN, seven or eight years old, enter. They look at BOB, then go over to SERGEI's bed.)

BOB: Is he a relative of yours? Are you in his family? Are you not allowed to talk to strangers?

(The CHILDREN look at SERGEI's things on his bedside table. They pick up his flowers and throw them on the ground.)

BOB: Hey, stop it. I'm calling people in here, stop that, get out of here.

(The CHILDREN start stripping SERGEI's bed and pushing the body around.)

BOB: WHAT ARE YOU DOING? STOP THAT! Okay, I'm going into the hall and....

(One CHILD produces a hammer and comes at BOB.)

BOB: What the fuck..... .

(He hits BOB *very hard with the hammer.)*

BOB: Shit, shit, stop it....

(The other CHILDREN *pull* SERGEI *off the bed and out of the room.* CHILD *with hammer exits.)*

BOB: What the fuck..... .

*(*DMITRI *and* VLAD *enter.)*

DMITRI: Who did this?

VLAD: What has happened here?

BOB: Huh?

VLAD: Answer me, what is going on?

BOB: They took him.

DMITRI: Who?

BOB: These kids.... I... hit me, with a hammer....

VLAD: You will wait here. *(To* DMITRI, *in Russian)* Please wait outside.

*(*DMITRI *exits.)*

BOB: What is going on here? Did you find those kids?

VLAD: What?

BOB: The children, they just....

VLAD: No one saw any children.

BOB: What are you talking about, there were five, maybe six kids....

VLAD: Many peoples in the corridor, no one saw any children. Now, Mr. Wills, you are feeling better?

BOB: I...

VLAD: You are feeling better, fever is gone?

BOB: Yes....

VLAD: Then I am going to ask you to leave.

BOB: But what about the old man?

VLAD: Is not your problem is my problem. You are going to leave hospital now, I think. I recommend that you leave Soviet Union soon. And I will recommend to authorities that they also suggest to you and to American embassy that you leave.

BOB: Excuse me, but aren't you a used car salesman?

VLAD: I work for hospital. My name is Vladimir.

BOB: We've met.

VLAD: No I have not seen you before.

BOB: Remember, I am a student here on an exchange program.

VLAD: We are exchanging you back then. You believe in nothing but your Mustang convertible, Mr. Wills. Black interior, white top, Model 1966. And that is the end when all you believe in is four wheels and a radio.

BOB: What are you talking about?

VLAD: I think you know.

BOB: Where do you get the authority to....

VLAD: Can I trust you not to cause more trouble?

BOB: I never believed anything you said on that boat for a second, I just want you to know that.

VLAD: All right.

BOB: Don't start getting superior with me, I'm going to leave. Are you happy?

VLAD: Ecstatic.

BOB: If I wasn't so mad at you, I would laugh at all this. The insanity of your country. The incredible stupidity.

VLAD: The horror, the horror. Joseph Conrad.

*(*VLAD *exits.)*

BOB: Very good, very cute. You know your literary quotes, I'm impressed. Everyone here is just too much.

*(*TOM *and* LONNIE*, in bear suit, without bear head, enter.)*

TOM: Hey, Bob, I'm double parked, let's book.

BOB: I feel a lot better now and I don't have time to talk, I'm sorry.

TOM: Let's go, Lonnie.

LONNIE: Really, Bob, don't you think this hospital business is going on a bit too long? We think it's time you got your shit together and get serious.

TOM: About your life.

LONNIE: We'll be outside if you need us.

TOM: We can fly you back to the ol' U S of A.

BOB: This place is incredible.

LONNIE: Everything you fear is true, Bob.

(TOM and LONNIE exit.)

BOB: Wait a minute. What's that supposed to mean?

(LUDMILLA enters.)

LUDMILLA: Mr. Wills, what is going on, everyone is very upset.

BOB: They told me to leave. *(He starts to get dressed.)*

LUDMILLA: No, I will see someone, okay? I will talk to my superiors....

BOB: No, I'm gonna talk to someone, I'm going to the American embassy.

LUDMILLA: Please, I can take care of this.

BOB: No, that's okay.

LUDMILLA: Are you sure you are all right?

BOB: What? Huh? Am I all right?

LUDMILLA: Maybe you should wait here....

BOB: Where?

LUDMILLA: Here! You should wait here, I will take care of this for you.

BOB: No, I got to get there before them. We'll work this whole thing out.

LUDMILLA: But....

BOB: I know we can do it, no problem. *(He exits.)*

LUDMILLA: But.... oh Boshi Moi *("Oh boy")*.

(Lights fade.)

Scene Five

(BOB stands in a street. YURI enters, walks up to BOB.)

YURI: Hey.

BOB: What? Are you talking to me?

YURI: Hey, hey you. You are American.

BOB: No, I'm a Canadian. We look and sound just like Americans but we're different. Canadians are not the same as Americans. In fact, most Canadians get very insulted if you confuse them with an American. We're not Americans, eh? I'm not so uptight about it, but most get upset.

YURI: No, you are American. I watch you for a while you are American, right. You don't fool me.

BOB: No, I'm a Canadian. Don't tell me what I am.

YURI: How is Canadian different from American if you are this Canadian person?

BOB: Well we, we use vinegar on our french fries and other things.

YURI: You try to fool me, but I watch you, you are American for sure. My English good, huh?

BOB: Your English is very good, yes.

YURI: You got blue jeans?

BOB: What?

YURI: American you got lots of blue jeans. Got Wrangler, Calvin Klein?

BOB: No, I don't wear blue jeans.

YURI: I got blue jeans on, see? Got leather coat, this coat one hundred percent leather, feel, go ahead.

BOB: Very nice.

YURI: You take me to your room we do business.

BOB: What are you talking about?

YURI: You give me blue jeans, I give you many roubles, okay.

BOB: No. Look, I don't have any blue jeans.

YURI: Okay, you are American businessman, you want trade. You want to make business, I understand. I am businessman, we bargain, we trade. What you want, I have lots of roubles. *(Shows wad of bills)*

BOB: Put that away, will you?

YURI: Just so you know I am serious. Okay. What you want for jeans? I pay big price.

BOB: I told you, no jeans.

YURI: It's okay, we're doing business, now what you want, whatever you want I can get. You want tapes? Cassette tapes? I get them for you, discount, or we trade. I got everything. You want Prince? Phil Collins? I got Wham, Frankie Goes Hollywood, Elvis Costello? You want Bruce Springsteen? You want Boss? I got tape and record BORN IN U.S.A. I got that.

BOB: No thanks.

YURI: Okay, you want icons? All Americans want real Russians icons from trip to Soviet Union, show off what they got. Good deal on real icons, fourteenth century, got church pews, got stained glass, altars, how about furs, Russian furs?

BOB: You are unreal.

YURI: No. I am serious, okay American businessman, you want hashish from Asia? Excellent stuff, opium, heroin, cocaine? How about girls? You want real Russian girls?

BOB: No, listen....

YURI: You want boys? Real Russian boys, do anything, take pictures, huh? Video cassettes?

BOB: I'm calling the police.

YURI: No police here, we are safe.

BOB: Stop it, let go of me....

YURI: What do you want American, huh? What do you want to trade? What you got to trade me? Let's go to your room right now.

BOB: No, dammit, get your fucking hands off me.

YURI: We haven't done business yet.

BOB: I don't want to do anything with you. GET OUT OF HERE, GET LOST.

YURI: Okay, okay, don't get so upset. You want something, you come to me. You find me here we trade or I give you lots of roubles. You give me trouble I go to police and tell them you try to sell me dollars and then you go to jail for a long time, nobody hear from you. But listen, I'm a nice guy and I understand American business and you think about what I got and you meet me here tomorrow. Da Svidanya.

(YURI exits.)

BOB: Holy shit. Who was that guy?

(SMALL CHILD appears.)

BOB: Hey kid, you lost? What do you want? Hey, stop staring at me....

(Other CHILDREN appear.)

BOB: Oh, no get the fuck away, you guys just stay away, I mean it.

(First CHILD pulls out a hammer and moves toward BOB.)

BOB: Get the fuck away from me. I'm gonna shout. I'M SHOUTING NOW, HELP! HELP ME!

(He starts to run, the other CHILDREN grab hold of BOB. BOB struggles, the CHILDREN all produce hammers and start savagely hitting BOB. BOB screams and disappears in the mass of CHILDREN.)

(Lights fade.)

Scene Six

(Hospital room. LUDMILLA *enters.* TATIANA *follows.)*

LUDMILLA: Where is he?

TATIANA: Who?

LUDMILLA: Mr. Wills. Robert Wills.

TATIANA: The American?

LUDMILLA: Yes. I heard he was being brought to this room.

TATIANA: He is being brought here.

LUDMILLA: I need to speak to him, it is very important. Oh. I feel terrible, I should have insisted on him taking a taxi or getting a ride....

TATIANA: Or spending the night.

LUDMILLA: I was.... I would like to talk to Vladimir, please, Tatiana.

TATIANA: Vladimir does not work here anymore.

LUDMILLA: Since when?

TATIANA: Vladimir was transferred. He requested a transfer to another city. Something about family problems. I have been promoted.

*(*BOB *is wheeled in by an* ORDERLY. *His arm is in a cast and his face is heavily bandaged.)*

LUDMILLA: Oh, Robert, you look terrible.

BOB: Thank you.

LUDMILLA: This is all my fault. I feel terrible.

BOB: Don't be silly, I fell down the stairs to my step-up toilet.

TATIANA: That is what happened, I believe. Ludmilla Petrovna, would you wait for me outside. I have some things to say to you in a minute. We will be joined in my office by some others.

LUDMILLA: Of course.

BOB: I'm fine, Ludmilla, great. I just love this hospital.

LUDMILLA: Oh. I feel terrible about this.

BOB: It's not your fault.

LUDMILLA: You are not getting accurate pictures of my country.

BOB: Well....

LUDMILLA: You have dinner with me. I will cook you nice Russian meal and so you will have better feeling about Soviet Union.

BOB: But I'm leaving tomorrow. They're kicking me out.

LUDMILLA: This is terrible. There is no reason for this.

TATIANA: Please wait outside.

LUDMILLA: *(To* TATIANA*)* Is this true?

TATIANA: I asked you to wait outside.

LUDMILLA: *(To* BOB*)* Then you come tonight.

*(*LUDMILLA *exits.)*

BOB: Is she in trouble?

TATIANA: Not as much trouble as you, I'm afraid. You have not been here so long and accidents keep happening. People visit you or you visit and there is all this discussion and trouble and people get hurt. As was stated earlier we feel you have worn out your welcome.

BOB: You're asking me to go.

TATIANA: Yes that is correct.

BOB: Well I don't want to stick around where I'm not wanted.

TATIANA: Very good.

BOB: That would be very un-American of me, making a pest of myself.

TATIANA: I'm glad you understand. I don't expect any more problems from you. All right Mr. Wills?

*(*TATIANA *starts to exit.)*

BOB: Nice shoes.

*(*TATIANA *leaves, miffed.)*

(Pause. BOB *looks at the* ORDERLY. *He waves weakly.)*

BOB: Hi....

(No reaction from ORDERLY. BOB *sighs.)*

(Lights fade.)

Scene Seven

(Darkness. Sound of door opening. LUDMILLA *and* BOB *enter.* LUDMILLA *turns on apartment lights.)*

LUDMILLA: So this is my apartment.

BOB: Very nice.

LUDMILLA: Because of housing shortage I have to wait few years to get. It is not so big, but it's nice and it's mine. For a year I had to share this with my grandfather. He is dead now.

BOB: I'm sorry.

LUDMILLA: He had decorated the apartment in very bad taste. And over here is stereo.

BOB: You have a lot of records.

LUDMILLA: So now I can play lots of music. I should make you something to eat. I'll put on some music.

(She puts on ARETHA FRANKLIN'S GREATEST HITS, "Respect", *and goes into kitchen.)*

LUDMILLA: YOU KNOW THIS RECORD?

BOB: Yes.

LUDMILLA: WHAT?

BOB: YES.

LUDMILLA: YOU LIKE IT?

BOB: SURE.

LUDMILLA: ARETHA FRANKLIN, GIVE ME RESPECT. *(She sings along a bit with the song.)*.... Find out what that means to me... R-E-S-P-E-C-T, Hey Babe, TCB. What you got, Baby I want...

BOB: What are you making?

LUDMILLA: SOUP, I AM MAKING SOUP.

BOB: Listen, can we turn the music off?

LUDMILLA: Yes. *(She enters with tray.)* Here is black bread, pork, duck, and sirniki, uh, sirniki is fried cakes with cheese.

BOB: Thank you.

LUDMILLA: Also I have jam and cakes and potatoes and vodka and the soup will be done soon.

BOB: You didn't have to make all this for me.

LUDMILLA: I make all this every day. *(Pours vodka)*

BOB: I think I've had enough.

LUDMILLA: This is special occasion.

BOB: Well, a toast to your apartment and your generosity.

LUDMILLA: Okay.

(They drink.)

LUDMILLA: Everything is better at apartment. I can cook better than restaurants and I shop better, too. Eat.

BOB: It's very good.

LUDMILLA: Here, I'll put butter on this.

BOB: Ludmilla, you can relax. Everything is great.

LUDMILLA: I never have anyone over here. This is my home, I know it's small but I always think about if I have someone over what kind of food I make and I have vodka and now you are here and it's a party.

BOB: And we're having fun. I'm sorry I have to leave tomorrow.

LUDMILLA: *(She is getting quite drunk.)* Eat some more. Here is some vodka.

BOB: I haven't finished anything yet. This is great. Really.

LUDMILLA: I saw something today. At the bus stop. On the way to the hospital. There are maybe three or four people waiting with me. One man he keeps staring at the others and listening, and I think to myself he is watching everything a little too hard. He is so serious. And I think he is from the police, to listen what other people say. I think every day at bus stops are police watching and listening and today at this bus stop it is this man. I look quick at others waiting and they look at me, and I see in their eyes, in a tiny second of this look, that they know too. So we wait. Now we are getting very nervous. And we all think we must talk, so that we show we do not know that secret policeman is watching us. But we must always only talk about innocent things, stupid things. An old man comes up to the bus stop. It is hot out, and he is sweating and trying to breathe and he smiles at us and he says, "It is so oppressive I can't hardly breathe." We all look at each other. The policeman says to old man, "Yes it is, it is hard to breathe." We hold our breath. The old man, not knowing what is happening, says, "Yes, so hard to breathe." And the agent grabs the old man very hard by the arm and starts to lead him away. And old man and the agent disappear as they turn the corner. Because here there are certain words that cannot be spoken out loud. They take on bigger meaning. And everyone at the bus stop knows this and looks at their feet and are silent as the old man disappears, maybe forever. Then I began to fear that everyone at bus stop was watching me. Watching to see my reaction to this scene. This incident was performed for my benefit and the agent leaves so that people can then hear me express my reaction to this arrest. So I say nothing, I trust no one at the bus stop. And each of us is thinking the same thing. Each of those others must think I am an agent watching them. Everything is fear. They could be listening to us right now. Maybe they are. I tell you this so you understand what it is like to get up every morning and wait for the bus to go to work. *(Pause)*

BOB: Then you should leave.

LUDMILLA: Leave my apartment?

BOB: Leave the country.

LUDMILLA: Very easy for you to say with your American passport.

BOB: You should come to America. You could stay with me.

LUDMILLA: You don't know me. You don't know my life. I tell you about waiting for the bus you tell me to leave my country and run away. Even if I could, why?

BOB: To be free.

LUDMILLA: And I would be free in America?

BOB: Relatively. Sure, yes. You would be free. Free to think, free to express your opinions.

LUDMILLA: It is so easy for you to talk this way and then go. So easy to leave. And I would live with you.

BOB: If you wanted, for a time.

LUDMILLA: I don't trust you.

BOB: I'm not saying we should sleep together, I'm saying you could stay with me in America, till you found out what you wanted to do. I'm serious. I really am.

LUDMILLA: All right, you say you are serious. I can never leave and you know this and that is why you say so boldly leave Russia and live with me, and we'll go to baseball games together.

BOB: I'm very serious.

LUDMILLA: You drink too much vodka and I think the soup is ready.

BOB: Let me help you.

(They stand up together. BOB *stands very close to* LUDMILLA.*)*

LUDMILLA: You are standing very close to me, do you notice?

BOB: Thank you Ludmilla for asking me here for a party.

LUDMILLA: The soup needs to be.... Oh, you are very bad. You say these things.

(The phone rings.)

LUDMILLA: It is police, they are going to arrest me.

*(*BOB *stares.)*

LUDMILLA: Just kidding. *(She picks up the phone. Waits.)*

BOB: What is it?

LUDMILLA: No answer. There was... no answer. Maybe it was a mistake.

(Lights dim.)

Scene Eight

(Moscow Airport. A few announcements of flights in Russian over the loudspeaker. RODGER *stands onstange.* BOB *enters with suitcase.)*

RODGER: Bob over here. Hi, my name is Rodger Potter. I'm with the American Embassy. I believe you asked to see a representative from the Embassy.

BOB: I don't believe this. I'm at the airport, ready to leave. Where were you guys a couple of days ago?

RODGER: Well we just received your request. I'm sorry, you had an accident.

BOB: I was hit by a subway here.

RODGER: Wow....

BOB: Really.

RODGER: Gosh, how did that happen?

BOB: How do these things ever happen? Bad luck, I guess.

RODGER: My God, you're lucky to be alive.

BOB: So they tell me.

RODGER: Well, listen, you need anything, you let us know.

BOB: Next time they let me come back, I will.

RODGER: Right. You're back to the States.

BOB: That's it, Rodger.

RODGER: Boy, I miss it.

BOB: Can't get a good hamburger and fries here, huh?

RODGER: You know it.

BOB: It sure was swell of you Embassy people to rush on over here to see off a fellow American. I appreciate that, I do.

RODGER: That's what we're here for.

BOB: My tax dollars at work, right?

RODGER: Guess you could say that, though actually I'm eyeing for a position in D.C. The State Department. Sort of have to do some grunt work first. Pay some dues.

BOB: Dad put in a word for you?

RODGER: He made a few calls. Now listen, Bob, I've heard that you've made some contacts here among the natives, made a few friendships, I'm all for that, but now if you decided to come back here and, you know, talk to these people, these Russians, or if you kept in touch with them and oh, say they made contact with you, you know, these Russians dropped you a note and you heard something you think we'd like to know, you just feel free to pass it on and I think I can say it would be appreciated. You just drop me a line and I'll make sure the right people get a look.

BOB: The right people?

RODGER: What we call the right people. The people who could use that stuff. Who know, I might become on of those guys.

BOB: Really?

RODGER: Don't think I wasn't approached. The pay is for shit, but that's not what we're here for.

BOB: Well, good luck.

RODGER: Thanks. Here's my address, and well, now, remember, if you want to, you drop me a line, all right? And I hope you feel better.

BOB: Sure. *(He starts to exit, comes back.)* Rodger, how did you pick me out in this airport? How did you know I was me?

RODGER: I have a photograph, from before the accident. And I was told you'd be here going back Stateside and let's face it, an American can always tell another American from a mile away.

BOB: We can?

RODGER: That's part of my job, Bob. About your accident. Could have been worse. You're a lucky guy. Luckier than you think. I believe in luck. You believe in luck, Bob?

BOB: I'm not sure.

RODGER: Start believing. You know who you look like? *(Pause)* The Invisible Man. Remember Claude Rains in *The Invisible Man*? That's what you look like.

BOB: Swell.

RODGER: Have a nice flight. Hope you don't have any problems when they go through your bags here. They are very efficient.

*(*BOB *exits.* RODGER *pulls out cordless phone. Dials long, complicated number.)*

RODGER: Get me Larry. *(He looks at his watch.)* Larry? Rodger. Yeah. He's on his way.

(Lights fade.)

END OF ACT ONE

ACT TWO

Scene One

(International Arrivals Terminal, Kennedy Airport. BOB *in line, waiting to get cleared through customs.)*

(The person in front of BOB *is cleared.)*

LARRY: Your passport, please.

(BOB *hands over his passport.)*

LARRY: You are Robert Wills?

BOB: Right.

LARRY: Uh huh, Mr. Wills your name is on my list here.

BOB: Your list?

LARRY: My list of names. You were traveling in the Soviet Union, is that correct?

BOB: Yes, it says that in the passport and....

LARRY: I believe there was a request for you to leave?

BOB: No, look, I'm a graduate student, my field is Russian Literature, and I had this accident, you know, and I thought I should just come home, there was no problem really.

LARRY: Would you follow me over to this room, we'd like to ask you a few questions.

BOB: But I'm in America now.

LARRY: Yes you are.

BOB: And I'm an American.

LARRY: As far as we can ascertain that is correct.

BOB: So why do you want to ask me a few questions? What's going on here? I mean, I'm back in the United States, why do you guys need to talk to me?

LARRY: Please don't be difficult, Mr. Wills. Would you mind just stepping over here please.

BOB: Oh, shit.

LARRY: Mr. Wills.

BOB: SHIT.

(They move to another area of the stage.)

(Desk. Two chairs. BOB *sits in chair. Pause.)*

LARRY: You want some coffee?

BOB: No thanks.

LARRY: Okay. I'm going to get a cup, I'll be right back. *(Exits)*

BOB: Wait, but... great.

*(*DON *enters.)*

DON: Was Larry just in here?

BOB: Who?

DON: Larry, uh... you know.... No, I guess you wouldn't, tall, gray suit—what the hell happened to you?

BOB: Accident.

DON: *Wow.*

BOB: Yeah.

DON: What, a bus hit you or something?

BOB: You wouldn't believe me if I told you the truth.

DON: Try me.

BOB: A pack of little children armed with hammers.

DON: I believe that.

BOB: This was in Moscow. Moscow, Russia.

DON: I know where Moscow is.

BOB: You believe that?

DON: Kids armed with hammers? Sure, why not. I'm Don. Work with Immigration. And you are....

BOB: Bob, Robert Wills.

DON: You're Wills, huh.

BOB: Yeah.

DON: Well, I've got your file. Right here. You name came up.

BOB: So I gathered.

(LARRY *enters.*)

DON: Hi, Larry.

LARRY: Hi Don. You want coffee?

DON: No thanks.

LARRY: I already asked Bob here. He didn't want any. But I did, so I went out and got a cup.

DON: Good thinking. This could take a while.

BOB: Excuse me.

LARRY: Yes.

BOB: Why am I here?

DON: Your name came up.

LARRY: On our list.

BOB: Yes.

DON: So I punched up your file.

LARRY: On our computer.

DON: Punch, punch, out comes everything.

BOB: Everything?

LARRY: Everything.

DON: These things are terrific.

LARRY: Me, I'm scared to death of these things. Computers.

DON: Come on, Larry.

LARRY: That's why I let old Don here handle that end.

DON: They're very simple. Really.

LARRY: I'm sure they are Don, but they just freak me out. They're just so....

DON: What?

LARRY: Fast. Just so damn fast.

DON: Yes.

LARRY: They can write poems now, God knows what else.

DON: Well, there you are, Larry.

LARRY: Yes. Mr. Wills. You just returned from the Soviet Union, is that correct? What happened to your face?

DON: Little kids with hammers.

LARRY: You're shitting me.

BOB: I wish I was.

DON: What is the world coming to?

LARRY: The center cannot hold.

DON: Yeats?

LARRY: Got it in one, Don, very good.

DON: Larry lent me this poetry anthology, I'm supposed to read a new poem every day. His idea to broaden me.

LARRY: He's stuck behind that damn console all day. Uh, Don, top file.

DON: Sure.

LARRY: *(Opens file)* Mr. Wills. You are a graduate student at Columbia.

BOB: Right.

LARRY: Thesis in Soviet Literature?

DON: Left New York two weeks ago?

LARRY: I can read, Don.

DON: Sorry.

LARRY: Don here's out of practice with people.

DON: He does this all the time.

LARRY: Down, Spot.

DON: Okay, I'll keep my mouth shut.

BOB: Just exactly why am I here?

LARRY: Well your name...

BOB: Was on the list, I know, what list is my name on?

DON: The trouble list.

LARRY: Donald....

DON: Lips are sealed, Larry.

LARRY: Thank you.

DON: Not a *peep.*

LARRY: A Vladimir Gorinsky, administrator, said, I will recommend that you leave the Soviet Union as soon as possible. And I will recommend to authorities that they also suggest to you and to American Embassy that you leave.

BOB: Maybe he said something like that.

LARRY: Those were his exact words.

BOB: Really?

LARRY: If I tell you those were his exact words, you can believe me.

DON: Believe him, Bob. Doesn't he look like Claude Rains in *The Invisible Man*?

LARRY: He does kind of.... Don, hand me that file.

DON: This one?

LARRY: No, the file in my car, of course that one. Okay, Bob, why did you tell a Soviet citizen to leave the country?

BOB: I never...

LARRY: You said.... You should come to America. You could stay with me.

DON: Why did you say, quote, you would be relatively, unquote, free in America. Free to think to express your opinions.

BOB: I said that?

LARRY: Yes, Bob, you did.

BOB: Well... uh... it's true, isn't it?

LARRY: Of course it's true, but why did you say it?

BOB: Because.... I said that?

DON: You said I'm saying you could stay with me in America.

BOB: Ludmilla...

LARRY: Right, Bob, coming back now?

BOB: Sort of.

LARRY: Bob, you did a lot of talking. And you raised some problems. Remember, in a foreign country you represent America. At least I sure as hell hope you represent America.

BOB: I do, really.

LARRY: Because if you didn't, if we had the slightest doubt you did.... You know what?

BOB: What?

LARRY: You'd be in deep-fried shit, your ass would be grass.

DON: You went to Russia and you blew it. You just got on the list.

LARRY: On the shit list.

DON: So now we wanna know why.

BOB: Why what?

LARRY: Why you had to be a royal pain in the hynie. Huh, Bob, spill the beans.

BOB: Do I need a lawyer here or something?

*(*LARRY *and* DON *smile.)*

LARRY: You're not under arrest, Bobby, this is not a police station.

BOB: But I can't be questioned like this, can I? Am I charged with some thing?

LARRY: No, Rob, we're charged TO KICK YOUR FUCKING ASS!

DON: Chill out, Larry...

LARRY: You scared now Bob?

BOB: Yes.

LARRY: Good, then raising my voice worked. Don, you wanna just back off and let me handle this? Why, Bob?

BOB: Well... you want an answer.

LARRY: Before next week, yes I would.

BOB: Well, it just seemed scary and.... I don't know.

DON: You don't know.

LARRY: You were there for a thesis, for research, right?

DON: Subject of thesis Bulgakov. Mikhail Bulgakov. *(He punches computer, reads printout on screen.)* Mikhail Bulgakov, born Kiev 1881, son of professor of theology, died of neurosclerosis 1940. Bulgakov lived through Kiev's fourteen changes of power in the refuge of his family's apartment later transforming this experience into his first novel, THE WHITE GUARD (1925), later into a play, DAYS OF THE TURBINS (1926). Am I close, Bob?

BOB: On the money.

LARRY: You think the president is a crackpot wildman, huh?

BOB: What?

LARRY: You said our president was a fucking crackpot wildman.

DON: It says that right here. You also called him the Prince of Darkness.

LARRY: Why Bob?

BOB: I...

DON: What a mouth you got, Bobo.

LARRY: What kind of thing is that to say?

BOB: What else you got on file?

LARRY: What do you want to know?

BOB: What kind of car did my father have?

DON: *(Punching computer)* Mustang, red convertible, model '67, not '66 like you keep telling people.

BOB: My dog's name?

DON: *(Punches computer)* Ralph.

BOB: Name of my high-school football team?

DON: *(Punches computer)* Trojans. Colors were maroon and white. You ran track first two years. Junior year, varsity tennis. Not a bad season.

BOB: This is incredible.

LARRY: Like I said, R.W., it's these computers, very scary. And so fast.

BOB: Am I really in... deep shit?

*(*DON *and* LARRY *grin.)*

LARRY: Not yet. Not if you're careful. Not if you talk.

DON: Why Bob?

LARRY: Why?

BOB: About saying those things. I don't know.

LARRY: You don't believe half the shit you spew out, do you?

BOB: I don't know.

LARRY: What do you believe in Bob?

(Pause)

BOB: I.... I don't know.

LARRY: That's what we like to hear.

DON: We got it all, fellah, from start to finish.

BOB: But that's kind of impossible.

LARRY: Welcome to the eighties, Roberto. Run home, Bob, go back to school, back to the library and the card catalogue and don't be a troublemaker, this coffee is shit, Don, can we send out?

DON: Sure Larry.

LARRY: Got someone waiting for you.

DON: A Doug Baker. You go to Columbia together. Played tennis. Number two doubles. Good backhand. His thesis is on the animal imagery in the novels of Ayn Rand and he owns every issue of *Sports Illustrated* since 1971.

BOB: That's him.

(Pause)

LARRY: You can go, Bob. Nice shoes.

(Lights fade.)

Scene Two

(A restaurant. GARY *waits at table.* BOB *enters, nose bandaged.)*

GARY: Hey Bob...

BOB: Look, I can't really afford this place...

GARY: No problem I got it. Sit down.

*(*BOB *sits.)*

BOB: Okay. Thanks.

GARY: Bob, what happened?

BOB: With the nose? Hit by a hammer.

GARY: Fuck.

BOB: Absolutely.

*(*WAITER *brings menus, exits.* BOB *and* GARY *study the menus.)*

GARY: Got great salmon steak here. I recommend it.

BOB: Uh huh.

GARY: Still working on the thesis, huh?

BOB: That's right.

GARY: Always chained to those library stacks. I remember your nose buried in those bummer books. Tolstoy, Dostoyevsky, had to be at least 2,000 pages.

BOB: Turgenev, Pushkin, Gorky, Lermontov.

GARY: All those greats. Hey, remember the track team.

BOB: Uh huh.

GARY: Remember what they called you? Remember your nickname on the track team?

BOB: Not really.

GARY: Leadboots. Ha. They called you Leadboots. Remember your nickname on the tennis team, huh?

BOB: Spaz.

GARY: Right. Ol' Spaz. Great time on that team. You, me, and Doug. What a group.

BOB: Uh huh. Great.

GARY: So you're probably wondering why I called.

BOB: Thought you called to see how I was.

GARY: Oh, sure, yeah, that too. But more importantly, to touch base and say, Where have we come from where are we going, you know?

*(*WAITER *crosses stage with flaming skewer of meat.)*

BOB: Well, I'm almost done with my thesis...

GARY: Listen, it's great to get nostalgic and all, but when I tell you the news, I think everything's gonna change.

BOB: What news?

GARY: The new job.

BOB: Job?

GARY: It's gonna blow your mind, really.

*(*WAITER *crosses stage without the flaming skewer.)*

GARY: You remember in college, I was taking those political science courses.

BOB: Pre-law stuff.

GARY: We all believed that at the time.

*(*WAITER *crosses the stage with fire extinguisher and exits.)*

GARY: It was understood to be pre-law courses, like the minor in history.
It was all carefully planned out under their guidance.
See, I was approached early on.
I don't want you to think it was the money, that is not what we are discussing.
But by working my way through law, then politics, then hooking up with the re-election juggernaught, I'm helping them, looking towards the future.
Then this new thing happened.
The nod. The phone call. The pitch was tossed, because my record speaks, Bob. The work, the work I've done and that was for real, sure it was. But the pitch was what I was looking for all along. And I dangled it in front of them. I made the right hints and they bit.
The phone call from the White House. From the special counsel to the

fucking President, Bob.
From Ron to his staff to me. And we make it official.
The Pitch. I got the slot I go in I get the office down the hall from him, from the fucking president.
And we know what that means. For them. What it means now for down the road.

BOB: Excuse me, but what are we talking about?

GARY: It's okay, and I think for our conversations about your interests and the recent visit and the hopeful results of that visit, we can talk turkey.

BOB: Turkey?

GARY: When I was approached I thought I could never reveal what I was into to anyone. But Bob, welcome home. Here's my phone number, okay, this is the new office number. You let them know this is only the beginning, there is a lot on the horizon. I'm in now Bob. I'm working for the bastards on the inside, that's what we've been pushing for all these years and by Christ it's touchdown all the way and go for the gold, Bob.

BOB: Gary, uh.... Congratulations on the new job.

GARY: Thank you and remember the lunch is on me, that's understood, right?

BOB: Right.

GARY: You about ready to order?

BOB: Oh, yeah, sure. Look, Gary, maybe I'm a bit off here, I'm back a few weeks and I don't know, I'm still kind of out of it but what the fuck is happening here?

GARY: Here at the restaurant?

BOB: Here, now, you and me. I'm not connecting I'm sorry.

GARY: They told me after you got back from there to make contact. The way I figure you can make these trips every couple of months, and okay we'll have lunch before you go, and you just bring in what I get you. It's perfect, any way you look at it. Your profile is excellent, we have lunch, we make contact, I tell you where I stand and it's a deal.

BOB: What?

GARY: Comrades, huh, Bob? Helping the cause. Doing our part. For the future. And of course the money does not hurt, not at all.

BOB: I think you made a mistake here.

GARY: I don't think so, Bob, your profile is excellent. Don't be nervous, it'll be fine, I'm the one in the hot seat, I'm the one passing the shit. You just have to slip it in one of your magazines or journals or whatever and that's it.

BOB: You're from us, right? You're telling me you're from them but you're really from us, trying to trap me and say, yes, I'll work for them.

GARY: Now I'm lost here, Bob.

BOB: You're CIA, right?

GARY: Very funny Bob, order your lunch.

BOB: Oh come on, this was very obvious, using you, asking me to lunch, but it just won't work, and I won't fall for it. You guys tried tripping me up at the airport but no fucking way, and the idea that you, Gary, a friend of mine, would use that friendship, turns my stomach. Well, if that's what you think of me, just fuck you and fuck them and fuck us.

GARY: What are you talking about?

BOB: I'm not sure, but I am so incredibly pissed off.

GARY: Sit down, Bob.

BOB: NO I WILL NOT SIT DOWN. I will not be a tool and you can tell your bosses TO EAT SHIT AND LEAVE ME ALONE.

*(*BOB *exits.)*

GARY: Check, please....

(Lights dim.)

Scene Three

*(*HELEN *and* JEAN *are sitting at a bus stop. A* MAN *waits with them.* BOB *enters. They wait.)*

HELEN: *(Reading her paper)* Oh my gosh.

JEAN: What?

HELEN: This.

JEAN: What?

HELEN: A man walks into the smoking car of a train. Opens fire with a machine gun.

JEAN: Oh no.

HELEN: Twenty dead, fifty-two injured. The New Haven line.

JEAN: I've travelled that. I could have been on that train.

HELEN: Yes.

BOB: Excuse me, does the seventeen bus stop here?

*(*HELEN *and* JEAN *stare at* BOB. *Long pause)*

BOB: The seventeen bus.

HELEN: Yes?

BOB: Does it... uh, stop here?

(Long pause.)

HELEN: Yes it does.

*(*HELEN *looks at her paper. Pause.)*

BOB: Thanks. Thank you.

HELEN: Oh.

JEAN: What?

HELEN: Plane bombing.

JEAN: Where?

HELEN: Denver.

JEAN: How many?

HELEN: Two hundred dead. No survivors.

JEAN: Terrible.

HELEN: Yes. Look at this.

JEAN: Hmmm.

HELEN: Hotel fire. Arson.

JEAN: Where?

HELEN: San Francisco.

JEAN: How many?

HELEN: Five hundred and thirty-two dead, many more feared.

JEAN: Dig them out.

HELEN: Take days.

BOB: *(To* MAN*)* Do you have the correct time?

(All stare at BOB.*)*

BOB: The time.... What time is it?

MAN: You want to know what time it is?

BOB: Yes.

MAN: Right now, the time.

BOB: Yes.

MAN: It's ten to one.

*(*HELEN *and* JEAN *back to paper.)*

HELEN: My....

JEAN: What?

HELEN: Nuclear accident.

JEAN: Where?

HELEN: Billings, Montana.

JEAN: How many?

HELEN: Two to three million.

JEAN: Dead?

HELEN: At least.

JEAN: Goodness.

HELEN: Look at this...

JEAN: What?

HELEN: Woman buried alive twelve weeks gains weight.

JEAN: Huh.

BOB: Excuse me...

HELEN: Yes.

BOB: What paper is that?

HELEN: This?

BOB: Yes.

HELEN: *The Times.*

BOB: *The New York Times*?

HELEN: Yes.

BOB: Well, I read *The Times, The New York Times* this morning, it didn't have any of those stories.

HELEN: No?

BOB: You sure that's today's *New York Times*?

HELEN: Of course I'm sure.

JEAN: He wants to rob you.

BOB: I don't want to rob you, I'm asking about your paper.

HELEN: This is today's *Times*. Maybe you read the morning edition, this is the final edition.

BOB: It's impossible that all that stuff happened between the morning and the late edition. And that story about the woman buried alive? That's in *The Times*?

HELEN: Yes. And here's a story about movie stars who have taken trips on UFOs.

BOB: This is odd. I never noticed this stuff before.

HELEN: Well maybe you should read the newspaper more carefully.

*(*JACK *enters. Goes up to* MAN. JACK *is dressed in dark suit and mirror shades.)*

JACK: Okay, Bud, let's go.

MAN: Get your hands off me.

JACK: Don't fuck with me.

MAN: Get away.

BOB: Hey.

JACK: Don't get involved here, fellah. *(To* MAN*)* Let's go. You're in big trouble, don't get me mad.

MAN: I'm telling you, I don't know you. *(He starts to walk off.)*

JACK: Don't walk away from me.... Stop right there. Okay.

(He pulls out a gun, fires. MAN*'s chest explodes.)*

BOB: Oh my God! Oh Christ!

JACK: Stupid jerk.... *(*JACK *goes through* MAN*'s coat. Lifts wallet, looks at it.)* Oh shit. Wrong guy. Boy, I did it now. *(To* BOB*)* Look, little mistake here. You didn't see anything right? This guy looked like somebody I know. It happens, right? We'll just forget the whole thing, right? Official Business.

BOB: I....

JACK: Right. Have a nice day. *(He exits.)*

BOB: You see this?

HELEN: What?

BOB: All this.... Jesus.... They just can't blow some guy away. This is America!

HELEN: I was reading my paper.

BOB: What?

HELEN: Stop bothering me.

BOB: GIVE ME THAT! *(Grabs paper. Crumples it to his chest.)*

*(*BOB *looks at* MAN *on the ground.* BOB *starts to leave.)*

JEAN: Here's the seventeen bus. You wanted that?

BOB: Yes. Seventeen bus. Stops here. Yes. *(He exits.)*

HELEN: That man has an attitude problem.

(Lights fade.)

Scene Four

*(*BOB*'s apartment.* DOUG *and* BOB*.)*

BOB: How do you feel, Doug? They knew you were waiting for me at the airport. They even knew about your backhand.

DOUG: Bob, everybody knows about my backhand, it's no state secret.

BOB: And what about Gary? Working for the White House?

DOUG: Yeah, I know. It's great.

BOB: Doesn't it bother you?

DOUG: Bob, you have to get real here.

BOB: Get real. I'm getting real. I'm getting incredibly real.

DOUG: They are not after you.

BOB: I say to myself there are laws here, wars have been fought so that we do not have to live in total fucking anarchy.

DOUG: Right, in the meantime guys are watching you and the phone is tapped.

BOB: I mean, don't they need me to conspire or something to be involved in these things?

DOUG: Are they staked out across the street? Where are they, Bob? Under the ashtray? Maybe they're watching you through the T.V.?

BOB: I never said that.

DOUG: No, Bob, the guy who sings opera and talks to himself on the corner. Soviet agent.

BOB: Okay, you made your point. But you can't deny very weird things happening.

DOUG: The East Village is very weird, Bob. You step outside and there are people with green hair. People wandering the streets with boots made out of Clorox bottles. Grandmothers with mohawk haircuts. Of course it's weird. But, hey, it's wacky, New York Is a Summer Festival kind of thing. You come back here and start babbling about hit men and tapped phones and this thing with the kids blows my mind.

BOB: But it's true.

DOUG: Maybe there are bits of truth buried in the bizarre trip you're on. You have done nothing wrong.

BOB: I know.

DOUG: So they're not after you.

BOB: No, here's where I think we disagree.

DOUG: You're not listening. Watch my lips. They are not after you. They are not going to come bursting through the door.

(Door buzzer)

BOB: Who is that?

DOUG: Is that your door?

BOB: Yes.

DOUG: Who is it?

BOB: I asked you.

DOUG: You expecting someone?

BOB: No.

DOUG: How'd they get in?

BOB: Answer the door, Doug.

DOUG: Maybe its a killer rhino.

BOB: ANSWER THE DOOR, DOUG. ANSWER THE DOOR OR I'M GOING TO JUMP OUT THE WINDOW.

DOUG: Okay, calm down, I'm going to the door. Whoa, you are wound very tight, Bob.

(DOUG goes off.)

BOB: I can handle it, I can handle it....

(DOUG comes back.)

BOB: So?

DOUG: Yeah?

BOB: Who's there? Who's at the door?

DOUG: A woman.

BOB: Where is she now?

DOUG: In the hall, she was not carrying a bozooka as far as I can tell, can I ask her in?

BOB: Right, okay.

*(*DOUG *exits. He enters with* LUDMILLA.*)*

BOB: Ludmilla?

LUDMILLA: Yes.

BOB: Ludmilla, it's you.

LUDMILLA: Yes, it's me.

BOB: You're here in America. Ludmilla... I...

LUDMILLA: Yes?

BOB: You look really good. Are you here for a visit?

LUDMILLA: No, I emigrated.

BOB: And you are staying....

LUDMILLA: Here with you. You told me to leave Soviet Union and live with you.

DOUG: You told her this?

BOB: Yes. Ludmilla. Well. You're here.

LUDMILLA: Yes.

DOUG: She's Russian?

BOB: Yes.

DOUG: She's moving in? Outstanding!

BOB: Ludmilla. Well. So here you are. You made it to America. Well.

LUDMILLA: You are surprised to see me?

BOB: Yes. No. Of course this is sudden. But it's nice. What a great surprise. How did you get here?

LUDMILLA: I take airplane from Paris.

BOB: No, how did you....

LUDMILLA: I have defected. I got to Paris for medical conference and I defect. *(Pause)* So, this is your apartment.

BOB: Yes.

LUDMILLA: You have lived here how long?

BOB: Two years.

LUDMILLA: And you live alone?

BOB: Yes.

LUDMILLA: And your parents live in New Jersey?

BOB: How do you know that?

LUDMILLA: I think you tell me this.

BOB: I never said anything about my parents.

LUDMILLA: Oh. I thought you said this to me.

BOB: No, I never said that. I never said anything about my parents living in New Jersey. Which they do. In New Jersey.

LUDMILLA: And you grew up there?

BOB: Why are you asking me this?

LUDMILLA: I don't know.

BOB: You don't know.

LUDMILLA: No.

(Long pause)

BOB: Yes, well. Doug. Ludmilla. Here we are.

(Pause)

DOUG: Boy, this is great. Isn't this great?

(Lights dim.)

Scene Five

*(*BOB*'s apartment.* BOB *and* LUDMILLA *sitting in chairs, reading magazines. Silence. The phone rings. Nobody moves. The phone rings again.* LUDMILLA *looks to* BOB. BOB *does not react. The phone rings again.* LUDMILLA *wants to answer it. The phone rings.)*

LUDMILLA: Robert.

BOB: Yes.

(The phone rings.)

LUDMILLA: Your phone is ringing.

BOB: Yes.

(Phone rings.)

LUDMILLA: Aren't you going to answer it?

BOB: No, it's.... I'm sure it's a wrong number.

LUDMILLA: How can you tell?

(Phone rings.)

BOB: If it's important they'll call back.

(Pause. They wait for the phone to ring. Silence.)

BOB: See, it probably wasn't that important.

LUDMILLA: Robert, do not be upset, but have you thought of talking to someone?

BOB: We are talking now, Ludmilla.

LUDMILLA: No, Robert, talking to someone about the things that make you, uh, um... that are causing you to be upset.

BOB: I'm fine here, Ludmilla.

LUDMILLA: Robert, perhaps you should consider talking to a person who could relieve these tensions you are experiencing.

BOB: You saying I should see a psychiatrist or something?

(Pause)

LUDMILLA: Well... yes.

BOB: You think I'm losing it here or something?

LUDMILLA: No, Robert, but I am very nervous and you are making me more nervous, and I am suggesting an opportunity to talk with a person more qualified than myself concerning your fear of answering the phone.

BOB: I don't have a problem with the phone.

(The phone rings. They wait. The phone rings again.)

LUDMILLA: Do you want me to answer it?

BOB: No, no, listen... I... I can answer the phone.

(Phone rings.)

BOB: No problem, okay. *(He picks up the phone.)* Hello? Yes? Hello, Doug. It's Doug.

LUDMILLA: Hello. Doug.

BOB: Yes I'm fine, Doug. Ludmilla's fine too. She's here, she's fine. We're fine. Ludmilla, would you go into the kitchen for a second?

LUDMILLA: Robert, I'm sorry, I...

BOB: No, look, could you get me a beer from the kitchen?

LUDMILLA: Of course. *(She exits.)*

BOB: *(Quickly)* Listen, Doug, she's out of the room. No, I am not losing it. I just find it incredibly strange that she just shows up here. Well, yes, I invited her here. Yes. Yes, I can handle it.

(Door buzzer)

LUDMILLA: Is someone at the door, Robert?

(The door crashes open, JACK *bursts in, gun trained on* BOB.*)*

JACK: Don't move, scumbag!

BOB: Look, Doug, I gotta call you back, I got somebody at the door. *(He hangs up.)*

JACK: Okay, you are dead meat, asshole!

LUDMILLA: *(Off)* Is someone there, Robert?

BOB: No, no, I have the television on, everything's fine.

JACK: *(Pushing gun in* BOB*'s face.)* You are finished, you understand, you are gonna be wasted, I am gonna smear your brains all over the wallpaper, you lowlife dickhead.

BOB: Uh, I think you got the wrong guy.

JACK: Oh, Jesus.

BOB: Look...

JACK: Oh, son of a bitch, is this 312?

BOB: No, it's not, the number's off the door.

JACK: I am really, really sorry. I made a big mistake. Can I use your phone?

BOB: Sure.

JACK: Wow, I thought this was 312. It's ringing. *(To phone)* OKAY, YOU ARE DEAD MEAT, ASSHOLE. I AM COMING OVER RIGHT NOW AND YOU ARE FINISHED. I AM GOING TO SMEAR YOUR BRAINS ALL OVER THE WALLPAPER YOU LOWLIFE DICKHEAD. *(Hangs up)* Hey, have I seen you before.

BOB: No.

JACK: Look, really sorry about busting the door open.

BOB: No problem.

JACK: I'll just let myself out.

*(*JACK *starts out.* LUDMILLA *enters.)*

LUDMILLA: Robert, the beer is... oh!

JACK: Love to talk, but I got business. Have a nice day.

*(*JACK *exits.)*

LUDMILLA: Robert, that man had a gun.

BOB: Yes he did.

LUDMILLA: And he crashed through the door?

BOB: Uh huh.

LUDMILLA: What kind of a country is this, people crashing into your home with guns and who is this person? This is terrible. Robert, that man had a gun, isn't it illegal to.... Robert, what are you doing with my bag?

BOB: You're a doctor, right? You have drugs for emergencies. This is an emergency. I am looking for emergency drugs in your bag.

LUDMILLA: No, Robert...

BOB: Don't argue with me, Ludmilla. I am very calm right now, but you don't want to see me lose it. Ah, here we are. *(Takes out bottle of pills)* This is something I never heard of. Okay. *(He swallows pills.)* What did I just take?

LUDMILLA: This is medicine for premenstrual syndrome.

BOB: Very good. Does it take effect quickly?

LUDMILLA: Yes, but....

BOB: Very good.

LUDMILLA: He was going to shoot you.

BOB: Right.

(Phone rings. LUDMILLA *looks at* BOB, *then also swallows pills. Phone rings again.)*

(Lights fade.)

Scene Six

*(*DOCTOR*'s office. Two chairs. Bookcase with VCR. Desk with phone.* BOB *in chair. The* DOCTOR *sits behind her desk.)*

BOB: I'll be up front, Doctor Terrafirma, this wasn't my idea.

ADELE: Well I'm sorry if you feel uncomfortable, Robert, people usually do the first time. And please call me Adele.

BOB: I am just saying that I don't need to talk to someone like you. A psychiatrist.

ADELE: Well you mentioned you are feeling under great pressure, that you were tense.

BOB: Not exactly, but you know everybody feels like that on certain days.... Uh, Adele.

ADELE: Why don't we start with you telling me a little about yourself? You said you were working on your doctorate.

BOB: Yes, in Russian Literature.

ADELE: Any hobbies? Play any sports?

BOB: Well I used to play tennis, but you know...

ADELE: You played in college?

BOB: In high school mostly, but I started in college and then got interested in other things.

ADELE: Did you have a nickname?

BOB: Excuse me?

ADELE: In school, did you have a nickname? Like on the tennis team?

BOB: What does this have to do...

ADELE: Surely you must have had a nickname on the team, everybody does. What was it?

*(*BOB *mumbles.)*

ADELE: What was that?

BOB: Uh, Spaz. They called me Spaz.

ADELE: I see.

BOB: But actually I was a decent player, I wasn't professional caliber, but it was a kind of joke and, you know, I don't see what my nickname has to do with any of this.

ADELE: And now you're studying Russian Literature.

BOB: Yes.

ADELE: Tennis days are long over, eh, Spaz? Decided to stop the sports.

BOB: Yes.

(Pause)

ADELE: Any specific area of Russian Literature?

BOB: Early Soviet satire. Bulgakov.

ADELE: How wonderful.

BOB: You've read Bulgakov?

ADELE: One of my favorites.

BOB: Not too many people read him.

ADELE: Well, he is very difficult to get in my country.

BOB: I'm sorry...

ADELE: Yes?

BOB: What did you just say?

ADELE: About what?

BOB: Did you say it was difficult to get Bulgakov in your country? Which country would that be?

ADELE: I didn't say that.

BOB: Yes you did. You said, "In my country."

ADELE: I said his work is often difficult to get.

BOB: You said that?

ADELE: Yes I did, Robert.

BOB: I'm sorry, I thought you said something else.

ADELE: Now Robert, your friend mentioned that you also had a tendency to overreact like this.

BOB: Like what? Was I overreacting here?

ADELE: Now, if I went in the other room and called you, you'd have no fear of picking up the phone, on my desk.

BOB: This one here?

ADELE: Yes.

BOB: No, why would I be afraid of answering a phone?

ADELE: Well, maybe somebody would be listening in on our conversation.

BOB: Why would anyone want to do that?

ADELE: Good question, Robert, why would anyone be interested in what we're talking about? We're not anyone especially important or dangerous.

BOB: Right.

ADELE: So you would answer the phone?

BOB: Of course.

ADELE: Well, I'm going in the room down the hall from the office and call you and we'll talk on the phone, all right?

BOB: Do we really need to do that?

ADELE: Of course you don't have to, but just for me, would you mind doing that?

BOB: It's kind of silly, isn't it?

ADELE: You think I'm asking you to do something silly?

BOB: Well, no, sure, I'll answer the phone if that's what you want.

ADELE: Good. I'll be a minute.

(She exits. BOB *waits. Long pause. He gets up sits behind desk. Waits, looks casually at some papers on the desk. Picks up the phone, listens, nothing. Gets up, goes to door.)*

BOB: Uh, Adele, you out there? I'm ready to answer the phone, hello? Are you down the hall, hello?

*(*BOB *comes back, sits behind desk. Waits. Finally goes over to bookcase, glances at titles. Looks at T.V. and VCR. Slides back a panel next to T.V. Sees rows of cassettes.)*

BOB: Miller, Taylor, Seward, Wills, R. Wills R. Wills number 4, 5, 6. What is this?

*(*BOB *looks around, takes out a tape. Looks out the door then runs back and puts tape on machine. Playback on VCR:)*

BOB: But you can't deny very weird things happening.

DOUG: The East Village is very weird, Bob. You step outside and there are people with green hair. People wandering the streets with boots made out of Clorox bottles. Grandmothers with mohawk haircuts....

(Phone rings. BOB *drops tapes, looking around.)*

BOB: Holy, shit, I'm fucked. Right, time to get out of here, Bob. *(He looks at ringing phone.)* Okay. *(He picks up phone.)* I'm on to you, Adele! *(He runs out.)*

(Lights fade.)

Scene Seven

*(*Bob*'s apartment. Dim light.* Bob *in bed. A figure enters.)*

Bob: Who is that? All right, I know you're there. I can see you. I have incredible night vision and I can see you in the room. Stop where you are. Okay, I'm turning on the light now. *(Lights up)* Ludmilla!

Ludmilla: Robert, I...

Bob: I knew it would be you, Ludmilla, I just knew it. They've told you to take me, right? You gonna pump me full of drugs and make me disappear? Is that it?

Ludmilla: Robert, please do not be so upset.

Bob: No, why should I be upset? You're just lurking in the middle of the night ready to neutralize me or something.

Ludmilla: Oh, I am so... embarrassed you turn on the light.

Bob: I bet you are, that wasn't part of your plan!

Ludmilla: No. I do not want to hurt you or do these other things. No, I.... When I bring you to apartment in Moscow, and make dinner and tell you things, things I have never said to anyone, I like you very much and soon you are gone....

Bob: Yes?

Ludmilla: Yes. And I remember you say stay with me and I think about the night something maybe happen between us. And tonight you are alone but you act now like I want to hurt you.

Bob: What about you just showing up here?

Ludmilla: But you invite me, Robert, you tell me stay in America.

Bob: But you're always watching me.

Ludmilla: You are person I live with. You wish me to go? I cannot go to Russia, and I cannot find apartment. I cannot even take bus!

Bob: I don't want you to go back to Russia.

Ludmilla: ing. And everyone at the bus stop knows this and looks at their feet and are silent as the old man disappears, maybe forever. Then I began to fear that everyone at bus stop was watching me. Watching to see my reaction to this scene. This incident was performed for my benefit and the agent leaves so that people can then hear me express my reaction to this arrest. So I say nothing, I trust no one at the bus stop. And each of us is thinking the same thing. Each of those others must think I am an agent wk you are afraid of me because I am Russian maybe.

BOB: That's ridiculous.

LUDMILLA: Is it?

BOB: What do you think?

LUDMILLA: I don't know.

BOB: You don't?

LUDMILLA: I think you think if I was American woman I could not harm you then.

BOB: That's not true.

LUDMILLA: Then why do you watch me so hard?

BOB: Why do you want me to answer the phone?

LUDMILLA: Why are people running in here with guns?

BOB: Why did you want me to see a psychiatrist?

LUDMILLA: Why do you think I leave everything, leave my country to be with you? I must be crazy.

BOB: You think you're crazy?

LUDMILLA: You think I am crazy?

BOB: Who do we think is crazy here?

(Beat)

LUDMILLA: Robert, I have nothing except you. I know no one here, I cannot find job or apartment, and I care about you and I want you to care about me and I wish you to touch me and hold me and.... Now you say something.

BOB: I'm sorry, Ludmilla. I'm sorry I said those things.

LUDMILLA: Then you do not hate me?

BOB: No.

LUDMILLA: Would you hold me?

BOB: Yes. Yes. I'll hold you. Why don't you get into bed with me and I'll hold you. And I'll turn out the light.

*(*LUDMILLA *gets in bed,* BOB *turns out the light. Pause.)*

BOB: Ludmilla, did you kick me? Ludmilla?

*(*BOB *turns on light.)*

*(*SERGEI *stands next to the bed.)*

BOB: Oh God, who is this?

SERGEI: It's me, Sergei.

BOB: Oh.

SERGEI: It's okay, I died in Russia.

BOB: Yeah?

SERGEI: Yes. They burned me up and everything. Spread my ashes to the wind.

BOB: I'm sorry.

SERGEI: This is nice room, nicer than the room we had in Moscow.

BOB: Yeah but you got to pay for it here, you have to pay a lot. Sergei, they're trying to kill me.

SERGEI: Yes?

BOB: They chase me with guns, and listen in on my phone, and watch me. I came back here and found out they were after me.

SERGEI: They are after all of us.

BOB: You think so?

SERGEI: I know so. Robert, it doesn't matter whether they're really after you or not. If you think so, they have won. The government doesn't want trust, it wants control. For them trust is good, but control is better. Da svidanya. *(He exits.)*

LUDMILLA: Did you say something, Robert?

BOB: Ludmilla, we need to go.

LUDMILLA: What?

BOB: We need to pack and get out of here.

LUDMILLA: What are you talking about?

*(*SMALL CHILD *enters.)*

BOB: Oh, no, not again, WHAT ARE YOU DOING HERE?

LUDMILLA: How did this person get into the apartment?

BOB: How did you get here, this is America, Uncle Tom? I bet Uncle Tom flew you over!

LUDMILLA: Robert, please....

(Other CHILDREN *enter.)*

LUDMILLA: Robert, there are several children here.

BOB: I love you, Ludmilla.

LUDMILLA: Thank you, what are these children doing?

(They pull on BOB, *start to drag him off.)*

LUDMILLA: Stop that, all of you stop this.

*(*CHILD *raises hammer at* LUDMILLA.*)*

LUDMILLA: Oh my God!

BOB: I'm not dead yet, stop, you Soviet youth!

(The CHILDREN *suddenly stop and leave.* BOB *and* LUDMILLA *watch them exit.)*

BOB: Ludmilla, we've got to get out of here.

LUDMILLA: Where can we go?

BOB: They'll be watching the airports, Grand Central, even the Major Deegan. Wait a minute—there is a place—they'll never look for us there.

(Lights fade.)

Scene Eight

(Railing at the stern of the Staten Island Ferry: BOB *and* LUDMILLA.*)*

BOB: When we get to Staten Island, we take the bus to Tottenville, then into New Jersey and disappear off the face of the Earth. Feeling better?

LUDMILLA: Yes.

BOB: There it is. Statue of Liberty.

LUDMILLA: Yes.

BOB: I've never actually been to the Statue of Liberty. Lived here all my life, never been there.

LUDMILLA: It is very nice.

BOB: Everything is going to be okay.

LUDMILLA: Really?

BOB: Sure. Everything is fine.

*(*DOUG *enters.)*

DOUG: Hi, Bob.

BOB: Doug, what are you doing here? On this boat?

DOUG: You guys just ran off. I've been trying to get ahold of you. What kind of thing is that, just running off, not telling people where you are. People get worried.

BOB: What people are we talking about, Doug?

DOUG: Oh, like your family.

(MOTHER, TOM, *and* LONNIE *enter.)*

MOTHER: Robert, you never told us you were living with a Russian woman.

TOM: That makes us look bad.

LONNIE: Like you don't trust us or something.

MOTHER: Do the Immigration people know about this? I ought to report this person to the authorities, you might be harboring this person illegally.

BOB: What are you doing here, Mom? How did you get on this boat?

DOUG: I told them you'd be here.

BOB: You what?

LUDMILLA: What does she mean about reporting me?

LONNIE: Look at the Statue of Liberty.

(MOTHER, TOM, *and* LONNIE *move off as* GARY *enters.)*

GARY: Bob, big guy, how you doing?

BOB: Gary, how did you get here?

DOUG: I told him, Bob. I thought we should get together for a talk.

BOB: I can't believe you would do this, Doug. You had no right to do this.

DOUG: But I'm your friend.

GARY: We're all your friends.

DOUG: You got to trust your friends.

BOB: Gary, would you go away, please. I'm having a very bad time now. And Doug, you should go too. Everyone should leave.

GARY: Isn't that your mother over there? You know something? She works for us, yes she does. Bet you didn't know that. Yes, we recruited her years ago. What would your mother be doing, working for us? To keep an eye on you. Been doing it for years, most of your family works for us. Tom, Lonnie, even Doug. Everyone you knew at school worked for us. Those guys on the tennis team? Sent us reports on you, typed, double spaced, very neat.

BOB: Mom, is any of this true?

MOTHER: Robert, what a silly question.

BOB: This is not happening.

(DON *and* LARRY *enter.)*

LARRY: Doug told us you'd be out here, with a Russian. You and this Russian woman are in big trouble. Want to get an Eskimo Pie, Don?

DON: Eskimo Pie! You bet!

(DON and LARRY move off.)

BOB: What are you all doing on this boat at this particular time?

DOUG: We thought you needed to get serious about your life.

BOB: Ludmilla, doesn't this seem strange to you?

LUDMILLA: It is very very strange.

(JACK enters.)

JACK: Been looking all over for you, now I got you.

MOTHER: Oh, there's Jack, I bet he wants to smear Bob's brain all over the wallpaper.

BOB: All I need now is for those kids to show up.

(The CHILDREN appear.)

BOB: Aaaaaaah! This has gone too far.

TOM: Brought those kids over, Bob. Special fare.

LONNIE: We couldn't pass it up.

LUDMILLA: Robert what can we do?

BOB: I'm having a major breakdown.

(SERGEI enters.)

BOB: Sergei, thank God you're here.

SERGEI: I have never seen Statue of Liberty.

DOUG: Isn't it great. Don't you feel like an American?

SERGEI: Bob, you look upset.

BOB: Sergei, what do they all want from us?

SERGEI: Do you feel in danger?

BOB: Yes!

LUDMILLA: Yes!

SERGEI: Well, Bob, what can you do?

BOB: Say you were on a boat, crossing the ocean, and you see up ahead this iceberg, and you know you're going to crash into it. You turn to the passenger next to you and say, "Excuse me, isn't that an iceberg we're headed towards?" "Yes." the passenger says. And that means we're in danger. Our lives are in danger. We only have a moment to make a decision. Maybe we should jump off the boat, I think. Granted we're in the middle of the ocean and jumping off we could be killed but it's better than staying put and slamming into a couple of tons of ice. Now Sergei, rationally speaking, what would you do? You gonna stay put on the boat or jump?

SERGEI: I'm not on the boat anymore.

BOB: Exactly. *(He clambers over the ferry's rail.)*

LUDMILLA: What are you doing?

BOB: Jumping.

LUDMILLA: Into the river?

BOB: That's right.

(The crowd rushes toward BOB.*)*

MOTHER: Stop him.

DOUG: Don't jump....

LONNIE: WAIT!

TOM: You're crazy to jump.

BOB: I'm crazy to stay.

(They try to hold him back.)

BOB: I'm jumping now..... .

LUDMILLA: I'm jumping too!

(Upstage the ICE CREAM MAN *appears.)*

ICE CREAM MAN: GET YOUR ESKIMO PIES!

CROWD: Eskimo Pie.

(They all—except LUDMILLA*—rush upstage to get ice cream, shouting, forgetting about* BOB *at the rail.)*

BOB and LUDMILLA: Okay, we're jumping now, we're going to jump.

(They jump off and disappear. The Others stop shouting for ice cream, turn around, and see that BOB *and* LUDMILLA *are gone. They stare out.)*

DOUG: Bob! Ludmilla! *(Beat)* Hey, things aren't that bad... are they?

(Lights fade.)

END OF PLAY

THE WHITE DEATH

Daniel Therriault

ABOUT THE AUTHOR

Daniel Therriault's first play, BATTERY, was awarded the Wigmore Foundation Production Grant and premiered at Theatre at St. Clement's featuring Holly Hunter. BATTERY has been produced across the country and in Europe, awarded six Drama-Logue Awards, optioned for a film and translated into German. Mr. Therriault's one-act, FLOOR ABOVE THE ROOF, commissioned by the Wigmore Foundation, was a winner in Chicago's Play Expo Competition, was co-produced by the Victory Gardens and Body Politic Theaters in Chicago and then produced by the Working Theatre at the Henry Street Settlement House in New York in 1989. THE WHITE DEATH, his second full-length play, has been awarded the Arthur Foundation Grant in New York, the Hawaiian Committee for the Humanities Grant and seven Drama-Logue Awards. Mr. Therriault has been the American Exchange Writer to Ireland, is a returning playwright-in-residence at the Sundance Institute and is an elected member of New Dramatists in New York City. All of Mr. Therriault's plays are available through Broadway Play Publishing.

To Bill and Lowry

THE WHITE DEATH premiered in Honolulu at Kumu Kahua, with Dennis Carroll, Executive Director, on 23 January 1986. The cast, in order of appearance, was the following:

KITTY KALUA .... Lei Kaniaupio
KANAKA .... James Grant Benton
KIMO .... Dave Lancaster
REV HUNTER .... Allen Cole
THE CARDINAL CODE .... Walt Robertson
TOURIST .... Frank B. Shaner
LIONEL HARDING .... Christopher Ivanyi
OMURO .... Dennis Chun

Director .... Dando Kluever
Scenery and lighting design .... Stephen Clear
Costumes .... Loletia Williams
Production stage manager .... Christopher Ivanyi

THE WHITE DEATH opened in Los Angeles at the CAST Theatre through Appian Way Productions and Ted Schmitt for the CAST Theatre on November 23, 1987. It was produced by Lisa James, Linda Bernstein, and Cheryl Bascom. The cast, in order of appearance, was the following:

KITTY KALUA .... Shuko Akune
KANAKA .... Henry K. Bal
KIMO .... Alberto Isaac
REV HUNTER .... Gregg Henry
THE CARDINAL CODE/TOURIST .... Royce D. Applegate
OMURO .... Rob Narita

Note: There was no actor for LIONEL HARDING in the L.A. production, they used a dummy.

Director .... Charles G. Davis
Set design .... Kevin Adams
Costumes .... Martha Ferrara
Lights .... Brian Gale
Sound .... Stephen Shaffer
Production stage manager .... Shawn LaVallee

CHARACTERS

KITTY KALUA, *female, Hawaiian*
KANAKA, *male, Hawaiian*
KIMO, *male, Filipino-American*
REV HUNTER, *male, white*
THE CARDINAL CODE, *male, in his sixties, white*
TOURIST, *male, in his fifties, white*
LIONEL HARDING, *male, white*
OMURO, *male, Japanese*

The role of THE CARDINAL CODE *is a voice over the telephone.*

If necessary, one actor can play the roles of THE CARDINAL CODE, TOURIST, *and* LIONEL HARDING.

The entire action erupts in the Volcano Bar, built on the rim of Kilauea Crater in the village of Volcano on the island of Hawaii. The action takes place within twenty-four hours.

The time is the present.

GLOSSARY

Pronunciation of Hawaiian

Vowels:
a like a in above
e like y in city
i like y in city
o like o in sole
u like oo in moon

Rising Diphthongs:
ae like y in my
ai like y in my
au like ow in how
ao like ow in how
oi like oi in oil

Exception: The first e in Pele and in hele is like e in bet.

′ *(in word itself)* A glottal stop, similar to the sound between the ohs in English oh-oh. ′ *(in pronunciation key)* A syllable accent.

HAWAIIAN

aloha (a-lo′-ha) Love, hello, goodbye.
Halemaumau (Ha′-le-mau′-mau) A volcanic crater.
haole (how′-ly). White person. Caucasian. Foreigner.
hapu'u (ha-poo′) A tree fern.
hele (he′-ly) To go, come, move.
Hilo (hi′-lo) The largest town on the island of Hawaii.
hukilau (hu′-ki-lau) To fish with a seine. A fish feast.
hula (hu′-la) Hawaiian dance.
ka The.
kalua (ka-lu′-a) 1. To bake in a ground oven, baked. 2. Pit.
kanaka (ka-na′-ka) Human being, man, Hawaiian, mankind.
kane (ka′-nay) Male, man, husband.
kapu (ka-pu) Forbidden.
Kilauea (Ki′-lau-ay′-a) Volcanic crater ruled by Pele.
koa (ko′-a) Indigenous tree and wood from that tree.
kukae (ku-kae) Feces.
lei (lay′-i) Necklace of flowers, leaves, shells, feathers.
lolo (lo-lo) 1. Crazy. 2. Stupid.
lua (lu′-a) 1. Toilet. 2. Hole that has a bottom, pit.
luau (lu′-au) Hawaiian feast.
mahalo (ma-ha′-lo) Thank you.

mahu (ma'-hu) Homosexual.
maile (mai'-le) A shrub with fragrant leaves used for leis.
makua 'uhane (ma-ku'-a u-ha'-ne) Catholic priest.
mauka (mau'-ka) Inland.
Mauna Loa (mau'-na lo'-a) Long mountain. Volcanic mountain that contains Kilauea Crater.
'ohana (o-ha'-na) Family.
okole (o-ko'-le) Buttocks.
ono (o'-no) Good, delicious.
pau (pow) Finished, done, ended.
Pele (Pe'-ly) The volcano goddess.
pilau (pi-lau') Stink, stench, bad smell, rot, decomposed.
po'i 'uhane (po'-i u-ha'ne) Soul snatching, to capture souls.
pua'a (pu-a'-a) Pig, hog, swine.
puka (pu'-ka) 1. Hole (perforation), puncture; opening.
Puna (pu'-na) Region on the island of Hawaii.
pupule (pu-pu'-le) Crazy, insane.
wahine (wa-hi'-ne) Woman, lady, wife.
wikiwiki (wi'-ki-wi'-ki) Quick, fast.

SLANG

brah (bra) Brother. Term of affection, like man or amigo.
Buddaheads (Bud'-dha-heads) Derogatory term for Japanese people.
bugger (bug'-ger) Man, guy, thing.
chee (gee) An expression of awe, confusion.
da kine (da kine) The kind, the thing, the type meant.
eeha (ee'-ha) An expression of rejoicing.
eh (ay) Hey.
Flip A derogatory term for Filipino.
garans (gar'-ans) Guaranteed.
Kanak (ka-nak') Short for Kanaka.
lava-lava A tight, wrap-around skirt, usually a floral design.
makee (ma'-kay) A Japanese word meaning dead.
manong (ma-nong') A derogatory term for Filipino.
max Maximum, limit.
Pake (Pa-kay') Chinese.
poi dog (oi as in oil) Mutt, mixed breed, not pedigree.
Portigi (paw'-ti-gee') Derogatory term for Portugese people.
shaka (sha'-ka) Good, great, all right, everything is cool.
sharkbait 1. White people. 2. Johns, customers.
wen Went.
Yakuza (Ya'-ku-za) Japanese organized crime gang.

(The Volcano Bar is a dive. Plastic leis hang on hooks, Hawaiian dolls in grass skirts wiggle, and giant artificial palm leaves loll from the ceiling with cardboard coconuts and outsized pineapples. Bottles of liquor, set in racks to protect against earthquakes, stand behind the bar itself. Barstools and a few tables with chairs inhabit the place. There is at least one window. A single door is the only public entrance. Directly opposite this entrance, another door, with the sign "Private" above it, leads to the backroom. The tavern is dirty; its walls are cracked, colors faded, and darkness rims the room.)

*(*KIMO *is Filipino-American, small and wiry, with a fool's grin that often bursts into nervous laughter. His eyes constantly change from harmless innocence to an idiot's terror. He moves quickly about the bar and calls out in a thin, impotent voice.)*

*(*KANAKA *is full-blooded Hawaiian. On first impression, he appears to be ignorance in motion. His laugh is grotesque and he submits to an uncontrollable habit of scratching all parts of his body because he is physically diseased. He dresses in heavy work boots, long pants, and a tee shirt.)*

*(*KITTY KALUA *is a fiery, part-blooded Hawaiian. Tousled black hair falls past her shoulders and her green eyes sparkle like polished olivine. Make-up and Japanese-Hawaiian clothes highlight her best features with a sexual slant.)*

*(*REV HUNTER *is white and sits at the far table with a drink in his hand. His face is completely blocked from the audience and he remains on the outer circle of the action.* KANAKA *holds* KITTY'*s wrist as she struggles to get free. He controls her easily, touching her as much as possible.)*

(Refer to GLOSSARY for Hawaiian pronunciation guide and dictionary of terms used.)

KITTY: Pele gon erupt this volcano! She gon explode 'cause of you, Kanak! Let me go! Pele gonna blow Kilauea 'cause of what you trying for do to me! No force me!

KANAKA: Pele no can erupt nothing.

KIMO: Please, Kanak, stop!

KITTY: Pele gon erupt this whole crater 'cause of what you doing!

KANAKA: The crater gonna blow, eh, but not because of some make-believe goddess named Pele.

KIMO: Let her go!

KITTY: The crater is saying no do this to me!

KANAKA: I gotta do it!

KITTY: Not to me!

KIMO: No force her!

KANAKA: I no scared of the mountain. Let the mountain do what it gotta do and let me do what I gotta do.

KIMO: Let her go now!

KITTY: It's against the rule.

KIMO: Against the rule!

KITTY: How many times already.

KIMO: You break the rule!

KITTY: And you know it.

KIMO: The rule!

KANAKA: The rule says I get her for free!

KITTY: You lie!

KIMO: Please, brah.

KANAKA: Nobody can stop the crater from shooting out lava. And nobody can stop me. I gotta blow, too.

KITTY: Me and Omuro made the deal. Everybody but you, brah. That's the rule. You the only one.

KIMO: You the only one!

KITTY: You know how come? Me and Omuro figure it out. You one pig. Pua'a. *(Beat)* And I no do pigs.

*(*KANAKA *wraps one arm around her neck. He presses himself against her; his mouth is close to her face.)*

KANAKA: I'll break your neck.

KITTY: Pigs no can break necks. They just eat and lie in the mud. Get your infested body off me.

KANAKA: I'll crush your ribs, then.

KITTY: Wild boars jus' squeal and run away. Go oink and hide in the hapu'u. Get out of my face. You stink. Your breath pilau. *(Vehemently)* Never, Kanak. Never with you.

KANAKA: My ancestors royalty.

KITTY: Then you one Prince of the Pigs.

KIMO: I get customer. For my sake, Kanak. Easy, brah. *(To* REV HUNTER*)* Having fun, sir? *(Beat)* Sit back and relax. *(Whispering)* Sorry about this guy. This never wen happen before. *(Beat)* But everything okey-dokey. Drink up and enjoy the local color.

*(*REV HUNTER*'s hand, holding a drink, rises and disappears into the darkness.)*

KANAKA: Okay. We sit down like nice people. Good, eh? We nice people.

*(*KANAKA *and* KITTY *sit.)*

KIMO: See, Kitty? He no touch you. I wen make him stop, yeah?

KANAKA: We talk business. Straight and simple. *(He takes out a small envelope from his pocket and slides it toward her.)* I get something you like. I can get more. Plenty more.

KITTY: I get one avalanche of cocaine. For me, every night she snow. Come back spring thaw. *(She pushes the packet away.)*

KANAKA: I pay then. Here! *(He slaps money onto the table.)*

KITTY: I no like your filthy money.

KANAKA: What--more? *(He slams down more money.)* Eh, I pay three time more than any tourist! Four time! *(He slams down more money.)*

KITTY: Your money more stink than you.

*(*KANAKA *runs his hand down her arm. She pulls away from him.)*

KITTY: No touch me.

KIMO: No touch her, Kanak. Everything but touch her.

KANAKA: Shut up.

KIMO: You can do anything. As long as you no touch her. Kapu for touch her.

*(*KANAKA *rubs the back of his hand along her jawline. She hits his hand away.)*

KITTY: Leave me alone.

KANAKA: You gotta do it with me. You know why? 'Cause me, I one Yakuza. And you the Yakuza whore.

*(*KITTY *slaps* KANAKA *in the face. He smiles and rubs his cheek.)*

KITTY: Don't you ever call me that again. Never. You hear? I ain't no whore. *(Pause)* I one prostitute. *(Beat)* Professional. This my body. My body my business and I the ace executive. President of the corporation. I call the shots. Hold the meetings. Run the machine. I decide what for sell and when, who for advertise to and what stocks for exchange. Eh, no get confused. I use who I like. Nobody uses me. Get that through your fat skull. Nothing but business. I take the dollar, no give a cent, and no feel a nickel's worth.

You understan'? *(Beat)* I'm one prossy. I no feel nothing. I run this body my way and this corporation does great.

KIMO: Kanak, what's the matter with you, eh? You never with her before. How come now?

KANAKA: Eh, Kimo, where the cash you owe us?

KIMO: First of the month tomorrow.

KANAKA: Oh, yeah? Well, it's three minutes after midnight. This the first of the month. Tomorrow is today.

KIMO: That no make sense. Please, not now. I get customer.

KANAKA: Then nail your lips shut. Runts that owe money get no right for talk.

KIMO: Please, brah. Shhh—

KANAKA: Keep your nose outta this. Go wash some glasses.

KIMO: *(Washing glasses; to* REV*)* Having good time, sir? You like something, jus' scream. Pretend this guy not here and enjoy. Okay?

KITTY: You hog.

KANAKA: Get in the backroom.

KITTY: Eh, I gon tell Omuro. You break the rule and you out, brah.

KIMO: Leave the bar, now.

KANAKA: I said shut up. I make you leave.

KITTY: Kimo say for get out. Jus' do what he say. You ugly pig.

KANAKA: Get in the room.

*(*KANAKA *shoves* KITTY *toward the backroom.)*

KITTY: No! One customer can come for me any second.

KANAKA: *(Shoving her again)* You get one customer already. Me, I your customer. *(He scratches himself.)*

KITTY: One real customer. One with no diseases. Look at you. You get every skin sickness you can think of. You get eczema and psoriasis. Rashes, warts, fever blisters. Who knows what else.

KANAKA: I don't get no V.D.

KITTY: You one typhoon of germs. One infected human being. I just think of you touching me and I get sick. If we make business, I for sure puke. No joke. That's how come we made the rule!

*(*KANAKA *smacks her in the face.)*

KITTY: Eh, if you gonna hit me, no hit me in the face.

KIMO: Pau already!

(KANAKA hits her in the face again.)

KITTY: I told you, hit me any place you like. But not in the face. I get bruise. Bad for business.

KANAKA: Men that rent your face no care about bruises.

KITTY: Jus' no hit my face!

KANAKA: But if one bruise gon make you break—

(KANAKA clamps a hand on KITTY. His other arm cocks back a steel fist.)

KITTY: Not my face!

(REV HUNTER emerges from the darkness. His face is visible for the first time. He dresses entirely in black. Even his fedora is jet. The white square of his Roman collar stands out boldly and reveals that he is a priest.)

REV: Didn't your mother ever tell you not to hit girls?

KANAKA: Sit down before I knock you down.

REV: For the love of Christ, let the woman go.

KANAKA: If I like see one comedian I go to Honolulu. *(Seeing the collar)* Eh, what we get here? Ah! Makua 'uhane, Kitty. Look. One operative in this joint. Think of that. In this dump. What a joke. More better you run home to your rectory, Padre, I hear your mother superior calling.

REV: Release her.

KANAKA: Get me mad, I step on your face. The CC never do nothing about nothing. Go play with your 'feminary' friends, Father. In your little parish. Your cave. This real life. Nothing for do with you. Say Mass and pray for sinners. Pray for me. Yeah. Offer up your whole life for me. Just leave me alone.

REV: Let the lady go.

KANAKA: This not one wahine. This one mouth. And one—

REV: I know what she does and I know what you are. A hog in human clothing. Let her go. Pigface.

KANAKA: I gonna turn your other cheek.

(KANAKA swings. REV ducks the punch, pulls out a .45-caliber revolver from a shoulder holster and knocks KANAKA's feet from under him, slamming him to his knees. REV's one hand grips KANAKA's hair while the other presses the gun to KANAKA's temple.)

REV: You're right. I do pray for pigs like you. I pray that God gives me the control not to murder you goons. I want to blast your brains all over this bar. Think about it. In two seconds you may never think again.

KANAKA: Ahh!

REV: How's this steel feel? One twitch of my finger and you're shaking hands with the devil.

KANAKA: What?

REV: I want to go all over the world and kill pigs like you. That would make so many people happy. Got that, pal?

KANAKA: Who are you?

REV: Cut out your tongue. Pop your ears. Break your snout. Chop your hands. Blind the eyes of your breed. Clear enough, muscle-brain?

KANAKA: Yes, Father.

REV: I want to kill you so bad. I can feel it. The trigger's almost pulled. I'm gonna desecrate your temples.

KANAKA: No kill me!

REV: I'm gonna blast you. Shoot you. Kill you.

KANAKA: Have mercy!

*(*REV *tears his eyes from* KANAKA *and looks searchingly to heaven.)*

REV: My God. I implore you. Let this temptation pass.

KANAKA: Let it pass! Let it pass!

*(*REV *becomes calm.)*

REV: Thank you, Father, for your army of angels to battle against the Satan within.

KANAKA: Thank you, Father. Thank you.

REV: *(With ironic command)* I save souls, mister. That's my business. If I'd 'a' rubbed you out, you would have been cast into everlasting damnation. That's against my conscience. I rescue souls. My curse, your luck. So I'm going to baptize you. *(Beat)* I can kill you then.

KANAKA: What?

REV: I'll be doing you a favor.

KANAKA: Huh?

REV: Once you're dead and baptized, you'll go to the big sty in the sky.

KANAKA: No!

REV: Straight to hog heaven. Do you reject Satan? *(He jerks back* KANAKA*'s head.)* Say I do.

KANAKA: I do.

*(*KANAKA*'s head falls forward.* REV *delivers the following sequence extremely fast. He jerks* KANAKA*'s head back just before each "I do".)*

REV: And all his works?

KANAKA: I do.

REV: And all his empty promises?

KANAKA: I do.

REV: Do you believe in God, the Father almighty, creator of heaven and Earth?

KANAKA: I do.

REV: Do you believe in Jesus Christ, his only son, our Lord, who was born of the Virgin Mary, was crucified, died and was buried, rose from the dead, and is now seated at the right hand of the Father?

KANAKA: I do.

REV: Do you believe in the Holy Spirit, the holy CC, the communion of saints, the forgiveness of sins, the resurrection of the body, and life everlasting?

KANAKA: I do.

REV: This is the faith of the CC. This is what the CC organization believes. I give you the Christian name of Aloysius. Pigface for short. Do you acknowledge this name?

KANAKA: I do.

REV: Blink and I'll blow you to hell in self-defense. *(Pouring liquor onto* KANAKA*'s head)* I baptize you in the name of the Father, and of the Son, and of the Holy Spirit. You are now born free from sin. A new creation. Alleluia, alleluia. Your brown soul is now white. Stay white. Don't become a white death. *(He blesses* KANAKA*, using his revolver to make the sign of the cross, during the following Latin.)* In nomine Patris, et Filii, et Spiritus Sancti. Amen. You're a member of the CC.

(He aims his revolver at KANAKA *and begins to squeeze the trigger.* KITTY *and* KIMO *let out a scream.)*

REV: Na. Heaven's too good for you. You deserve a tougher sentence. I give you life. *(He lowers his gun.)* Now scram. Before I shove you on a spit and barbecue.

KANAKA: Yes, Father. *(Tripping over his feet and moaning like a wounded animal, he exits through the front door.)*

KIMO: That was something. That was really something.

REV: Just another conversion.

KIMO: I never seen anybody handle Kanak like that. In fac', I never see anybody handle anybody like that.

REV: With God on your side, miracles happen.

KIMO: Not like that. Chee.

REV: *(Sliding his revolver into its holster)* Saving souls is tough nowadays. Sometimes you have to resort to brute force. *(To* KITTY*)* Join you?

KIMO: Join her! Sit down. Relax.

REV: *(To* KITTY*)* Can I buy you a drink?

KIMO: Drinks on the House!

REV: *(To* KITTY*)* Mind if I sit with you for the free drink?

KITTY: *(Clearly not enthralled)* Whatevers.

*(*REV *sits at her table.)*

KIMO: Alright! One Jack Daniels on the rocks. Two shots worth. Boy that Tennessee whiskey best!

REV: Easy on the ice this time. And no stir. I don't like my booze bruised.

KIMO: Okey-dokey!

REV: *(To* KITTY*)* I don't like anything bruised. Especially people.

KIMO: Shame on you, Kitty! How come you no say mahalo to the Father? Thank him for step in. *(He makes the drinks.)*

REV: You don't have to say anything.

KITTY: That's right. I never gotta say nothing. What I gotta thank you for anyway? That's no big deal. Eh, you like see some roughhouse, stick around here one Saturday night. We no need nobody for step in for us. Me and Kimo can handle anything. He's my protector.

REV: Heck of a job.

KIMO: Kitty, he save you.

KITTY: Save me how? Everything gonna be more bad when Kanak come back and this collar no stay.

KIMO: Now, Kitty.

KITTY: People like you always sticking their noses into other people's business. Think they can help, when they no even understan' what's going on. Always judge and try fix. Make their mark someplace they no belong, on people they don't even know. Try make you think like them. Act like them. Come off like they do you one favor. Stand up for the little lady. Pull out their gun and their conscience. Eh, I no need it. Believe me, brah. We can handle him. *(Beat)* Anyway, Kanak one nice guy when you get to know him.

REV: But I wasn't saving you. I was saving him. I save people from themselves. It's not my job to save a person from another person. That's police work.

KITTY: *(Taken off guard)* Well, good you no step in for my sake. Get me mad everytime, people try save me.

REV: I wasn't even thinking of you and for that I'm sorry. Accept my apology?

KITTY: What you trying for be? One knight in shining collar? Never mind.

REV: Thank you.

KITTY: Jus' keep your conscience in your holster, that's where it belongs.

KIMO: *(Carrying a tray of drinks to the table)* Eeha! Everybody make up! Everybody happy! Champagne for the lady. Jack Daniels—light ice, no stir—for the operative. Rum and pineapple juice for me. I like make one toast. To this operative that come to us outta the darkness.

(They drink. He makes a grand gesture.)

KIMO: Aloha. This the Volcano Bar. *(He bows.)* My name Kimo. That's Hawaiian for James.

KITTY: James English for Kimo.

KIMO: You can call me Jimmy. It's more easy for the visitors.

REV: Glad to meet you, Kimo.

KIMO: I the owner of this bar. I Filipino descent but I not member of the CC. My family somehow slip through the crack, yeah. *(He laughs, then is suddenly terrified.)* But you no try baptize me, now, Father! Please!

KITTY: No be stupid, Kimo.

KIMO: And this Kitty Kalua.

REV: My pleasure.

KITTY: I'm sure.

(Beat)

REV: What's kalua mean in Hawaiian?

KITTY: To cook underneath. But one word in Hawaiian can mean many things. Ka lua means the toilet. And I sure take a lot of kukae.

KIMO: How come you no act nice? So please, Father, what's your name?

REV: Hunter. Rev Hunter.

KIMO: Rev for reverend.

KITTY: Or revolver?

REV: Revolution. The number of revolutions per minute.

KIMO: Like rev-up!

KITTY: We never get one operative in this joint before.

KIMO: Never! *(Beat)* So where you staying?

REV: Halemaumau Hotel.

KIMO: Oh, right down the road. Eh, maybe you get lucky, gon see the eruption. Kilauea getting ready for blow. The scientists say that the pressure stay up, you know. This bar, eh, Father, she built right on the edge of the crater. In fac', half this building stay on stilts, hanging right off from the rim, into the crater. So real volcano bar, you know. You can see the whole crater right through this window over here.

(He indicates an invisible picture window that lies between the actors and the audience. When the characters look through this window, they look out onto the audience.)

KIMO: But it kinda dark, now. You no can see nothing. You ever see the crater before?

REV: No.

KIMO: The dark hide what you no can imagine. Tomorrow bring light.

KITTY: Pele gonna blow in revenge.

KIMO: That's one treat for see the eruption! Unreal.

KITTY: She not take trash from nobody.

KIMO: Your heart bust outta your chest. You get this feeling in your guts. You always remember your first eruption. Kinda like sex. You lucky man you see that, eh, Father.

KITTY: She jus' shoot out when somebody go mess with her.

REV: What's she talking about?

KIMO: Blood Hawaiians, you know, they believe that Kilauea crater stay ruled by Pele. That she makes all the eruptions.

KITTY: She da kine woman. She wen make this crater. *(Pointing out the picture window)* Right outside this bar she made Kilauea for her fiancé. But then she saw him and her own sister making sex on the rim. She wen explode with lava and the eruption wen kill them both. Now, everytime Kilauea blows, it's Pele against something.

REV: I used to like ghost stories, too.

KITTY: Eh, no way. Pele real.

REV: My God forgives all sinners.

KITTY: Some things jus' no can be forgiven. Watch it, makua 'uhane! Pele gonna erupt 'cause you make your home on her volcano, stink up the air with that Latin and dirty her altar with baptizing Kanak!

REV: *(Deadpan)* I'm trembling.

KIMO: Please, Kitty. The operative stay our guest. Be nice. He saved you.

KITTY: He saved Kanak!

KIMO: Alright. *(Whispering to* KITTY*)* Be happy. *(Loudly)* I get more drinks. One more round on the House. *(To* REV*)* She get crazy with this Pele stuff. Gibber jabber all the time. Pele this, Pele that. This Kitty turn into one mynah bird. Pay no attention, Father. But you come back here daytime and I'll show you the crater. Magnificent view from my window. *(Emphatically)* The best view on the island! You see the sulphur shooting from the lava vents. Look like the steam trying for blow the lid off the crater. Like one rice cooker. *(He laughs.)* You see tomorrow.

REV: Is that what I smell, sulphur?

KIMO: Sulphur.

REV: Whole area reeks of it.

KIMO: More drinks coming up! *(Whispering to* KITTY*)* Cheer up.

*(*KIMO *makes the drinks.* REV *places a photograph on the table.)*

REV: You know this guy?

KITTY: Never seen him before in my life.

*(*REV *shows the photograph to* KIMO.*)*

REV: Ever seen him?

KIMO: President of the Hilo Sugar Company. Come in here all the time. But not for drink; for Kitty. *(Scolding* KITTY*)* What's the matter with you? How can you tell him you no know this guy? Everybody in town know you know him! *(Confidentially to* REV*)* He get killed yesterday. She one nice girl. Leave her out of it.

REV: He have a date with her yesterday?

(KIMO *nods.)*

REV: And got it right after.

KIMO: I don't know nothing.

REV: Thanks. *(To* KITTY*)* One of your customers. That's tough.

KITTY: Not. Life's one big luau.

REV: Who iced him?

KITTY: What my clients say to me stays secret, padre. You know the game. Like confession. My body's my church. They worship in it. I give them sanctuary, too. My breast the altar; my lips the gateway to paradise. You promise heaven. *(Beat)* I deliver.

REV: There ain't no heaven on earth, darlin'. And I don't care who's been ramming your sanctum.

KIMO: *(Serving the drinks)* You no can act right or what?

KITTY: How come you like for know about this guy?

REV: I'm on assignment from Rome. They can smell sin all the way to Italy on this thing. *(Beat)* I find the killer, convert him, and save his soul.

KITTY: But how come this haole death?

REV: What's haole?

KITTY: You haole.

KIMO: Haole's white.

REV: White death.

KITTY: You waste your time. The CC get no business over here. More better you work on one tan.

REV: I hate the sun.

KITTY: I love it. You wen convert our Queen. Then the soldiers came and took our islands for the U.S. With guns. When you kill one people's god, you kill the whole culture. First the church, then the soldiers. That's how it always works.

REV: If I wanted a sob story, I'd go to an orphanage. *(Crossing to the telephone booth)* Besides, that wasn't us. That was the Protestants.

KIMO: You can use my phone behind the bar. No charge.

REV: Private call. *(He goes into the booth and dials. It rings.)*

(The CARDINAL CODE *is a voice over the phone.)*

CODE: The Cardinal Code.

REV: *(Into the phone)* Hunter.

CODE: Where are you?

REV: In a whiskey shack over an active volcano.

CODE: You have a nose for the hot spots.

REV: I tracked down the best prossy on the island. Took a shot in the dark that this corpse knew her. Bull's-eye. He was with her just before he punched out. She's my only lead.

CODE: I wish I could yank you off that crater. Those islands mean nothing.

REV: Rome thinks they do.

CODE: Burn Rome. Hawaii could fall to the Hare Krishnas and I wouldn't blink. *(Beat)* Chicago gave us some good times, huh, Rev?

REV: I miss the darkness. The cold. The slush.

CODE: It's all still here. Get your butt out of Rome and come back to the Windy City.

REV: I'm just checking in.

CODE: All right, I won't push. Racism's always in vogue. Let's go down that alley.

REV: I'll shoot out some streetlights. See who runs.

CODE: Watch out for falling glass.

REV: Always do.

CODE: Life everlasting.

REV: Amen. *(He hangs up and goes to the bar.)* One more Jackie D., Kimo, and have one on me.

KIMO: Mahalo. But on the House! *(He serves the drinks.)*

KITTY: When the haoles took over--

REV: Oh, Jeez.

KITTY: They made us grow only sugar cane. Now companies buy foreign sugar for more cheap. Our business go bust. Sugar killing our islands. We call it the white death.

REV: The Irish got stuck with potatoes. What else is new? *(Beat)* Listen, I hate to be a killjoy, but I gotta catch up on my jet lag.

KIMO: You come back here tomorrow. I go show you the crater. We have some laughs like that.

REV: It's a date.

KITTY: How's about a date with me, Father?

REV: There're always women who fall for the collar. I never pay for it.

KITTY: I wouldn't kiss your rosary beads.

REV: And I wouldn't leave Volcano if I were you. You're the last person to feel that dead man alive. You stay put, sister. *(He throws down the rest of his drink.)* Goodnight, Kimo. Thanks for the hooch. *(He exits.)*

KIMO: That Rev Hunter's some haole bugger, yeah? He wen make Kanak beg for mercy like that.

KITTY: Slice that hog into ham.

KIMO: Make him squeal like one stuck pig.

KITTY: Okay, now. I gonna rest up before the Hotel closes. Maybe one customer make tracks over here, yeah. Knock two times if sharkbait come in. I let you get one drink outta him, then I come out ready.

KIMO: Routine.

KITTY: Shaka, brah. *(She exits into the backroom.)*

KIMO: Chee, that Rev Hunter, boy, he get some da kine, eh. Power. Wonder how it feel be like him?

*(*KANAKA *enters with a drawn, long-bladed fishing knife.)*

KANAKA: Where the operative?

KIMO: He no stay.

KANAKA: He went?

KIMO: Pau already.

KANAKA: Good, then, brah. Oooee! That haole, he do me to the max. No lie. *(He inserts the knife into a leather sheath hanging from his belt.)* How's it? Where the puka?

KIMO: C'mon, Kanak, no start up again.

KANAKA: I gonna do her.

KIMO: You no can do nothing.

KANAKA: Where she went?

KIMO: What's the matter with you?

KANAKA: *(Throbbing)* I'm a man. That's what's the matter with me. I decided tonight I'm a man. *(Whispering)* A man. *(Matter-of-factly)* Nothing for get excited about. Simple. No big deal.

KIMO: How come you acting lolo tonight?

KANAKA: I gonna get her. That's how come. *(Emphatically)* I need her. You know?

KIMO: You know you no can get her.

KANAKA: Gimme one beer!

*(*KIMO *gets him a beer.)*

KANAKA: Eh, Kimo, me, I just one regular guy, yeah. No different. The same like whoever. Anybody you like me to be. Everybody. Nobody. Yakuza.

KIMO: She free to all the Yakuza, but not for you, you know why, 'cause you full of disease. She catch and spread them.

KANAKA: Shut up about my diseases! *(Beat)* You no can catch nothing from me. I not contagious. When you touch me, you no become me. I keep my diseases inside, brah. In my blood. You never can catch that. Besides, me and Kitty both Hawaiian. She no can catch what she already get.

KIMO: You're crazy, you know that.

KANAKA: I just common everyday kinda guy. After work joe, eh. I get one regular need. You know, da kine. I like slip my blade into her sheath. Simple. No big deal. Okay? Everybody can get her. Well, so should I. No take that away from me, too. Not that. *(In confidence)* So Kimo, what you think, eh, you can fix me up with her or what? Maybe I let you slide on one of your payments, you know. Get her for do it with me. I know I nothing special. But maybe if you pretend I'm some Korean or tourist. Anything but me. Maybe if you, Kimo, you go send me in there, she go do it with me, then. You do that for me, brah?

KIMO: I ain't get nothing for do with her like that. Anyway, Kitty no stay.

KANAKA: Where she went?

KIMO: She wen split. I dunno. So calm down.

KANAKA: I no need calm. I need Kitty.

(A TOURIST *enters. He is middle-aged and costumes himself in a gaudy aloha shirt, loud bermuda shorts, a hat, and thong slippers. A flowered lei and a camera hang around his neck. He's a fast talker. To the* TOURIST*, everything exists for his pleasure.)*

TOURIST: *(Loudly upon entrance)* Howdy!

(Recognizing the bait, KIMO *snaps into a coolie act. He dumps ashtrays, wipes the bar, nods his head, and laughs whenever the* TOURIST *laughs.* KIMO *smiles so much that it hurts.)*

KIMO: Please, come in, sir!

TOURIST: Dang, it's colder than a cow's teat in a blizzard. I thought this was Hawaii.

KIMO: We get you hot right away.

TOURIST: Now you're speaking my language.

KIMO: *(Making a grand gesture)* Aloha. This the Volcano Bar. My name's Kimo. That's Hawaiian for James.

TOURIST: Gimme that again.

KIMO: Kimo.

TOURIST: That's hilarious! I'll never remember that. I'll just call you Jimmy-boy. It's shorter. Well, this is some kind of decor. *(Pointing)* Pineapple, right? You people really know how to do a place up. Something to write home about. *(Confidentially and quickly)* Well, listen, Jimmy-boy, mind if I don't introduce myself? Gotta keep things under cover. I've had my nose to the grindstone for a full year so I'm entitled to a little fun. My wife's asleep and what she don't know won't hurt her. I hear you can give me the vacation I'm looking for.

KIMO: *(With theatrical charm)* No worry, sir. You wen enter your Polynesian Palace of Pleasure! Home of the Big Island Princess. Exotic excitement, garan ball bearin's. She come out couple minutes.

TOURIST: Hey, I ain't buyin' no warn-out mare. I'm lookin' for a filly bitin' at the bit.

KIMO: She not busy that way. She be wikiwiki.

TOURIST: Wikiwiki. You people always say things twice. That kills me. That means quick, don't it? Wikiwiki means quicky-quicky. Well, that's what I'm here for. *(He laughs.)* Get it? See, I speaky-speaky that Hawaiian stuff! *(He laughs, as does* KIMO.*)* The bartender at the Hotel said she was a real volcano, make a dead man erupt. I'll take her.

KIMO: You like, you get.

*(*KIMO *knocks twice on the backroom door.* KANAKA *snaps his head toward* KIMO, *glares at him intensely, and then looks away.)*

TOURIST: What's her name?

KIMO: Kitty.

TOURIST: Ah, a purrin' kitty-cat. I like that fine.

KIMO: What you like for drink, sir?

TOURIST: Don't want to diminish my love potential.

KIMO: One drink minimum, Tourisan.

TOURIST: One drink might just grease the pump, won't it. What's that funny drink you got here?

KIMO: Mai Tai?

TOURIST: That's the one. Like my tie. Get it? My tie. *(They both laugh.)* You fellas don't wear ties, though, do you?

(The TOURIST *puts money on the table.* KIMO *serves the drink and takes the money. The drink is garnished with a large slice of pineapple.)*

TOURIST: Yep. You all got a beautiful little country out here. I'm thinkin' of settlin' down 'round these parts when I retire. Florida's so darn crowded. Might just park my butt on this island to die. *(Beat)* What do you think of Americans?

KIMO: I stay American.

TOURIST: I'm sure you're a citizen and everything, but I mean the folks who were born here.

KIMO: I stay born here.

TOURIST: *(Taken off guard)* In the U.S. of A.? *(Beat)* How come you talk like that?

KIMO: I always stay talk this way.

TOURIST: Oh! You mean you were born here in Hawaii. Oh! But you're not from.... Let me ask you this then. What do you think of like Americans from Iowa? I been there and it ain't much different from Nebraska. Lotta hogs instead of cattle. I'm from Grand Island, Nebraska, myself. Born, raised, and stuck. The center cut of this great country of ours. What do you think of folks like us?

KANAKA: *(In a low, rumbling voice)* What does he think of real Americans.

TOURIST: Yeah—well no, not real—you know what I mean—hey, that's funny! *(He points at* KANAKA *and laughs.)* A real kidder. You Hawaiians are the funniest dern people, that's why me and the missus just keep on coming back!

KIMO: You mean mainlanders.

TOURIST: That's the word I'm lookin' for. Thank you, Jimmy-boy. I'm a mainlander. You're island Americans. Gee, it's funny to think of America as an island, ain't it?

KIMO: I think mainlanders are great.

TOURIST: That's all I wanted to know! You think we're great. Beautiful. *(To* KIMO*)* I can tell you're a real Hawaiian. Injun blood.

KIMO: No, I not.

TOURIST: You sure as heck look Hawaiian.

KIMO: This guy over here, Kanaka, he stay full-blood Hawaiian.

TOURIST: You're an honest-to-God native? No kidding? I gotta get a picture of this. *(He takes a picture of* KANAKA. *To* KIMO:*)* Could you snap one of the two of us together?

*(*KIMO *takes the shot.)*

TOURIST: Much gracías, amigo.

KIMO: The lady you gonna stay with, she get blood Hawaiian, too, you know. But she kinda poi dog. Mixy-mixy blood.

TOURIST: Woooeee! I'll have to get a picture of her, too, for my private collection. Know what I mean? A genuine souvenir. Gonna teach that little girl how to hula Nebraska style. *(He winnies.)* We went to a black sand beach today. I know the sign said and the tour guide said, but no one on the bus took any, so why not? I'm only one person. What the heck, I grabbed some. *(He takes out a small plastic bag full of black sand.)* Pretty stuff black sand, don't you think? Crushed lava rock. Gonna show it to the folks back home. I love this country. Even like the stores. Like those naked posters of Pele. Fine-looking goddess. Wouldn't mind dippin' into her crater. *(He sniggers. Abruptly:)* While I think of it, how would either of you boys like a job? I know all you *(Winking)* kanes are always on the rampage for some wampum, right? Well me and the missus need a driver just 'til the end of the week. All you do is take us where we want, from one hotel to another, load and offload our suitcases. Oh, I don't have to explain. You boys must do it all the time. Any takers? It's good money. If you're smart you could save enough money to vacation in Nebraska. Think about it. Bet you need a new surfboard or something. Anyhow, when I finish branding this filly, you give me your answer. Speaking of business, where is that little geisha girl?

*(*KITTY *enters, ready to act her role. She is barefoot and dressed in a Ti leaf skirt, a Hawaiian-print bikini top, and a maile lei. Colorful sea shells encircle her ankles, wrists, waist, neck, and head.)*

KIMO: *(Proclaiming)* Here she comes! Princess of the Volcano! Our own lava flow! Kitty Kalua!

KITTY: Aloha, Mac. Welcome to my mountains. I like haole boys. I like you. How you like for plunge into my volcano?

*(*KIMO *flips a switch and recorded Tahitian drums play. The music is fast and pounding.)*

TOURIST: Woooeee! Aloha my jungle kitten!

*(*KITTY *dances Tahitian, swinging her hips back and forth with the beat of the drums. She begins teasingly and sensuously, then builds to a furious pitch. At the peak, on cue,* KIMO *shuts off the music.)*

KITTY: I get so hot when I dance. I don't know why I wear so much clothes. I go get more comfortable. When I'm ready *(Pointing to a light above the backroom door)* the light goes on. We talk business, then we make business for how you like.

TOURIST: Darlin', my eyes ain't gonna stray from that there bulb.

KITTY: Aloha for now. *(She exits into the backroom.)*

TOURIST: Oh my Lord, Lord, Lordy. Whatcha say her name was? Pussy?

KIMO: Kitty.

TOURIST: Same thing. In Hawaiian that's Pussy-Pussy, ain't it?

(The TOURIST *howls.* KANAKA *looks the* TOURIST *dead in the eyes for the first time. He has lost his hysteria; what remains is an intense focus of purpose.)*

ANAKA: Take off your pants.

(Pause)

TOURIST: Sorry, buddy, I didn't catch that.

KANAKA: Take off your pants.

(Silence)

TOURIST: *(Bursting into laughter)* You people say the strangest things! You really do. Take off your pants. Oh, I gotcha. Take'em off now before I go in with the lady. Some kinda custom. Well, I been through the hukilaus. Skip the pants number. Tell you the truth, you put a scare into me a second there.

KANAKA: Haole no understand English? Take. Off. Your. Pants. *(Lifting his knife from its sheath)* Now.

(The TOURIST *takes off his pants.)*

KANAKA: Throw them to the bartender.

(The TOURIST *does.)*

KANAKA: This Kimo. Say hello Kimo.

TOURIST: Hello Kimo.

KANAKA: Kimo nice name.

TOURIST: Kimo nice name.

KANAKA: Stop the coolie act, Kimo. No tourist talk. Stay the manong you are. How much?

KIMO: Eight-hundred dollars.

KANAKA: You dumb haole.

TOURIST: I'd like to know—

KANAKA: So you like our island, yeah, cowboy?

TOURIST: Very much.

KANAKA: What you like? *(He clips the* TOURIST*'s hat off his head with the knife.)*

TOURIST: I like everything.

KANAKA: You like the flowers? *(He cuts the lei from his neck. The flowers drop to the floor.)* You like for take pictures of the natives? *(He slices the strap and the camera falls to the floor.)* You like aloha shirts?

(He runs the blade down the TOURIST*'s shirt, slicing the buttons off in one smooth stroke. He takes the shirt off the* TOURIST*, revealing a body naked except for a pair of boxer shorts with the word ALOHA! printed across the front.)*

KANAKA: You wear what you think look Hawaiian down to your underwear. You dress up like this for mock us?

TOURIST: No.

KANAKA: If not for make fun, then you like for be us.

TOURIST: I want to be like you.

KANAKA: You like the beaches? *(Offering the sand)* Eat.

TOURIST: What?

KANAKA: We get the islands deep inside. More deep than your heart. Only way you get the beaches inside you, haole. You like be Hawaiian? Eat the sand. Ono.

(The TOURIST *eats the sand. He chokes.* KANAKA *drags him behind the bar and puts a bottle to the* TOURIST*'s mouth. The* TOURIST *drinks and stops coughing.)*

TOURIST: If it's money you want, take it.

KANAKA: I no like your stink money.

TOURIST: This joke has gone far enough, boys.

KANAKA: Say 'boys' one more time and I cut out your tongue.

KIMO: No, Kanak, please.

(The bar conceals all action below their waists. KANAKA *cuts off the* TOURIST*'s underwear and throws them in front of the bar. The light above the back room switches on red.)*

KANAKA: Without our clothes you're naked.

TOURIST: I'm sorry if I said something wrong. Maybe I stepped outta line. I got a couple of kids. I'm just a regular guy.

KANAKA: If I go to Nebraska, you let me act like you? No way, pally. Me, I regular guy jus' like you. Two things different. I get the knife. And this not your island.

(He clamps a hand around the TOURIST'*s throat. The* TOURIST'*s body accidently hits the switch and the Tahitian drum music comes on.)*

KANAKA: Repeat. I love your island for steal from.

TOURIST: I love your island to steal from—

KANAKA: Your goddess for make fun.

TOURIST: Your goddess make fun—

KANAKA: Your men for carry my bags.

TOURIST: Your men carry my bags—

KANAKA: Your women for do it to.

TOURIST: Do it—

*(*KITTY *enters, wearing a kimono.)*

KANAKA: How you gonna do it to our women without this?

KIMO: No!

(The hand wrapped around the TOURIST'*s neck disappears below the bar, followed by the swift knife. The* TOURIST *screams.)*

KANAKA: How you gonna do anything with no life?

*(*KANAKA *plunges the knife seven times into the* TOURIST. KITTY *screams.* KANAKA *lets the carcass fall to the floor behind the bar. He becomes drained of all energy and dazed. Pause.)*

KITTY: What you wen did?

KIMO: I try to stop him.

KITTY: You stupid or what?

KIMO: He never listen to me.

KITTY: How dare you butt into my business?

KIMO: How dare he kill in my bar!

KITTY: You get no right for touch my customer.

KIMO: He get no right for murder in my bar.

KITTY: You dummy!

KIMO: Blood all over!

KITTY: Stupid idiot!

KIMO: Stink in the air.

KITTY: That's my customer!

KIMO: It's my bar!

KITTY: Mongoloid!

KIMO: Blood bad for business!

KITTY: He's dead before he paid me!

(KANAKA throws the TOURIST's money into the air. KITTY picks up some bills.)

KIMO: The House rule says no murder in my bar!

KITTY: You get no right for cut my stuff.

(KANAKA switches off the music.)

KANAKA: You no even dance Hawaiian. You dance Tahitian.

KITTY: I dance for get more money from him.

KANAKA: *(Almost inaudibly)* This not his island.

(Silence)

KITTY: We gotta make one plan.

KIMO: That's what we need!

KITTY: We gotta act fast.

KIMO: I get dead tourist in my bar! *(He laughs hysterically.)*

KITTY: Stop it! *(Beat)* Burn his clothes in the rubbish can out back, then throw the ashes in the hapu'u. Scrub this bar so hard one dog no can smell one whiff of blood. But first put the body into one pineapple sack. Hele! Now!

(KIMO runs behind the bar and crouches down to the corpse, out of sight.)

KIMO: He still bleeding!

KITTY: Kanak, you go dump the body.

KIMO: What I gonna do with—his—da kine?

KITTY: Throw it in the bag with the body. Stupid!

(KIMO runs around like a madman. He collects the TOURIST's clothes and throws them into a bag, except for the camera. He shoves as much money as he can into his pockets and begins to scrub the top of the bar with a sponge.)

KITTY: Eh, remember. Kanaka never came back here tonight. *(To KANAKA)* I no cover up for you, pig. I protecting Kimo. Not you, porker.

KIMO: *(Wiping the blade and* KANAKA*'s hands clean)* I gon bury the knife.

KANAKA: My knife.

*(*KANAKA *slides the knife into his sheath and comes out from behind the bar with the bag full of body. He drags the burlap load unconsciously as if it actually were a sack of pineapples. The sack leaves a trail of blood behind.* KIMO *squats with the sponge and follows the bag across the room, wiping up the path of blood and whimpering to himself.)*

KITTY: Shh. Listen. *(She looks out the picture window.)* Kimo, stop crying. Shut up!

KIMO: *(Trying to control himself)* What?

KITTY: One beautiful sound.

KIMO: I no hear nothing.

KITTY: Beautiful nothing.

KIMO: You going lolo now, too?

KITTY: No eruption.

KIMO: No Pele.

KITTY: Not. Pele's here. But she no making no noise. She not mad for what you did, Kanak.

KIMO: Pele say Kanak good?

KITTY: She say yes. She never like the tourist either!

KANAKA: Pele get nothing for do with it. This jus' the still before the storm.

KITTY: No matter what you say, Pele love you for killing the tourist. She thought he was one dumb haole, too. *(She laughs. Suddenly, in a silky voice:)* Kanak. Go quick. Anybody can walk in.

KIMO: *(Quietly)* Take care yourself, brah.

*(*KITTY *approaches* KANAKA *impulsively. She gently touches his lower lip with one finger and rubs his lip smoothly back and forth.)*

KITTY: *(Directly into his eyes)* Try stay safe.

KANAKA: Eh, Kimo, I sorry for mess up your bar. And thanks for mop-up. Kitty, I sorry for mess up your customer. And thanks for touch my lip.

*(*KANAKA *exits with the body.* KIMO *continues to clean as the lights fade to a blackout, then immediately come up on* KIMO *setting up the bar for the new work day. It is dawn. The sun rises during this scene, though the bar remains dim since the small window is filthy. Edgy from paranoia and giddy from no sleep,* KIMO *is a mess. He sniffs around the bar.* KITTY *inhales a line of cocaine.)*

KITTY: Stop sniffing all around, Kimo! Scrub, sniff. Scrub, sniff. This place one bar, all right. One bar of soap! *(Beat)* Time for quit. Get some sleep.

KIMO: The sun wen come up already. Okay. Me, I pau. Nobody gonna know what happened here last night.

KITTY: Especially that demon with the gun.

(The backroom door flies open. KANAKA *bursts in.* KIMO *screams.)*

KIMO: You scare me, Kanak! What, you lolo come busting into my bar like that?

KITTY: No come through my room! What's the matter with you? What if I get one customer? What if I by myself?

KANAKA: Forget it.

(Beat)

KITTY: You wen get rid of it?

KANAKA: Yeah. I wen did it. *(Beat)* Then I talk to Omuro. He say no problem. His goons in the police gon bury the case. Jus' another dumb tourist accident.

KITTY: With knife holes in the body?

KANAKA: I wen take care of the knife pukas. Me, I fool everybody. No worry. *(Beat)* But let me tell you about this devil in one collar! Look like we get one important bugger here. You should see Omuro's face when I wen tell him the name Rev Hunter. That yellow man turn white. *(Beat)* Hunter get big reputation. But watch it, brah. He's dangerous. Master of conversion. *(Beat)* When Hunter catch you break the law, he no tell the police. That's too easy, eh. He shuts up about your sin. Not even one judge in court can make him talk. No, what Hunter do to you more bad than the death penalty. *(Beat)* He change you. *(Beat)* He make you believe in things you no believe in. Make you act like people you no like. *(Beat)* He's one conversion machine.

KITTY: Hunter no can make me different.

KANAKA: He brainwash you so bad, brah, that you wake up years from now, look around, and you get one wife, three kids, and one boring job.

KITTY and KIMO: No!

KANAKA: Yeah! *(Beat)* Hunter wen baptize me, eh. But me, I no different. Look how I wen did the tourist.

KIMO: You not changed.

KITTY: You the same.

KANAKA: Force-baptism. That no count. *(Beat)* He's one thief. But what he steals is your soul.

KITTY: Po'i 'uhane!

KANAKA: How I wen did that tourist, Hunter can do to your soul. He stabs right through your chest, more deep than your heart and rips your soul right out from under your flesh.

*(*KITTY *and* KIMO *gasp in terror.)*

KANAKA: I never touch one soul. *(Beat)* The Yakuza protects you and pays you, yeah?

KITTY and KIMO: *Yeah.*

KANAKA: The CC kills your soul, then asks for money.

KITTY: He never get me.

KANAKA: Me neither! *(Beat)* He jus' like one shark. Sleeps with his eyes open. Always on the hunt for one more soul for eat.

*(*KIMO *glances out the window and shrieks.)*

KIMO: Eh, the bugger coming!

(They all scream.)

KANAKA: *(Having scared himself)* I gotta get outta here! *(He runs toward the backroom.)*

KITTY: No go through my room!

KANAKA: I collect tonight, Kimo! Pay you then, Kitty!

KITTY: Go out the front!

KANAKA: Eh, I not sharkbait!

*(*KANAKA *exits through the backroom.* REV *enters through the front door.)*

KIMO: Ah! Famous man in my bar! You one big shot.

REV: Where'd you hear that?

KIMO: Everybody know you one big wheel.

REV: I couldn't sleep. Sometimes I just can't keep my eyes closed.

(Beat)

KIMO: You hungry? Like small fish? No look at me.

KITTY: *(Whispering)* Stupid, Kimo.

REV: How about a nightcap, instead?

KIMO: On the House for the big cheese.

REV: Surprised to see your lights on. You having an early day or late night?

KIMO: I no can sleep. Business been slow. This place real murder last night. *(He mispours a drink.)* Oops! I spill. No worry. I mop up. I good for mop things up. *(He tries to subdue a laugh but fails.)*

REV: You ever been to a morgue? Never smells clean. Always the antiseptic trying to cover up the stink of death. *(Beat)* You've doused this place with ammonia.

KIMO: I do big clean-up every once in a while. *(Innocently)* How come you here?

REV: Our date, remember? There it is. *(Looking through the picture window)* Would you look at that. What all the tourists come to see. Kilauea Crater.

KIMO: Best view on the island!

REV: You mean that, don't you. Last night I had no idea this thing was so big. *(Abruptly)* Who came in here after I left?

*(*KIMO *drops his drink.)*

KIMO: Oh, boy. I so clumsy this morning. Ah. No body. No body after No body after you. No. *(Beat)* Body. *(He cleans up the mess.)*

REV: That's funny. I was closing down the Hotel bar when in came a woman screaming that her husband was gone. Bartender said he sent the poor guy over here.

KITTY: No need cover for me, Kimo. Tourist come in, make business and split. So what?

REV: He's dead.

KITTY: What do you know.

REV: That's my question.

KITTY: Nothing.

REV: Even a corpse gets sanctuary, huh? The living are sacred, honey, not the dead. Police dogs found him at the botton of the crater. Cops were on him like lice. I couldn't get a good look at him.

KIMO: Hard for tell when the body in the bag.

*(*KITTY *shoots him a look.)*

KIMO: They throw the body in the bag real quick. Police body bag. Or was the body out of the bag? In the bag or outta the bag? Body. Bag.

REV: You need some rest, Kimo. *(Beat)* Or better, a drink. *(To* KITTY*)* Go dress your face. Kimo and I want to talk.

KITTY: There's no secrets with me and Kimo.

REV: Man talk.

KITTY: I bartend for you, Kimo, get some sleep.

KIMO: We go talk man to man. *(Strongly)* Go to your room.

KITTY: *(To* REV*)* You think you're real tough, yeah, Hunter?

REV: That makes two, darlin'. You're a regular black widow spider. A date with you and you're dead.

KITTY: Watch him, Kimo. Mahu, I think. You boys have fun. No kissing.

(She exits into the backroom.)

KIMO: Be nice! *(Suspiciously)* How come you like talk with me?

REV: Just taking you up on the free drink.

KIMO: Celebrate you top dog!

REV: I like you by yourself.

KIMO: I good company. Me alone. You like Kimo! Whiskey, sir?

REV: Now you're talking. But don't call me sir. You say sir too much. What are you having?

KIMO: Too early I think. Well. Maybe tiny one. *(He gets the drinks.)*

REV: That a man. *(Looking around)* Must've felt great when you bought this place. Local boy makes good. To your bar.

KIMO: My bar.

(They drink.)

REV: Too bad you don't run it.

(Beat)

KIMO: What you mean? I stay here all the time.

REV: You serve drinks. That's all. You don't run this bar. Kanaka owned this place last night. Kitty runs the show at times. And I bet there're others.

KIMO: I the owner. What I say goes.

REV: You don't even charge for drinks. How much booze have I drunk in here for free? You're even a coolie to your customers.

KIMO: I like you. I let people I like get away with things.

REV: You're impotent.

KIMO: I not impotent!

REV: A joke in your own joint.

KIMO: It's not my fault.

REV: Of course not. You're not naturally weak inside.

KIMO: No, I not.

REV: It's bad influences.

KIMO: Bad people.

REV: Bad conditions.

KIMO: The Yakuza!

REV: Ah. That's a tough jam.

KIMO: Nobody go up against the Yakuza. They Japanese but they get some Hawaiians, now. Was more better before the Yakuza wen get Kitty. When it jus' me and her. We jus' did what we like. *(Strongly)* I not one pimp. I never get no cut. I even give her free room. And never wen sleep with her. Not one time. Me and Kitty, we stay like brother and sister. 'Ohana.

REV: Is that why she treats you like you have no—

KIMO: *(Interrupting)* Yakuza give her lotsa coke. She half outta her mind, now. We gotta do what the Yakuza like.

REV: Last night Kanaka said you owe money.

KIMO: Protection pay.

REV: From who?

KIMO: The Yakuza.

REV: Who do you pay?

KIMO: The Yakuza.

REV: You pay them to protect you from themselves?

KIMO: I not supposed to tell you this.

REV: Just think if you said to Kanaka "Leave my bar." And he answers, "Whatever you say, boss," and leaves.

KIMO: *(Laughing)* For you he go; for me, never.

REV: It could happen. But you need an organization with muscle behind you. Just like the Yakuza. No man can stand alone. He needs conglomeration. Just think. You walk into this bar, your bar, and with one shot, clear out the whole joint.

KIMO: Never.

REV: You'd be the big shot.

KIMO: I always like get one class place. But I make one big mistake from the start. I never get no rules. This place complete chaos. Now I gotta serve criminals, prostitutes, and tourists. *(Beat)* But I still get dreams, eh. Sometimes I think like this place is one first-class restaurant. But jus' gourmet Filipino food. Spicy beef with almonds in the peanut sauce. Ooh, the best in the world. The backroom over there, that the kitchen. All good, modern appliances. I stay cooking back there. And when I become one big success, I can teach one young kid my style and how for make good like me. Then I serve my original drinks, Kimo Specials, in long-stem, crystal snifters. The whole bar look like the Philippines. Get like jungle everywhere. Lace drapes. Chandeliers. Son of a gun. The Maitre d', he in one white tuxedo. And the Filipino waitresses in brocade sarongs and transparent silk blouses. Boy. Not a lot of tables, jus' choice ones. All private. Nice, polished koa wood and each chair one tiny throne. Reservations months in advance. And somebody say something stupid I no like, I jus' tell my bouncers, eh, throw him out, jus' like that. No tourists. Jus' good people. Locals. Then I get respect. Hold my head up. Then I can be one big shot.

(Beat)

REV: You can have that.

KIMO: What?

REV: Just join the CC.

KIMO: What you talking about?

REV: You can have your restaurant.

KIMO: How?

REV: I baptize you. Then you refuse to pay the Yakuza.

KIMO: I no can do that!

REV: You can if you're a Soldier for Christ. The Yakuza is only one country. The CC is all countries. I make one phone call and a platoon of Italian Specials are here in twenty-four hours. Emergency? A planeful of Mexicans in the time it takes to untangle a scapular. These Buddha-thumping Japanese are nothing. Let us take care of you, James. Don't be afraid. Follow me.

KIMO: I will.

*(*REV *dips his fingers into his drink and sprinkles* KIMO*'s head.)*

REV: James, I baptize you in the name of the Father, and of the Son, and of the Holy Spirit. Your brown soul is now white. Stay white. Don't let your soul become a white death. *(He takes a drink, then looks at* KIMO *calmly.)*

KIMO: That's it?

REV: That's it.

KIMO: I member of the CC?

REV: Is the Holy Spirit a bird?

(Beat)

KIMO: Me and you on the same side, now? Me and famous person! No more Yakuza. I get my restaurant. More drinks!

REV: It's not that simple. You're whitewashed. But now you've got to go further.

KIMO: Where?

REV: One complete revolution. You've got to rev up. *(Beat)* You can do it, James. You're as tough as a steel crucifix.

KIMO: Whatevers.

REV: A Soldier can't be a weak, sniveling idiot. You have to face yourself. There's something about that tourist last night.

KIMO: Please. I—

REV: This cup won't pass from you. The tourist.

KIMO: Father—no—

REV: People never tell their real sins in confession. I'm gonna tell you yours. You do whatever people expect of you. You're a sucker for the Yakuza. You butt-kiss any tourist. You don't even have the guts to be a pimp. So you're a eunuch and a free ride to a coked-up prossy. *(Beat)* You're not a pretty picture, James. The tourist came in. What did he do?

KIMO: He wen make me mad.

REV: That's it.

KIMO: Push my face for grin. Make my hands serve him.

REV: Deeper. Go on.

KIMO: I love the tourist. But I like for kill him. He pay me for smile. I keep him happy. I eat. Buy clothes. Stay zero. When all's pau, the tourist make me nothing. *(Beat)* The knife wen stab his stomach. My mouth say no, but my eyes go yeah. The tourist wen scream. Me, I happy. His blood run down. Beautiful. His screams was music. The knife push. He wen jump like one little puppet. He go dance for my tune. Jus' this one time. *(Beat)* But I no wen did it. I no get the guts. I'm always stay one coolie. I wen wrestle with the body, mop up the blood, cover the stink. Even when he's dead, I still serve the tourist. I love Kanak for kill the tourist. But I tell you something. I never gonna mop up for nobody again. Nobody. Never.

(The front door flies open. Blazing white light from outside shatters the darkness of the bar. A body flies mid-air through the doorway, hits the floor, and rolls to a halt.

REV *pulls out his revolver, spins to the window, and looks out. He moves toward the door but as soon as he hits the white light, his body freezes, caught in the brilliance. Covering his eyes, he struggles toward the opening and rolls out of sight through the door way.* KITTY *enters and runs to* KIMO *in amazement.)*

KITTY: Kimo, what, you stupid? You wen squeal on Kanak.

KIMO: I did? No, we was talking about me. Not Kanak. How you know? Stay listen at the door?

KITTY: Yeah. And you said Kanak wen did him.

KIMO: I did? He one operative. He no can say nothing. Look, another dead body in my bar! I did? Did I?

KITTY: How do all the dead haoles find this bar?

*(*REV *enters and approaches the body, which is sprawled in an unnatural position. The corpse is white, handcuffed, barefoot, and dressed in an expensive lounging robe. The head is covered with a black hood; a shank of rope is tied around its neck.)*

REV: *(Dazed from the sun)* Couldn't see a thing. Sun blinded me.

KITTY: Up the volcano the sun strong, yeah. What's the matter, operative? You no can take Pele's light? Her truth too powerful? You lose sight of your aim? Pele rob you of your vision?

KIMO: Father, a note.

KITTY: If jus' the sun blind you, wait 'til Pele blow the crater. She make you fry, haole, like one white chunk of fat.

REV: Read it.

*(*KIMO *takes the note from the face of the hood.)*

KIMO: 'Rev Hunter: Leave these islands or you'll be the next white death.'

*(*REV *loosens the rope and removes the hood from the corpse.)*

KITTY: Lionel Harding.

KIMO: President of Puna Sugar.

REV: *(Giving* KIMO *a business card.)* Just in case something happens to me, here's The Cardinal Code's phone number. Trust him like sunrise. But right now, call the police. Tell them the head of Puna Sugar just dropped in. Let them know you run things around here. For the first time you'll be telling the truth. *(Slipping on a pair of sunglasses)* You're with me now, kid.

*(*REV *starts for the front door as the lights fade to a blackout, then immediately come up on* KITTY *and* KANAKA*, counting money. It is twilight. The sun slowly disappears during this scene. The bar becomes darker as night descends, and hotter as the volcano boils.)*

KITTY: Crater ready for blow. Pele mad at something.

KANAKA: Sun going down but it more hot. Me, I sweating like one pig.

KITTY: Smell like one, too.

KANAKA: Then give me back that stink money coming from my smelly hand. But no, you sniff Yakuza pay like it's perfume.

KITTY: If this perfume, it's cheap. This only half what my pay's supposed to be.

KANAKA: Omuro say he get cut on your personal customers.

KITTY: That not the deal we made.

KANAKA: The deal's what Omuro say the deal is.

KITTY: Not with me. I trick all Yakuza for free. But my personal clients stay mine. I think Yakuza doing it to me more ways than one.

KANAKA: What you crying for? You jus' get three-thousand dollars worth of free cocaine, eh.

KITTY: That ain't one snowball to the sex blizzard I been giving.

(Beat)

KANAKA: Eh, Kitty. How come you no do da kine with me, eh? I been thinking. You do it with haoles, Flips, Pakes, Portagis, Buddhaheads, even Samoans. Everybody. Except Hawaiian. Eh? That's how come you no do it with me. Not because of my diseases. Not because of my smell. It's something else, ain't it, Kitty. It's because of my blood. *(Beat)* Maybe you look at me and see you. Like look in one mirror. You see your eyes in mine. What, if you do it with me, you think it be like doing it to yourself? *(Beat)* Look what they do to you every night. *(Beat)* You diseased, too. C'mon, Princess, that's how come, eh. You Hawaiian like me.

*(*JAMES *enters.* KIMO *has become* JAMES. *He wears long pants, shiny shoes, and a long-sleeved shirt that is crisp and buttoned at the top. He carries a full sack of religious items and a Bible.)*

JAMES: *(Simply)* Kanak, get out my bar.

*(*KANAKA *turns, sees* JAMES, *and bursts out laughing.)*

KANAKA: That's funny, Kimo. Some kinda costume? You think it Halloween, dress-up like one haole? Or you do da kine stand-up comedy?

JAMES: My name James.

KANAKA: James?

KITTY: Your name Kimo.

KANAKA: Oh, you little haole boy? You go eat potato now instead of rice?

(JAMES *hangs a large steel crucifix on the wall. He takes various religious articles out of his sack and places them around the bar. He has statues, vigil lights, scapulars, etc. He takes down various "heathen" adornments such as half-naked Hawaiian dancers and Tiki statues. He begins to convert the bar into a shrine.)*

KITTY: What you doing to the bar?

KANAKA: No matter how flipped out you are, Flip, you still owe us money. Pay day for us, but pay-up day for you.

JAMES: How come I owe?

KANAKA: You no pay, I broke your leg, that's how come.

(JAMES *puts a piece of paper on the bar.)*

JAMES: Pay-up day for you. This your bill.

(KANAKA *rips it up.)*

KANAKA: What bill? *(He laughs grotesquely.)*

JAMES: *(Writing another bill quickly)* This bill. One-hundred forty-five dollars and thirty-three cents. Tax included.

KANAKA: You been smokin' or what, brah? Gimme one beer.

JAMES: No more free drinks for nobody.

KITTY: That's it, Kimo. You tell him. It's about time this pig start paying. Thing's gonna be different around here, you piece of bacon.

JAMES: No pay, no drinks.

KITTY: Tell it like it is, brah.

JAMES: No rent, no room.

KITTY: What?

KANAKA: Huh?

JAMES: You gotta move outta the back room. No more prostitutes in my bar.

(Beat)

KANAKA: One more time, brah.

KITTY: No act, Kimo.

JAMES: Not. I no like stay ugly no more. I like one pretty place. Good people. Happy, safe life. Nice things for once. Clean dreams.

KITTY: You make me feel dirty.

JAMES: Maybe you gotta feel dirty so you can wash and come clean.

KITTY: You like rent, I pay rent.

JAMES: Too late. I like you out.

KITTY: We been together for so long. Seem like all our life. I can't remember not knowing you.

JAMES: And all that time you use me. Like one bar rag. No more.

KITTY: This not you talking. Those not your eyes. Tell me you no mean this. No do this. Stop when you still can, Kimo. Run from that Hunter. Run free.

(Beat)

JAMES: Free like you? *(Beat)* You one whore. *(Beat)* I look at you and I like for throw-up.

(Silence)

KITTY: *(Deeply hurt)* When you like me out?

JAMES: Tomorrow. I like start my new life now.

KITTY: That's what you like, that's what you get.

KANAKA: *(Burning)* Eh, manong, you cracked or what? You no talk to Kitty like that. You in big trouble, pally. She Yakuza. Omuro no gonna like this. You better think twice or go buy some crutches. Last time, Flip. Keep Kitty! Gimme beer! Gimme money!

JAMES: Go rot in hell.

KITTY: Kimo!

KANAKA: Okay, cripple. You no pay-up, you get bust up.

(KANAKA grabs JAMES violently.)

KITTY: Leave him alone!

KANAKA: I hate for do this to you, you mop up for me, but this gonna hurt.

(KITTY jumps on KANAKA's back. REV enters through the front door with his revolver drawn.)

REV: Freeze.

KANAKA: Get outta here, shark. This my job.

REV: This my job, too. James is CC. Let him go.

KANAKA: What?

KITTY: Hunter wen convert Kimo!

KANAKA: No wonder he acting lolo.

REV: I'm here for you, Pigface. Taking you in for the tourist murder.

KANAKA: I never murder nobody. I never even seen the guy.

REV: Oh, yeah? You look like pals in this picture. *(He holds up a photograph.)* Snapped right before you butchered him in cold blood.

KANAKA: Kimo! I kill you! You turn into one canary for the CC? You convert from coolie to stoolie!

REV: *(Strongly)* Let him go or I shoot.

*(*KANAKA *releases* JAMES.*)*

JAMES: I wen give him the picture of you and the tourist for your own good. And I gonna testify in court against you for save your soul.

REV: Let's go. You've got a date with an iron cage.

KANAKA: Uh-uh. Wait one minute. Something the matter here. Yeah, I know. The CC protects murderers from the law.

REV: Only through confession.

KANAKA: Whatever that is, I do it!

REV: No dice.

KANAKA: Eh, you wen baptize me, brah. I CC. You gotta confess me!

(Beat)

REV: Guess you've caught me on a technicality. *(Beat)* Pay James or no absolution. *(To* KIMO*)* Add a bottle of white wine to his bill.

KANAKA: Eh!

*(*KANAKA *pays* JAMES. JAMES *puts a bottle of white wine on the bar.)*

REV: Keep your accounts clean, Kanaka, in heaven and on Earth. Two glasses, please, James.

*(*JAMES *places the glasses next to the wine.)*

KANAKA: *(Suddenly terrified)* You ain't gonna change me, yeah? No do me like you wen did Kimo. Lock me up if you gonna try make me not me.

REV: Mind if we use your bar, James?

JAMES: I go out front, keep customers out.

REV: All churches should be bars. Attendance would go up.

KITTY: Send mine 'round the back, eh?

JAMES: I no do that no more.

KITTY: I forget. Habit, I guess. I gotta go pack anyway.

*(*JAMES *exits out the front door.)*

KITTY: Dig one hole and watch them fight for jump in. I like kill you for convert Kimo. You wait, haole. The lava gonna fly.

*(*KITTY *exits into the backroom.* REV *holsters his revolver and takes the wine and glasses to a table. He sits.)*

REV: Sit.

*(*KANAKA *sits at the table.* REV *takes out a small pouch and removes a communion host.)*

REV: This is my body. Eat me.

(Pause)

KANAKA: You make me puke.

REV: *(Breaking the host in two)* Eat it.

*(*KANAKA *eats half,* REV *the other.* REV *pours wine into the glasses.)*

REV: This is my blood. Drink it.

KANAKA: I not one vampire.

(They both drink.)

REV: Give me some money.

*(*KANAKA *gives him a couple of dollars.)*

REV: I've gotta say Mass. That's how I collect.

KANAKA: More better for bust bones.

REV: *(Placing a stole around his neck)* Relax. It's really wine. Who's killing the sugar men?

KANAKA: What's that gotta do with the tourist?

REV: I'm running this confession! You want protection or a steel box?

(Beat)

KANAKA: Unifac owns the sugar companies. The companies go broke. So Unifac's gotta sell them. Yakuza like for buy. But Unifac, they no like for sell to the Japanese crime, yeah. So the Yakuza knock off Unifac's top men one by one until they sell them to the Yakuza. Simple. No big deal.

REV: Why does the Yakuza want the cane fields?

KANAKA: They no tell me that stuff. I jus' crack necks.

REV: You didn't kill those sugar men. They were executed clean. One bullet through the brain. You're messy. They murder with the mind. You kill with your heart.

KANAKA: I gotta believe in what I do.

REV: One question. The tourist's body was punctured with what looked like boar tusks.

KANAKA: You like that one, eh? Well, me, I figure I fool everybody, yeah. I put the dead body inside the bag, then throw the haole into the back of my pick-up truck. I drive to the garbage dump. I could get rid of him inside the compacter, but no, I get more better idea. I wait in the dark for the wild boar for come. I know she come to the dump at night. And then I hear one. Bugger come real slow, yeah. Sniff out for humans. She no smell me. Bugger come near. I make my move. The pig scared, squeal, run. I jump on her back. Pull out my knife. Cut her neck. Ooh, the bugger let out one big wet groan. I grab the tusk. Pull the neck back. Snap. Limp. Makee. *(Beat)* The moon bright. I cut out one tusk. Take the body out from the bag. In the moonlight, I stick the tusk into the pukas the knife we make in the haole. I go back to Kilauea. Shove him down the throat of the volcano. Feed him to the crater. The haole like it here so bad, he can stay for good. This not his island.

REV: But the body was naked. If you wanted to fool everyone and make it look like the guy was attacked by a wild boar, he would have had some clothes on.

(Beat)

KANAKA: Oh, yeah. *(Beat)* Eh, sometimes I think I more better go up Mauna Loa. Live on berries and game. When I go up the mountain all my allergies stop. My skin come clean. The air different. Me, I allergic to everything. Alcohol. Cigarettes. Haoles. Before the haoles come, there was no disease. Not even the common cold. Can you think of that? But the haoles come bring their white death. Now everything infection. I think more better, me, I live before the haoles. My ancestors was royalty, you know. Now everything die. Not that many full-blooded Hawaiians left. One doctor tell me, eh, I allergic to myself. But not when I go mauka, up the mountain. When I come to town, that's when I like get everything I no can have. Like Kitty.

REV: Why do you want Kitty?

KANAKA: 'Cause I no can have her. *(Beat)* I never can get no woman. Not even one prostitute. Nobody like touch me. Nobody. Sometimes me, I get this feeling deep inside of me and I jus' like for explode. Like one volcano. Like last night. My skin crawl then I bust out. I think maybe if somebody jus' touch me once in a while, I'd be all right. You know? When I go touch Kitty, she yells and moves away. But when I hit her, she stay still. She no let me hug her, but she let me hit her. So I hit her for touch her. She no like me hit her in the face, so I try not to. But if somebody jus' let me touch them, eh, I no try hit Kitty. Maybe. *(Beat)* I get this one dream about Kitty, always stay the same. Over and over again. I know what's gonna happen. It's Kitty. She walks up to me real slow. Then puts one finger on my lip, and rubs, back and forth. So soft. Like nobody I ever know. Then last night. In real life. She wen touch me. No kidding. Jus' like that. In this bar. I thought dreams was just dreams. You know, the thing that never comes true. But last night, my dream come true. Kitty wen walk up and touch my lip like that. Jus' like my dreams.

REV: You don't want to sleep with Kitty.

KANAKA: Yes, I do.

REV: I don't think so.

KANAKA: I'm a man. She's everything I like.

REV: I think you just want her to look at you. Like you. Touch your lip once in a while.

KANAKA: I like her for look into my eyes and see me.

REV: You want her to dream of you, like you dream of her.

KANAKA: I like her for dream of me.

REV: You're not the same as everyone. You're different. You want to be different to her. You want to be special, like she's special to you. Kitty's not just anyone.

KANAKA: She's special to me.

REV: She's not just a woman. She's Kitty. Not no one. Someone. Different. Like you. You're different.

KANAKA: Me, I different. I not the same.

REV: Everyone sleeps with Kitty. It's different not to sleep with her. Only certain special people don't sleep with Kitty. Like Kimo.

KANAKA: Kimo and her stay close.

REV: Kimo doesn't sleep with her. You want to be close to her. You don't want to sleep with her.

KANAKA: Yeah, I different, eh. 'Cause me, I no like sleep with her. 'Cause then I special to her.

REV: The unique doesn't sleep with her, only the common do.

KANAKA: See, me, I feel close to her. She's special to me. I love her. What? What I wen said? I love her. I no like sleep with her, I jus' like for love her. Protect her. Like Kimo. But Kimo not Kimo no more. I try be like Kimo. And I can really protect her. You'll see. And we'll be special for each other. I no go hit her and then maybe she go touch my lip. I love her.

REV: Was Omuro in on this alone?

KANAKA: Him and some fat cat from the mainland. *(Beat)* Eh, what I wen said? I mixed up with this love stuff.

REV: What does Kanaka mean in Hawaiian?

KANAKA: Human being.

REV: For the record, did you kill the tourist?

KANAKA: Yeah.

REV: *(Blessing him)* I forgive you in nomine Patris, et Filii, et Spiritus Sancti. I bury your sins within my heart. Go in peace and sin no more. That means don't kill any more tourists.

KANAKA: Okay. I protected or what?

REV: Yeah.

KANAKA: All right. Eh, Father, thanks for straightening me out about Kitty.

REV: Comes with the collar.

*(*KANAKA *runs to the backroom and pounds on the door.)*

KANAKA: Hey, Kitty! We 'ohana now. Special.

*(*KITTY *enters, wearing a lava-lava and a print top.)*

KITTY: What's the matter, you stupid or what?

KANAKA: I finally figured it out. Everything good. I no hit you no more. I protect you. I go do anything you say.

KITTY: *(To* REV*)* You wen did him, too, eh.

REV: And he told me all about you and that fat cat from the mainland.

KITTY: *(To* KANAKA*)* Pupule! *(To* REV*)* So what, I wen did that guy Red one time. What you gonna do, call the cops?

(A storm breaks. Lightening scratches across the bar through the picture window. Rain falls. Thunder. JAMES *is pushed into the bar.* OMURO *enters. He is Japanese, dressed in a three-piece suit with silk tie and handkerchief, and carries a submachine gun.)*

OMURO: His piece.

*(*KANAKA *takes* REV*'s revolver and points it at* REV.*)*

OMURO: I warn you once with that note. Patience running out.

REV: Didn't catch the name, pal.

KANAKA: This Omuro.

OMURO: *(Raising the gun)* Hear my confession.

REV: When an operative's in a jam, he hears confession. Spill it.

OMURO: What you think this all about? Drugs. What else? Japan call it the white death. Here call it cocaine. Cane fields front for drug trade. Dope in the sugar shipments. Sugar can go everywhere, baby. Make the whole world sweet. Locals keep job cut cane. We build the Buddhist temples. Everybody get fat, happy, and Buddhist. Forgive me, Father, for I am going to sin. *(He cocks the machine gun.)*

REV: *(Blessing* OMURO, *deadpan)* I absolve you in the name of the Father, and of the Son, and of the Holy Spirit.

OMURO: Amen. Now that you forgive me, you are harmless. You cannot tell one soul. The CC most wonderful corporation. Go home, Hunter, there no more game for you here. *(Taking out a large bag of cocaine)* Here kitty, kitty, kitty.

*(*KITTY *offers him her open mouth. He licks his finger, dips it into the cocaine, and rubs it onto her gums.)*

OMURO: Nice kitty. You go to Buddha study?

KITTY: Once a week.

OMURO: Kanaka?

KANAKA: Me, too.

OMURO: Excellent. Only Buddha can save you, baby. *(Looking out the picture window)* Ah! And the Buddha getting ready erupt his crater. Maybe I turn this bar into temple in honor Buddha's volcanic power. Statue Buddha look excellent where that crucifix hangs. This his island, now. And the Buddha is happy.

KITTY: Pele still live here.

OMURO: Nobody convert to Pele. She washed up. Jesus, too. But Buddha doing excellent.

KITTY: I no like the cut you take on my personal clients.

OMURO: Standard for Yashiwara. All Tokyo, Honolulu chicks.

KITTY: My clients stay mine. That was the deal.

OMURO: Deals change, baby.

KITTY: Not with me. This not your body.

OMURO: *(Erupting)* When I tell Kimo pay, he pay, Kanaka collect, he collect, Hunter forgive, he forgive. When I tell you trick, you trick.

KITTY: Buddha no sit on this crater. Pele gon blow your Buddha back to Japan. Shoot the hot lava under his fat okole.

*(*KITTY *dumps the bag of cocaine onto* OMURO*'s head. He knocks the bag away, spins his machine gun around to everyone, then aims at* KANAKA. KANAKA *is pointing* REV*'s revolver at* OMURO. *Silence.)*

OMURO: Put down gun, Kanaka.

KANAKA: No. *(Beat)* Bust your own bones. This not your island.

OMURO: Tsk, tsk, tsk. You better hide deep in the hapu'u, pig. You sign your own contract, baby. *(To* KITTY*)* And you, pussy-cat, you work nowhere. Not Honolulu, San Fran, L.A., D.C. Not all Kittys have nine lives. *(To* REV*)* Hunter. You're so cool. Don't you ever see Red? *(Smiling)* Shaka, brahs.

*(*OMURO *backs out the door, still aiming the machine gun at* KANAKA, *and exits. When the door is opened, the wind whistles, rain falls, thunder.* REV *goes to the phone booth and dials. It rings until the* CARDINAL CODE *picks up.)*

KANAKA: That Buddhahead mean business. And the crater. Come with me, Kitty. I protect you. We go mauna, hele, up the mountain.

KITTY: With you? You lolo? I no need run from the crater. Pele no gonna hurt me. She protect me, not you, hog. This my last night in the Volcano Bar. I stay right here. You say you go do what I say, Kanak? Well, I say split.

KANAKA: If that's what you like. *(He exits through the backroom, still carrying* REV*'s revolver.)*

KITTY: Eh, not through my room! *(To* JAMES*)* I forget. Not my room no more. *(She sits and takes cocaine.)*

CODE: *(A voice over the phone)* The Cardinal Code.

REV: *(Into phone)* Hey. Red.

CODE: Yes?

REV: Hunter.

CODE: *(Laughing)* No one has called me Red since—

REV: Your last trip to Honolulu. Stiffs are piling up down here. The heat's up.

CODE: Then I'll pull you out right now. Three murders in three days is a burn.

(Beat)

REV: What three murders? *(Beat)* Wrong response, Code. *(Beat)* I never told you about Talbot. Or the tourist. *(Beat)* Did I? *(Beat)* But then I didn't have to. *(Beat)* Just had a little chat with your buddy. Old Buddha-breath. Force-confession from a Buddhist? Jeez, that's no inside job, huh? You write that cute little note or did Omuro come up with that himself? I don't like threats on my life. Especially from my boss.

CODE: I don't know what you're talking about.

REV: Maybe Rome does. Life everlasting—

CODE: Wait. Calm down. *(Beat)* All right. *(Beat)* The Chicago Chancery owns the sugar land. *(Beat)* We lease to Unifac. They went bankrupt; now we'll lease to the Yakuza. They'll do well; we get a cut. Progress is made by compromise, Rev. Like all corporations, self-preservation is first. Then, we can do good. You know that. We'll feed and clothe the poor with this money. We can't stop human nature, but we can utilize conversion. Clean dirty money. Convert bad into good. *(Beat)* Rome sent you to investigate because they want the deal for themselves. *(Beat)* Stick with us. You're still an American. I'll make it worth your while. *(Beat)* How did you know it was me?

REV: I didn't. *(Beat)* About my assignment. How do you convert the CC? *(He rips the phone out of the booth. Thunder booms.)*

JAMES: You all right, Reverend? *(Beat)* We gotta go. The eruption.

REV: I'm not going anywhere, Kimo.

JAMES: My name James.

REV: You're as Hebrew as pork.

JAMES: You wen baptize me.

REV: To get information. *(Beat)* The game's up. The whole thing's a bust. *(Beat)* Listen. You went for the restaurant, pal. Don't come off thinking it was something else.

JAMES: But—

REV: Get outta here. Beat it. Before I deconvert you. Yeah. Maybe that's what I should do. Go back across the world and deconvert my converts. *(He takes a big drink from a Jack Daniels bottle.)*

JAMES: You turning on the CC?

REV: Maybe I've always been a double-agent and never knew it. You hear me? Get outta here.

JAMES: You tell me get out my own bar? *(Beat)* This all been one act? You wen lied to me this whole time?

(Beat)

REV: Yeah.

(Beat)

KITTY: When you grow up, you wanna be jus' like Rev Hunter, yeah, Kimo?

(Pause)

JAMES: You both go to hell. *(He exits.)*

KITTY: Kimo!

*(*Rev *slams the bar.)*

Kitty: You one messed-up haole bugger.

Rev: An accomplice to my own murder case. Sent here to find who? Myself? Hunter hunts Hunter. But what do I convert myself into?

Kitty: How come you gotta convert people, anyhow? I no like other people for believe in Pele. She my goddess. But you, you hold a gun to other people's temples.

*(*Rev *takes a drink from the bottle, then pours into a glass with no ice.)*

Rev: I think I just excommunicated myself. So it's all history. Wanna drink?

Kitty: I stick with this. *(She snorts a line of cocaine.)* I wen quit, too. No more Yakuza for me. I never get one pimp; I no need no corporate pimp, now. I stand by myself. Again. No more organization.

Rev: That's me. Un-organized.

(She does another line of cocaine.)

Kitty: Y'know, think about it. Me and you, we get the two oldest con-jobs in the world. *(Beat)* Only one thing different. I give them what they pay for.

(Kilauea erupts. There is a deep explosion. The Volcano Bar shakes. Bottles rattle. The bar reflects the scarlet motion of the shooting lava. A red glow shows through the cracks in the floorboards. They watch the eruption through the picture window and are bathed in red light.)

Kitty: The eruption. *(Beat)* We stay above the flow; we're safe.

Rev: *(Watching the eruption)* So that's how this island is made. Burning it down and building it up. And men killing each other over it. For their gods. *(Beat)* What if a volcano was just a volcano? Wouldn't it all be a sin?

*(*Kanaka *enters, carrying* Rev*'s revolver and covered with snow. The crater continues to erupt.)*

Kanaka: The sky bust open! Snow blizzard. Ice cubes. But the crater still erupt. The volcano crazy. Come with me, Kitty.

Kitty: We're safe now.

Rev: I'm sorry for everything I did to you, Kanaka.

Kanaka: You no did nothing to me. Come, Kitty.

Kitty: Not. I'm okay here.

Rev: *(Suddenly antagonistic)* Yeah. That's right. She's with me. Mine.

(He grabs Kitty.*)*

Kanaka: What you doing?

REV: I take what I want from here. Like everybody else. And I'm taking her. What are you gonna do about it?

(REV twists KITTY's arm behind her back.)

KITTY: Oww. What's the matter with you?

KANAKA: No do that.

REV: Why not? You're not going to stop me. You don't have the guts anymore.

KITTY: Let go.

KANAKA: *(Raising REV's revolver)* Stop.

REV: You're not gonna pull the trigger. You're gonna let me yank the tusks right outta your mouth. Aren't you, Pigface.

KANAKA: Let her go.

REV: What are you waiting for? Or did I do you like you did the tourist? Huh? Do it. I dare you.

(He pushes KITTY away and shoves his forehead right to the barrel of the revolver in KANAKA's hand.)

REV: Do it. Do it!

(KANAKA pulls the trigger. The revolver clicks rapidly, slows down, and then stops.)

REV: That's the old Kanaka I know. *(Beat)* My gun's never been loaded.

(Beat)

KITTY: What?

REV: Fifth Commandment. I play by the Book. I don't kill anyone. No matter how much good it does.

KANAKA: You wen baptize me with no bullets?

(Beat)

REV: *(To KITTY)* Sorry about getting rough with you.

KITTY: I can handle one collar.

KANAKA: I wen stand up to Omuro with a toy gun?

REV: It's all a bluff. All of it. A big, big bluff.

(A man in a hooded raincoat bursts in through the backroom. REV turns toward him. The man raises a gun and fires. REV and KITTY fall to the floor. KANAKA runs, opens the front door, and just as he's about to exit—)

MAN: Stop!

*(*KANAKA *freezes.)*

MAN: Turn around. Hele!

*(*KANAKA *faces him. The man drops his hood. He is* JAMES.*)*

JAMES: Kanak. Leave. My. Bar.

KANAKA: Whatever you say, Boss.

*(*JAMES *smiles and raises his gun.* KANAKA *jumps through the front door as* JAMES *opens fire.* JAMES *runs to the door and fires into the darkness, snow, and wind. He closes the door, then takes off his raincoat. He is dressed in an elegant tuxedo. He lights a cigarette which is at the end of a long cigarette holder, and takes a puff. He goes to the bar phone, takes out the card, and dials. It rings.)*

CODE: *(A voice over the phone)* The Cardinal Code.

JAMES: *(Into the phone)* James.

CODE: Is it done?

JAMES: Yes.

CODE: Deconversion can't be tolerated. He knew that. Your namesake was an apostle, James. A fisherman. Would you like to be a fisher of men?

JAMES: I do what you say, your Eminence. *(Beat)* I wen did Kitty. Omuro say.

CODE: She was a good girl. I absolve you in nomine Patris, et Filii, et Spiritus Sancti. I hold your sins within my heart. Go back to Omuro. He'll take care of everything. You'll get your restaurant. Life everlasting.

JAMES: Amen. *(He hangs up the phone. Standing over* REV:*)* It's. My. Bar. *(Beat)* Mine. *(He goes to* KITTY.*)* I'm sorry, Kitty. *(Beat)* But I'm forgiven. *(He backs away.)* I'm forgiven.

*(*JAMES *exits through the front door.* KANAKA *immediately enters through the back room. He kneels beside* KITTY *and props her dead body against himself.)*

KANAKA: Look, Kitty. The volcano no cry for you. It jus' lava. *(Beat)* I go up the mountain now. No Buddha. No Jesus. No Pele. Jus' the crater. I take you with me. *(He picks her up.)* Sleep, Princess. You safe, now.

*(*KANAKA *exits with* KITTY*'s body through the front door.* REV *sits up. Then stands. He takes off his jacket, then his clerical collar and vest. He touches where the bullets hit the bullet-proof vest. He looks out the picture window.)*

REV: First thing you learn in the seminary is how to play dead. *(He discards the collar and vest. He wears a black tee shirt. He watches the eruption through the picture window as crimson washes over him.)* Best view on the island. *(*REV *finishes the Jack Daniels in his glass and exits through the backroom as the blood-red lights slowly fade. Blackout.)*

END OF PLAY

HARM'S WAY

Mac Wellman

The music to the songs in this play is contained in the acting edition published by Broadway Play Publishing Inc.

ABOUT THE AUTHOR

Mac Wellman is a poet and playwright living in New York. His recent productions include CLEVELAND, presented by BACA Downtown, under the direction of Anne Bogart; DRACULA, at River Arts Rep in Woodstock NY, under the direction of Len Jenkin; CELLOPHANE, also presented at BACA Downtown, under the direction of Jim Simpson; and WHIRLIGIG, for which he received a NYSCA commission. Mr Wellman has edited two anthologies of new American drama: THEATER OF WONDERS published by Sun & Moon, and 7 DIFFERENT PLAYS published by Broadway Play Publishing in 1988. Sun & Moon will also publish THE FORTUNETELLER, his first novel, and A SHELF IN WOOP'S CLOTHING, his third book of poems. Wellman is the 1989 recipient of both McKnight and Rockefeller fellowships. He is a member of New Dramatists.

HARM'S WAY is for Yolanda, with love

HARM'S WAY premiered on 13 November 1985 at the LaMama ETC Annex in New York, with the following cast:

MOTHER	Tom Costello
FISHEYE	Sheila Dabney
SANTOUCHE	Stephen Mellor
ISLE OF MERCY	Deirdre O'Connell
BY WAY OF BEING HIDDEN	Zivia Flomenhaft
CROWSFOOT	Gregg Daniel
WIZARD	Shelia Dabney
BLACKMANGE	Tom Costello
PRESIDENT MCKINLEY	Jeff Shoemaker
CHORUS	Tuwanda Coleman, Amy Sobin, Lute Ramblin'

Director	George Ferencz
Set design	Patrick Kennedy
Costumes	Sally Lesser
Lights	Howard Thies
Stage manager	Virlana Tkacz

Bob Jewett and Jack Maeby composed the music, which they performed along with Jeremy Kahn.

CHARACTERS

(in order of appearance)

MOTHER, *a firm believer in parental discipline*
CHILD, *a petulant brat*
FISHEYE, *a friend to*
SANTOUCHE, *an angry person*
ISLE OF MERCY, *his lady*
BY WAY OF BEING HIDDEN, *a person of curious identity*
CROWSFOOT, *an entrepreneur*
CROWSFOOT'S HELPER, *ditto*
POPSTAR, *an enterprising musician*
A MAN, *with a puzzling sense of humor*
WIZARD, *a specialist in an unlikely profession*
BLACKMANGE, *a man with important information*

and a CHORUS *of musicians in many guises*

Scene One

(An alley between darkened tenements. The MOTHER *is chasing her* CHILD *about in an attempt to get him to eat a sandwich she is holding in one hand. She has a revolver in her pocket.)*

MOTHER: Ugly kid. Eat!

CHILD: Witch. Go stuff it.

MOTHER: Watch your mouth.

CHILD: Don't want that crap. It's crap.

MOTHER: Good American cheese. Real baloney
on Wonderbread. Eat it. Or else.

CHILD: Crap.

MOTHER: You don't eat it and I'll whip you good.

CHILD: Crap sandwich.

MOTHER: I'll show your ass.

CHILD: Stuff it up your ass, witch.

MOTHER: You don't eat that sandwich and I'll kill you good.

CHILD: Suck my dingus, witch.

MOTHER: Lemme at you, I'll bust your chops.

CHILD: Nyah! Nyah!

MOTHER: Kid don't talk to his mother like that.
I'll teach you, little son of a bitch.

(She shoots and kills him.)

MOTHER: No respect...

*(*FISHEYE *enters.)*

FISHEYE: What's going on?

MOTHER: Little shit-ass wouldn't eat his sandwich, and I showed him.

*(*SANTOUCHE *enters.)*

SANTOUCHE: Hey, you.

MOTHER: No goddam respect...

SANTOUCHE: What's happening here? Who's the stiff?

MOTHER: Kid, that's all. None of your business.

SANTOUCHE: What happened, Fisheye?

FISHEYE: She and the kid were
fighting and then she
pulls the gun out and
shoots him, Santouche.
I never seen anything
like it.

SANTOUCHE: Fucking monster...

MOTHER: Guess I showed him.

FISHEYE: Santouche, what's wrong?

SANTOUCHE: Shut up.

MOTHER: No fucking respect.

SANTOUCHE: You really do that?

MOTHER: No fucking respect.

SANTOUCHE: Lady, I was talking to you.

MOTHER: HE DIDN'T HAVE NO FUCKING RESPECT.

SANTOUCHE: I asked you a question, bitch.

FISHEYE: Santouche...

SANTOUCHE: Shut up.

MOTHER: Leave me alone, big shot.
You got no respect either.

SANTOUCHE: I'll show you respect, bitch. *(He shoots and kills her.)*

FISHEYE: Santouche!

SANTOUCHE: Fucking unnatural cunt. I can't stand 'em.

FISHEYE: Santouche, are you crazy?

SANTOUCHE: Killed her own flesh and blood.
Won't eat his sandwich, my ass!

FISHEYE: Santouche, let's get the hell out of here.

SANTOUCHE: All in good time.

CHORUS: *(Crying out)* What's going on? What's all the noise? Someone's been shot.

SANTOUCHE: Let's haul ass
out of here.

FISHEYE: Santouche...

SANTOUCHE: Move it, Fisheye, move it!

Scene Two

(The interior of a small, sparsely furnished house. ISLE OF MERCY *is seated at a table.* SANTOUCHE *is pacing back and forth.)*

ISLE OF MERCY: What's wrong?

SANTOUCHE: I've got to go away for a while.

ISLE OF MERCY: Why?

SANTOUCHE: I killed somebody. Had to. Didn't
particularly want to, but I did. So
I've got to go someplace where I'll
be safe. Quiet.

ISLE OF MERCY: How long?

SANTOUCHE: Don't know.

ISLE OF MERCY: What am I supposed to do?

SANTOUCHE: Not your problem, Isle of Mercy.

ISLE OF MERCY: Don't call me that.

SANTOUCHE: It's funny. Isle of Mercy.
A pretty name for a pretty woman.
(He moves to embrace her.)

ISLE OF MERCY: It's not my name.

SANTOUCHE: It's your name if I say it is.
You got a better one?

ISLE OF MERCY: You know it.

SANTOUCHE: I need money. I'll have to sell
my things. Need money quick.

ISLE OF MERCY: How long?

SANTOUCHE: Lay off? I'm hassled enough.

ISLE OF MERCY: I am simply trying to figure out
what to do. That's all. How can
I know what to do otherwise?

SANTOUCHE: Talk too much. I need money.

ISLE OF MERCY: We don't have it.

SANTOUCHE: Have to sell something.
You have to sell something
for me.

ISLE OF MERCY: What? But what?

SANTOUCHE: The watch.

ISLE OF MERCY: It's broken.

SANTOUCHE: It's a gold watch.

ISLE OF MERCY: It stopped working a long time ago.

SANTOUCHE: You never wound it. It runs. It's a
gold watch. A thing like that's got
to be worth something. Where is it?

ISLE OF MERCY: Here. In the box.

SANTOUCHE: Let me see it, stupid.

ISLE OF MERCY: Watch what you say.

SANTOUCHE: Let me see the damn watch.

ISLE OF MERCY: It's broken.

SANTOUCHE: You never wound it right.

ISLE OF MERCY: How do you wind a watch wrong?

SANTOUCHE: You wound it backwards. I saw you.

ISLE OF MERCY: I never touched it.

SANTOUCHE: You did too.

ISLE OF MERCY: I never touched it. It's yours.

SANTOUCHE: I'll wind it up.

ISLE OF MERCY: Go ahead.

SANTOUCHE: Shut up.

ISLE OF MERCY: Leave me alone.

SANTOUCHE: It won't wind.

ISLE OF MERCY: I told you.

SANTOUCHE: You told me nothing. It's broken.

ISLE OF MERCY: I told you.

SANTOUCHE: I need money. What am I going to do...

ISLE OF MERCY: Sell it anyhow. It's gold, like you say.

SANTOUCHE: Not worth crap.

ISLE OF MERCY: Sure it is, even broken.

SANTOUCHE: Shut up.

ISLE OF MERCY: It's worth something. I'll sell it for you.

SANTOUCHE: I've got to get out of here.

ISLE OF MERCY: It'll be all right.

SANTOUCHE: Easy for you to say.

ISLE OF MERCY: I'm trying to help.

SANTOUCHE: Big help you are.

ISLE OF MERCY: I'll sell the watch and get the money to you.

SANTOUCHE: They'll throw me in the can.
I won't go again. Had enough.
It's too much. They'll have to
kill me first.

ISLE OF MERCY: Shut up.

SANTOUCHE: I won't go.

ISLE OF MERCY: Won't have to go if I sell the watch.

SANTOUCHE: I'll try it.

ISLE OF MERCY: Cheer up.

SANTOUCHE: How long will it take?

ISLE OF MERCY: A couple of days at most.

SANTOUCHE: Meet me at the Fair. Take the boat cross the river.

ISLE OF MERCY: How long?

SANTOUCHE: Two days. At sundown. By the Fair.

ISLE OF MERCY: All right.

SANTOUCHE: Bring the money. I'll be hiding.

ISLE OF MERCY: How'll I find you?

SANTOUCHE: I'll find you. I'll look different.

Isle of Mercy: I'll be there with the money.

Santouche: I'm all packed.

Isle of Mercy: Santouche.

Santouche: That's all. Have to get the hell
out of here. Bring the money. Once
the heat's off I'll be back. Maybe
I'll be lucky.

Isle of Mercy: Santouche...

Santouche: Have to go now. Don't bother me...

Isle of Mercy: Who'd you kill?

Santouche: Don't give me any trouble. I can't
take it. Just bring me the money. And
don't you mess around while I'm gone
or there'll be trouble, real trouble.

Isle of Mercy: Santouche!

Santouche: Told you I have to go.

(He leaves. She examines the watch more closely.)

Isle of Mercy: No wonder it's broken. There's some
kind of big, long hair in here. All
tangled and twisted up. Funny-looking thing.
(She pulls out the mainspring.)
Now look what I've done. It's more
broken now than it was before.

Scene Three

(A nightmarish hillside. Dim fires and explosions in the distance. There are three tall poles, or posts, on top of which are mounted wagon wheels. By Way of Being Hidden *and two dummies are strapped, respectively, atop each of these.)*

Santouche: What are you doing up there? Hey, you!
They must be some apples in that tree...

By Way of Being Hidden: Sombitch, let me down
outta here, hey stupid!

Santouche: Who're you calling stupid?

By Way of: You, asshole. Let me down.

SANTOUCHE: And what if I don't want to?

BY WAY OF: For Christsake, man!

SANTOUCHE: How come you got up there
in the first place?

BY WAY OF: It's all part of the show.

SANTOUCHE: What show?

BY WAY OF: Never mind. Just let me down.

SANTOUCHE: Why should I bust my ass?

BY WAY OF: Look, I'll do good by you, you'll see.
You let me down and I'll even it up,
don't you worry about that. A man like me
you can trust, I swear.

SANTOUCHE: Well, how do I get you down?

BY WAY OF: I'll show you...

SANTOUCHE: What about them?

BY WAY OF: Croaked, you numbskull.

SANTOUCHE: I don't know about this...

BY WAY OF: Chickenshit, dumb chickenshit!

SANTOUCHE: What, who are you calling chickenshit, you?!

BY WAY OF: You, chickenshit, you're afraid
to climb this pole.

SANTOUCHE: Hell if I am.

BY WAY OF: You are.

SANTOUCHE: What's your name, anyhow?

BY WAY OF: By Way of Being Hidden.

SANTOUCHE: No, I asked for your name.

BY WAY OF: By Way of Being Hidden. That's my
name. Now get a move on, chicken-
shit, or come dark and the rats'll
gnaw my eyes out.

SANTOUCHE: Shit if I care. What kind of name is that?

BY WAY OF: Son, what is your name?

SANTOUCHE: Santouche.

BY WAY OF: Santouche, my friend, much as I
enjoy the pleasures of conversation,
and like yourself, no doubt, would never
presume upon the honorable disinterest
of a true friend.

SANTOUCHE: Get to the point.

BY WAY OF: Are you going to let me down, chickenshit?

SANTOUCHE: All in good time. You got money?

BY WAY OF: You think if I had money I'd've
got myself strapped up here, like a
goddamn human scarecrow?

SANTOUCHE: You said it was part of the show.

BY WAY OF: Santouche, I swear I will
richly repay your generosity if you
only shinny up this pole and cut these
straps, you'll see, I'm not bullshitting.

SANTOUCHE: Well, all right, just let me figure
out a safe way of getting up there.

BY WAY OF: For Jesus Christ's sake, there isn't
any safe way of getting up here.
Don't think, Santouche. Just do it.
Don't you have no spirit of adventure?

SANTOUCHE: By Way of Being Hidden, my ass. *(Pause)*

BY WAY OF: I'm a girl. *(Pause)*

SANTOUCHE: Be right up.

Scene Four

(A small group of circus wagons and a tent in a clearing in the forest. The CHORUS *comes on stage and acts as an audience for* CROWSFOOT*'s exhortations.)*

CROWSFOOT: Ladies and gents! This is the final call!

ISLE OF MERCY: What's going on here?

CHORUS: We're waiting for the Guyanousa.
They've got one in that tent...

CROWSFOOT: Ladies and gents! This is the final call
for to get a glimpse at one of the most
astonishing marvels ever presented 'neath

the blue of God's welkin; a creature so
rare it has never come across another
like it, a creature so fabulous it has
never even heard tell of itself, a creature
so lopsided—with the feet longer on one
side than the t'other—that it can graze
on the steepest mountain slope; and—
Ladies and gents, there is so much more
to be gleaned about this creature: some of it
scandalous, some of it horrifying, and all
of it amazing, at the very least! And
two bits, a measly one-quarter of a dollar,
will buy you admission to the tent, where
even now the creature is snorting and
stamping and shaking his shaggy locks. So,
if there's anyone out there who'd still
like a ticket he'd better holler because,
ladies and gents, this is the last call. And
them that miss this shot to see the fabulous
one-time-only legendary Guyanousa may have to
wait twenty, thirty, who knows how many years before
another such opportunity presents itself. So it's last
call, ladies and gents. Last call! Last call!
Last call!

ISLE OF MERCY: Sir, I'd like a ticket. Me, I'd like a ticket.

CROWSFOOT'S HELPER: Mr. Crowsfoot...

CROWSFOOT: Yes, my dear, you come right over here, and I'll give you your ticket.

CROWSFOOT'S HELPER: Mr. Crowsfoot!

CROWSFOOT: Yes, Mr. Suggs?

CROWSFOOT'S HELPER: Hot damn, Mr. Crowsfoot! The Guyanousa am loose!

CROWSFOOT: Holy Jesus Mother of Mary I'm getting out of here!

CROWSFOOT'S HELPER: AYEEEEE!

CROWSFOOT: Last time it got loose it ate up
the whole town of Dead Snake Junction,
dogcatcher and all!

CROWSFOOT'S HELPER: The Guyanousa am loose!

(Crowd flees, screaming.)

CROWSFOOT'S HELPER: The Guyanousa am loose!

*(*HELPER *runs into the tent.* ISLE OF MERCY *stays.)*

CROWSFOOT: The Guyanousa am loose! *(Pause)*
Little lady, hadn't you better
run off, too? You don't want to get
eaten up, or—God forbid!—molested... *(Pause)*
by an ugly, evil-smelling,
hellfire-breathing, tree-uprooting
creature with no respect, that
ain't never been housebroken,
tamed, or other wise civilized,
now do you?

ISLE OF MERCY: I paid my quarter. I want to see
The Guyanousa.

CROWSFOOT: We can't hold it off forever,
can we, Mr. Suggs? Mr. Suggs?
The Lord be praised, it must've
already ate up Mr. Suggs!
You'd better haul ass out of here,
young lady. Creature's got a strange
hankering for the innards of young
girls. Terrible things happened
in the last town, I assure you...

ISLE OF MERCY: I paid. I want to see.

CROWSFOOT: Young lady wants to see the Guyanosa,
Mr. Suggs, ain't that rich!
The Guyanousa am loose!
Don't you understand, young lady?
You'll be killed, tore up, massacreed.
God, what a bloody mess there'll be:
gore and blood and ruination a-
hanging from the treetops.

ISLE OF MERCY: I won't go till I see the Guyanousa.

CROWSFOOT: She won't go, Mr. Suggs, do you
hear me? Till she catches sight
of the Guyanousa. Maybe we'd
just better oblige her. Do you
hear me, Mr. Suggs? She wants
to see the flaming Guyanousa! Suggs!
Pardon me, young lady, I'll just

tiptoe in the tent and see what awful
fate has befallen my colleague.

ISLE OF MERCY: There ain't no Guyanousa. You're a liar.

CROWSFOOT: Oh, now, don't say that.

ISLE OF MERCY: That was my last quarter.
I want to see the Guyanousa.

CROWSFOOT: You'll be ate up. Scram.

ISLE OF MERCY: You're a cheat.

CROWSFOOT: Beat it, bitch.

ISLE OF MERCY: Give me my money back.

CROWSFOOT: Get lost.

ISLE OF MERCY: I need the quarter. Otherwise
I can't cross the river.

CROWSFOOT: What river?

ISLE OF MERCY: Chagrin River.

CROWSFOOT: There's no river. Someone's diddled you.

ISLE OF MERCY: Sure there is. Chagrin River.

CROWSFOOT: It's part of the show. The con.

ISLE OF MERCY: Give me my quarter back.

CROWSFOOT: Go whistle for it.

ISLE OF MERCY: I don't have any money left.

CROWSFOOT: No skin off my teeth.

ISLE OF MERCY: You're a liar.

CROWSFOOT: Sucker born every day.

ISLE OF MERCY: I'm no sucker. Give me my money back.

CROWSFOOT: Get out of here.

ISLE OF MERCY: You're a crook.

CROWSFOOT: Honest as any man
can afford to be. A man's
got to live.

ISLE OF MERCY: Heard that before.

CROWSFOOT: Cynic. Beat it.

ISLE OF MERCY: Not till I get my money back.
I've got to have that quarter.

CROWSFOOT: I told you: there ain't no
such thing as any Anger River.
It's part of the show.

ISLE OF MERCY: Got to sell my watch and meet
my man on the other side.

CROWSFOOT: He must be part of the con, too.

ISLE OF MERCY: If he was here you wouldn't
say that.

CROWSFOOT: You don't beat it and I'll turn
the dogs loose on you.

ISLE OF MERCY: Why not the Guyanousa?

CROWSFOOT: What?

ISLE OF MERCY: You're a filthy liar.

CROWSFOOT: It's an honest day's work. That's all.

ISLE OF MERCY: I want my quarter back.

CROWSFOOT: There's other ways to get it.

ISLE OF MERCY: What do you mean?

CROWSFOOT: You're young yet. You can earn it
on your back.

ISLE OF MERCY: You cheated me.

CROWSFOOT: Nothing special about you.
Are you clean? Still, who'd
want to put it in you?

ISLE OF MERCY: I don't do things like that.

CROWSFOOT: Still, you're not much to look at.
You could be a gypsy and read
hands. Can you read hands?

ISLE OF MERCY: Give me my quarter.

CROWSFOOT: Look, bitch. I am trying to help you.

ISLE OF MERCY: Won't do it.

CROWSFOOT: If you had a beard.

ISLE OF MERCY: Just give me my quarter.

CROWSFOOT: Can you walk on your hands?

ISLE OF MERCY: Bastard.

CROWSFOOT: Here's my card. I am The Guyanousa.
Look, my dear, you'd better make up
your mind and make it up quick. If
you're not part of the show, you're
part of them that takes it all in,
and that's a fool. Think it over.

ISLE OF MERCY: What am I going to do?

CROWSFOOT: You're wasting my time.

ISLE OF MERCY: Bastard.

CROWSFOOT: Think it over.

(She sits down on the ground.)

Scene Five

(The POPSTAR *resembles a scarecrow tied to a stake. He holds an enormous guitar. As he sings he moves only his head and hands. Long pauses between stanzas. Again, the members of the* CHORUS *act as an audience. All are mounted on short stilts, and they lean together to form a human tripod. When the* POPSTAR *sings they moan and sway gently back and forth.* SANTOUCHE *and* BY WAY OF BEING HIDDEN *sit on the ground listening to the music.)*

POPSTAR:
You got to
You got to
You got to
You got to
You got to

You got to
You got to
You got to
You got to
You got to
Fry your head,
You got to
Fuck the dead.

You got to
You got to

You got to
You got to
You got to
You got to
You got to
You got to
Be what you
Think you want
To be if you
Want to know
Who plays what
Part in the show.

You got to
Get out
My way.
You got to
Move away,
You got to
Do what I
Say when I
Say what
My way is,
You got to
Do what I say
'Cause my way's
Harm's way.
(Repeat more softly, till end of scene.)

BY WAY OF: You like it?

SANTOUCHE: What say?

BY WAY OF: You deaf?

SANTOUCHE: What say?

BY WAY OF: You deaf?

SANTOUCHE: What say?

BY WAY OF: Dead head.

SANTOUCHE: After what I done for you, how come you're not more grateful?

BY WAY OF: Brought you to the show, didn't I? That's grateful.

SANTOUCHE: I am a man...

BY WAY OF: You ain't so special.

SANTOUCHE: Find yourself another. *(He gets up.)*

BY WAY OF: Hey, I didn't mean it.

SANTOUCHE: Fuck yourself. If this
is the show, it sucks.

BY WAY OF: Brought you to the show.
What did you expect?

SANTOUCHE: Music.

BY WAY OF: This is music.

SANTOUCHE: I mean music
music. This sucks.

BY WAY OF: What the hell do you expect from me?

SANTOUCHE: Nothing. I'm going. So long.
(He gets up.)

BY WAY OF: Hey, Santouche. Hey, man.
You gonna walk out on me?

SANTOUCHE: There's a place I've got to be at
by tomorrow. Other side of the river.

BY WAY OF: Other side of the river? You're crazy.

SANTOUCHE: I'm going.

BY WAY OF: What for? What for?
(He goes out.)
Shaddup!
(Music stops. Pause.)
Nobody runs out on me.
(Pause)
Wonder what's so hot
on the other side of the river.

Scene Six

(In front of an old saloon. Noise of conversation and merriment from within. As he attempts to enter, SANTOUCHE *bumps into* FISHEYE, *who is leaving. Later on in the scene, the* COOK *is played by a member of the* CHORUS.*)*

SANTOUCHE: Fisheye! What're you doing
this side of the river?
I thought you'd be long gone by now.

FISHEYE: Lucky I found you. You can't
go in there. Blackmange is having
a party. It's his birthday.

SANTOUCHE: Thought I smelled something
that stunk.

FISHEYE: You gotta be real careful.

SANTOUCHE: How many men's he got with him?

FISHEYE: Only nine.

SANTOUCHE: Armed?

FISHEYE: Knives, sidearms, grenades.

SANTOUCHE: Can you cover me
from the kitchen?

FISHEYE: You can't be serious.

SANTOUCHE: Fisheye, I'm going in there.

FISHEYE: They'll massacree ya.

SANTOUCHE: Not if you help.

FISHEYE: What's your plan?

SANTOUCHE: Go around back to the kitchen.

FISHEYE: Won't be a party to this.
(SANTOUCHE *pulls a gun on him.)*
Anything you say, Santouche.

SANTOUCHE: Remember all the good
I done ya.

FISHEYE: You're right. I ought to be more
grateful. We'll get 'em in the
crossfire.

SANTOUCHE: Blackmange! I don't believe it!

FISHEYE: It's him all right.

SANTOUCHE: After all these years!

FISHEYE: What happens if they decide
to bust out the back way?

SANTOUCHE: I'll cut 'em down before
they get to you.

FISHEYE: All right then.

SANTOUCHE: I'll start after you fire the
first shot, only lay off old
Blackmange himself. I want him.

(FISHEYE *rushes out as* BY WAY OF BEING HIDDEN *enters from saloon, slightly drunk.)*

BY WAY OF: Santouche, is that you?

SANTOUCHE: You clear out of here if you
want to stay alive.

BY WAY OF: It's a matter of some importance.

SANTOUCHE: Back off, bitch, or you're a dead
man.

BY WAY OF: You saved my life. I mean
I was only trying to help. But
seeing as how... *(She backs off.)*

SANTOUCHE: That's better. Now you just stay there
till me and my friend are finished.

BY WAY OF: Fine with me.

SANTOUCHE: Blackmange, you asshole!

(FISHEYE *begins to fire. Yells and screams from within.* SANTOUCHE *begins to fire through windows and doors of the saloon.)*

SANTOUCHE: Blackmange!

(BLACKMANGE *stumbles through the door. Slumps.* SANTOUCHE *shoots him several times.* BLACKMANGE *falls and lies motionless. Shooting subsides.)*

SANTOUCHE: Got him, Fisheye! I got him. Hey,
Fisheye, I got him. He's dead. Just
look at him. Stinking, ugly stiff.
Whoopee! Hey, Fisheye...

*(*COOK *enters.)*

COOK: He's dead.

SANTOUCHE: Dead? Fisheye?

COOK: The whole gang went busting out the
back way. You kept pluggin' the stiff.
They ripped him up good. He's dead. They're
gone. They'll come back for you, Santouche.

SANTOUCHE: Get lost.

COOK: They'll do a number on you. *(*COOK *goes out.)*

BY WAY OF: Santouche, hey.

SANTOUCHE: What is it?

BY WAY OF: Remember me?

SANTOUCHE: Beat it.

BY WAY OF: You saved my life.

SANTOUCHE: My friend's croaked, can't you see? Beat it.

BY WAY OF: Your lady's been abducted.

SANTOUCHE: What!

BY WAY OF: That's right.

SANTOUCHE: Who? Where?

BY WAY OF: Don't know.

SANTOUCHE: Shit if you don't know. Some kind of trick
this is. You don't tell me who's got her and...

BY WAY OF: Easy now.
I don't know who's got her,
but I do know who does know...

SANTOUCHE: Who's that?

BY WAY OF: Him.

SANTOUCHE: The stiff.

BY WAY OF: Yep.

SANTOUCHE: Blackmange?

BY WAY OF: Yup. You killed him.

SANTOUCHE: Why didn't you tell me?

BY WAY OF: I tried.

SANTOUCHE: You didn't try hard enough.

BY WAY OF: What am I supposed to do?

SANTOUCHE: Shut up.

BY WAY OF: But fortunately I have an idea.

SANTOUCHE: Shut up. How do I know
you're telling me the truth
about Isle of Mercy?

BY WAY OF: Don't believe me then. I don't give a crap.

SANTOUCHE: She was going to sell my watch.

BY WAY OF: Going around with all that money on her.

SANTOUCHE: So what?

BY WAY OF: All alone from what I hear.

SANTOUCHE: So?

BY WAY OF: You want to hear my idea?

SANTOUCHE: No. Beat it.

BY WAY OF: All right.
Just trying to be of use.
Didn't mean no harm.

SANTOUCHE: Get lost. Leave me alone. Beat it.

BY WAY OF: Be seeing you.

SANTOUCHE: What the hell am I going to do?

BY WAY OF: Want to hear my idea?

SANTOUCHE: Beat it, lady, or I'll lay you out
for the buzzards.

BY WAY OF: Okay. Okay. Just trying to help...
(She starts to go out and pauses.)
I got a friend who's got a friend as
can make that stiff talk. It's true.

SANTOUCHE: What'd you say?

Scene Seven

(A starry night. ISLE OF MERCY *sits on a boulder looking at the moon. She sings her song.)*

ISLE OF MERCY: This is
Isle of Mercy's song.
It won't be long.
She is very
very tough.
She got no inside,
got no outside.
Whoever told you so,
they lied.

(The two CHILDREN *are at first hidden in the shadows. They approach her gingerly, and only after a rather long pause.)*

FIRST CHILD: Hey, lady.
(Pause)

SECOND CHILD: Hey, lady,
what are you doing?

ISLE OF MERCY: Looking at stars.
(Pause)

SECOND CHILD: I said what are you doing?

ISLE OF MERCY: I said looking
at stars. Can't you hear? *(Pause)*
That light
up there.
That's a star.

SECOND CHILD: Ain't you lonely
sitting there?

ISLE OF MERCY: Nope.... Sometimes.
(Pause)

FIRST CHILD: I got a rock with a face on it.
(Pause)

FIRST CHILD: I got a rock with a face on it.

ISLE OF MERCY: I heard you the first time.
(Pause)

FIRST CHILD: You want to see it? *(Pause)*
You want to see it?
(Pause)

ISLE OF MERCY: Okay. Show me the rock
with the face on it.
(She examines the rock.)
That ain't no face...

SECOND CHILD: I told you that wasn't no face.

FIRST CHILD: Sure looks like it to me. *(Pause)*
The moon's got a face, see.

(They all look up briefly.)

FIRST CHILD: Sometimes he turns his face
to one side. Sometimes it's
straight on. I can't see
too good. It's awful far.

SECOND CHILD: He can't see straight.

ISLE OF MERCY: I was talking to him.
You don't need to butt in.

FIRST CHILD: The moon's a rock with
a face on it.

ISLE OF MERCY: Pretty big rock, if it's just a rock. *(Pause)*
Whose kids are you
anyhow? Crowsfoot's?

SECOND CHILD: Hell no...

FIRST CHILD: We borned ourselves
out of rocks.

ISLE OF MERCY: Kids don't come
from rocks, stupid.

FIRST CHILD: Shit, I know that.

ISLE OF MERCY: Where do they come from?

FIRST CHILD: You know...

*(*CROWSFOOT *enters.)*

CROWSFOOT: Well my dear, are my little
self-begotten bastards bothering
you? If they grieve you, take a
stone to 'em.

ISLE OF MERCY: Go back to the wagon, Crowsfoot.

CROWSFOOT: They's a customer. You come along.

ISLE OF MERCY: I am relaxing
with my friends.

CROWSFOOT: The Wheel of Possibility don't slow down
for nobody nohow, that's for sure.
You rattle your bones, and get a move on.
Hup, hup!

ISLE OF MERCY: Scram, Crowsfoot.

CROWSFOOT: Pretty lady, you are pushing me
to extreme acts of unkind coercion.

*(*ISLE OF MERCY *stands up on tiptoe and peers offstage as though to catch a glimpse of the prospective customer. Then she sits back down. Pause.)*

ISLE OF MERCY: I won't do it.

CROWSFOOT: Yes you will.

ISLE OF MERCY: No I won't.

CROWSFOOT: Yes you will

ISLE OF MERCY: Think you can tell me what to do!

CROWSFOOT: You'll do exactly what I tell you to. *(Pause)*

ISLE OF MERCY: Shit on you.

CROWSFOOT: Watch your mouth.

ISLE OF MERCY: I won't do it.

CROWSFOOT: Yes you will.

ISLE OF MERCY: You fuck him then.

CROWSFOOT: Now Mercy, cool down...

ISLE OF MERCY: You know who that is?

CROWSFOOT: He's just like everybody else.

ISLE OF MERCY: That is the devil himself.

CROWSFOOT: So? I'm not particular.

ISLE OF MERCY: I am.

CROWSFOOT: You can't afford it.

ISLE OF MERCY: Oh yes I can. Like
the man said, There is
some shit I do not
eat.

(Pause)

CROWSFOOT: You want me to give
you another one of my
speechifications?

(Pause)

ISLE OF MERCY: You win.

CROWSFOOT: Come along then.

*(*CROWSFOOT *leaves.* ISLE OF MERCY *gets up to go.)*

ISLE OF MERCY: So long.

BOTH CHILDREN: So long.

(Pause. ISLE OF MERCY *sits back down.)*

FIRST CHILD: Moon's where the ghosts go.

ISLE OF MERCY: Why do they do that?

FIRST CHILD: So no one can hurt them.

SECOND CHILD: Who can hurt a ghost,
stupid? A ghost's a dead
thing. It don't have to
be protected.
(Pause)

ISLE OF MERCY: Maybe the moon's a ghost...

SECOND CHILD: You ever seen a ghost?

FIRST CHILD: What do you mean by that?

SECOND CHILD: I'm getting scared.
Come on, let's go
back to the wagon.

CROWSFOOT: *(Offstage.)* Isle of Mercy!

ISLE OF MERCY: They ain't no such thing
as a ghost.

FIRST CHILD: Why'd you say that
about the moon being
a ghost.

SECOND CHILD: Let's go back, come on!

ISLE OF MERCY: I don't know.

FIRST CHILD: You talk funny. For a girl.

ISLE OF MERCY: You know what I'd do
if I was a ghost?

CROWSFOOT: *(Offstage.)* Isle of Mercy!

SECOND CHILD: I'm getting out of here!

FIRST CHILD: If I was a ghost I'd
fly away. Fly right smack
out of here. That's for damn sure.

SECOND CHILD: You're both crazy. *(*SECOND CHILD *goes out. Pause.)*

Scene Eight

(A clearing in the forest. BY WAY OF BEING HIDDEN, SANTOUCHE, *a* WIZARD, *and the corpse of* BLACKMANGE. *The* WIZARD *is dressed as the others except he sports a necklace of onions, garlic, and rattlesnake skins. His top hat is festooned with leafy twigs and switches. He carries a small black bag full of bottles and tins.* BY WAY OF BEING HIDDEN *carries a large suitcase. To revive* BLACKMANGE *the* WIZARD *kneads a paste from the flour, water, and whiskey. He then rolls the paste*

into a little ball, plants a garlic clove in the ball, and places it under the dead man's tongue.)

WIZARD: That's the corpse.

BY WAY OF: Yup.

WIZARD: How'd he croak?

BY WAY OF: It wasn't measles.

WIZARD: How'd he croak?

BY WAY OF: Shot. Ah. Several times.

WIZARD: Uhm. So you say.

BY WAY OF: Can you do it?

WIZARD: Maybe.

SANTOUCHE: Well? Can he do it?

BY WAY OF: Says maybe.

SANTOUCHE: Shit.

WIZARD: I'll need some
flour, water, and
a bottle of whiskey.

BY WAY OF: Coming right up. *(Rummages through the suitcase for these)*

SANTOUCHE: What you gonna do?

WIZARD: Like patching a tire.

BY WAY OF: Hear that, Santouche?
Like patching a tire!

SANTOUCHE: I hear it.

WIZARD: Is that the killer?

BY WAY OF: That's the killer.

WIZARD: Was there bad blood between?

BY WAY OF: You might say.

WIZARD: By Way of Being Hidden,
I don't want none of your
horse crap. This is serious
business. And you get that
man outta sight, hear?

BY WAY OF: Santouche, you get
out of sight, you hear?

SANTOUCHE: Why? I stand where I please,
as I please.

BY WAY OF: If the stiff sees you it won't work.

SANTOUCHE: Hell.

WIZARD: It's true, son.

SANTOUCHE: All right, all right, Shit, man!
Can't get no peace from a man
even by killing him no more.

WIZARD: This world
is full of dark souls
and wondrous things.

SANTOUCHE: What kind of sawbones
can bring a man back to life anyhow?

WIZARD: Young man, you are disturbing
me. This is America. Therefore
anything can happen...
Aside from which, the object is
not to restore the poor stiff
from across the murky deeps of
Styx, which is ridiculous;
but a more pragmatic and wholly
American one: namely, to bring
him temporarily back from across
the shadowy waters of Lethe.

SANTOUCHE: Afraid I lost you.

BY WAY OF: A stiff's a stiff.

WIZARD: What I mean is that all we need
is his memory. He don't have to
be alive, you dig?

SANTOUCHE: Yeah... but.

WIZARD: All we got to do is trick him
into thinking he's alive.

SANTOUCHE: Is that all....

WIZARD: That is the practical approach
to the art of undoing death.

SANTOUCHE: I'm afraid I still don't understand,
Doc, but I'll take your word for it.
All I want is results.

WIZARD: My sentiments exactly.

SANTOUCHE: By Way, I have a feeling he's bullshit.

BY WAY OF: Shut up, Santouche.

SANTOUCHE: That stiff don't know beans.

WIZARD: Shut up, killer.

SANTOUCHE: Only ones end up getting killed
have had it coming. Like him.

WIZARD: Oh yeah? What'd he do?

SANTOUCHE: Spit in my eye. Told me off
in front of people. Went and stooled on me good.

WIZARD: Concerning what?

SANTOUCHE: Never you mind. I spent some time
out of circulation on account of him.

WIZARD: So you killed him.

SANTOUCHE: Let's just say he got
his comeuppance.

WIZARD: Let's just say...

SANTOUCHE: You're a wise one, you are.

WIZARD: Gentlemen, we are about
ready to begin The Con.

SANTOUCHE: What's he talking about?

BY WAY OF: What con is that, doc?

WIZARD: Friends, we are about to
fool death himself. It's
all part of the show.

BY WAY OF: Hot damn! He's serious.

SANTOUCHE: The man is out of his mind!

WIZARD: What's his name?

SANTOUCHE: Blackmange.

WIZARD: Blackmange? What kind of a name is that?

SANTOUCHE: It's because he's so ugly.
(The WIZARD *cradles* BLACKMANGE.*)*

WIZARD: Blackmange, my friend, are you awake?

SANTOUCHE: Nothing's happening.

BY WAY OF: Shut up.

WIZARD: Blackmange, sit up now, you've been
asleep for a long time, why it's past noon,
the birds are a-singing, sun is a-shining away,
pretty girls are a-wiggling their asses out in the street,
ain't you ever going to get up? Ain't you hungry?

BLACKMANGE: Ahhhhhh.

WIZARD: Blackmange, I'm going to do right by you,
I swear it, I'll kill 'em myself, whoever
it was done this to you, you'll see, who was it?
Tell me, Blackmange, and I'll nail 'em good, you'll see.

BLACKMANGE: Ahhhhhhhhh.

SANTOUCHE: Jesus fucking Christ.

BY WAY OF: Shut up.

WIZARD: Who done it, tell me, Blackmange?

BLACKMANGE: Dunno...

WIZARD: The girl, who's got the girl? Maybe
he done it, I'll get him for you, you'll
see, come on, Blackmange.

BLACKMANGE: Ahhhhhhhhhhhhhh.

WIZARD: Her name's Isle of Mercy.

BLACKMANGE: Santouche girl. He done it. He killed me.

WIZARD: What about the girl? Who's got her?

BLACKMANGE: He done it. Ahhhh.

WIZARD: I'll settle his apples, you bet I will,
but that girl, who's got her? That guy that's
got her's in on it, I swear, him and Santouche,
I swear, who was it?

BLACKMANGE: Santouche... and him?

WIZARD: Who was it? He's the real one, he set you up,
I swear he did, he was laughing at you, come on,
who was it, old Blackmange, only way for me to get even,
no, don't go back to sleep without telling me,
who's the man who's got Isle of Mercy?

BLACKMANGE: Guyanousa's got her.

WIZARD: What's that? What'd you say?

SANTOUCHE: Did you hear what he said?

BY WAY OF: I don't get it: guy snoozing....
What's that? I don't get it.

SANTOUCHE: Can you make out what it is?

WIZARD: Who's got her? Who was it, Blackmange?
He done you in, that one.

BLACKMANGE: Guyanousa's got her.

WIZARD: Guyanousa's got her. Now it clicks.
The Guyanousa is a sideshow con.

BY WAY OF: That's right. Now I remember.

SANTOUCHE: He said the Guyanousa's got her...

BLACKMANGE: Ahhhhhhh... kill him.

WIZARD: Fuck you stiff! Go back to being
dead. We're going to feed you to pigs.
Santouche's here, take a look at him.

SANTOUCHE: Fuck you, Blackmange.

BLACKMANGE: Ahhhh...

BY WAY OF: He's dead again.

WIZARD: He always was. Now he knows it again.

SANTOUCHE: The Guyanousa.

WIZARD: Friends, I'll be going now. Please
don't hesitate to get in touch if
you should ever require my services
again. I also raise storms, debase coin,
cause floods, stunt crops, induce a few
miscarriages, and on a good day I can
throw a close election.

SANTOUCHE: Here's your money, beat it.

WIZARD: Be seeing you, kind gentlefolk, be seeing you. *(*WIZARD *takes up his bag and goes out.)*

SANTOUCHE: No one does that to me.

BY WAY OF: What are you talking about?

SANTOUCHE: The Guyanousa.

BY WAY OF: Now aren't you glad
for the favor I done you?

SANTOUCHE: I'll get him good.

BY WAY OF: You don't sound grateful.

SANTOUCHE: Shit on you. Beat it.

BY WAY OF: Last time I ever help you out.

SANTOUCHE: Leave me alone, understand?

BY WAY OF: All right, all right, I didn't mean
anything by it. I'm going, I'm going...
(She starts to go out.)

SANTOUCHE: Fucking sideshow con-man.

BY WAY OF: Knew a man like you
once. One day a little
blue bug came up and
bit him on the ass.
He went nuts.
Beat himself to death
with his own fist.
(Pause. She slowly turns and exits.)

Scene Nine

(A hillside by the river. The river is filled with smoke. A small, mullioned window is planted on the hill, and dim light shines through. Old gravestones and stuffed rats are scattered about. The MAN *is standing in a waist-deep grave he has dug on the hill. His companion, a dummy, is propped against a nearby tree. The dummy's chest is pierced by several arrows, and there is a hatchet buried in his forehead.* SANTOUCHE *appears from behind the hill. He is crossing the river on stilts, and is dressed fantastically so that he resembles a giant bird. After greeting the* MAN, *he climbs down to the earth.)*

SANTOUCHE: All on a-fucking-count of the goddam watch
that don't keep time, and that goddam woman
that couldn't tell the fucking time if the
goddam watch kept it. Wonder where the hell she is.

MAN: Hey, you! Shinbones!

SANTOUCHE: You talking to me, groundhog?

MAN: Yeah, you. Who'd you think I was talking to?

SANTOUCHE: What're you doing in that hole?

MAN: Well I'm not here
for my beauty sleep,
that's for sure. Come here.

SANTOUCHE: What's wrong with him?

MAN: Stiff. Can't you see? A fucking stiff.

SANTOUCHE: That much I can tell.

MAN: He was being difficult.

SANTOUCHE: What did you say?

MAN: It's why I killed him.

SANTOUCHE: I don't understand your meaning.

MAN: How would you, if I haven't
explained my meaning to you?

SANTOUCHE: Got a point there.

MAN: Thing is...

SANTOUCHE: Well, good day, sir. I think I'll
just mosey on down the road... .
It's been a real pleasure.
(The MAN *pulls a gun on* SANTOUCHE.*)*

MAN: Hold on, buddy.

SANTOUCHE: You meet such interesting people...

MAN: One step further and I'll drill ya.

SANTOUCHE: Just a figure of speech.
I wasn't really planning to walk off
like that. After all, we haven't even
been properly introduced. My name's Santouche.

MAN: Now listen, bud, and listen good... .
You listening?

SANTOUCHE: I'm listening. Real close...

MAN: This stiff is a stiff 'cause he won't
bury me. He wouldn't do it. So I
off him, and he still won't do it.
Seems simple enough to me. Shovel
a few yards of dirt over me. I told
him I'd lie real still, and not to
worry if I started to squirm around
once he got to my face. I told him
he could have my stuff. Shoes. Pack.

Good hat. And a couple guns. That's
not asking a whole lot, it seems
to me. Well, he had some kind of old-fashioned
ethical-humanist compunctions
about burying a living man. We talked
it over for a long time. He threatened
to take off without helping me out...

SANTOUCHE: I'll bury you, sure I will, no sweat.

MAN: Shut up. It's not polite to interrupt.

SANTOUCHE: Sorry. I was just trying to be neighborly.

MAN: I don't want you to bury me. I want him to.

SANTOUCHE: But he's dead...

MAN: That's where you come in.

SANTOUCHE: I'm afraid I don't get what you mean.
Or maybe I'm just thick.

MAN: He won't listen to me.

SANTOUCHE: No, it doesn't look as though he'll do
a whole lot of listening from here on in.

MAN: But you are listening to me.

SANTOUCHE: Oh yes, I certainly am, and it's a great
pleasure to do so.

MAN: Then you talk to him.

SANTOUCHE: What?

MAN: I said you talk to him, and convince him
he ought to do as I say.

SANTOUCHE: But, he's a stiff.

MAN: And you'd better be pretty goddam persuasive.

SANTOUCHE: You're pulling my leg.

MAN: Because if you don't talk that pigheaded
son-of-a-bitch into burying me, I'm likely
to get angry again, and I'll just have to
blow you away for sure, and bud, you'll look
as worse off as him. And that ain't good.

SANTOUCHE: No indeed, sir, it ain't good at all.

MAN: Well, what say, my young man?

SANTOUCHE: I guess I see it your way.

MAN: I'm so glad you listen to reason.

SANTOUCHE: Well, it's no trouble, my friend. I mean
I do like to be helpful, particularly to
one like yourself, who is so...

MAN: Persuasive...

SANTOUCHE: What's his name?

MAN: Cleveland. Mr. Grover Cleveland.

SANTOUCHE: Thanks.

MAN: You're welcome, I'm sure.

SANTOUCHE: You're fortunate I've got some recent
experience in this field....
Ah, Mr. Cleveland...

MAN: You don't need to be so formal.
A friend of mine's a friend of his.

SANTOUCHE: Oh, I see. Ah, Grover, old man.

MAN: That's better...

SANTOUCHE: Ah yes, Grover, my friend. I hear
you're unwilling to oblige our
common friend here, ah....
Might I ask what your name is, sir?

MAN: Surely. I'm called William McKinley.

SANTOUCHE: Ah, yes, Mr. McKinley here desires
that I do my utmost to convince
you of the folly of your ways, in so
willfully resisting his blandishments
to the effect that you assist him in his
ardent wish to be—er—interred at this
time, in this place...

MAN: That's very good.

SANTOUCHE: Thank you kindly, Mr. McKinley, I'll just go on.

MAN: Don't let me interfere.

SANTOUCHE: Now, my dear Mr. Cleveland, much as I do not
wish to presume to offer unsolicited advice,
especially in the case of so recent a friendship...

MAN: Very tactful. I like that....

(SANTOUCHE *kicks the gun away and grabs it.)*

MAN: Shit.

SANTOUCHE: Okay, stiff, get out of that hole, and get out of there quick.

MAN: It was only a joke.

SANTOUCHE: Joke my ass. Move!

MAN: Don't. Don't. Don't.

SANTOUCHE: Now grab that stiff, stiff, and throw him in the hole.

MAN: What're you so angry about? It was a
joke. It's all in good spirits I assure you.

SANTOUCHE: Now you get in the hole.

MAN: What are you going to do?

SANTOUCHE: Just what you said you wanted.

MAN: You must be crazy.

SANTOUCHE: Shut up, Mr. McKinley. *(Begins to shovel dirt over the* MAN, *who is by now back in the grave.)*

MAN: It was a joke, just part of the show.
I was bored. Have pity on me. The future
is boredom. I wouldn't have harmed you, I
swear! It was all part of the show.

(SANTOUCHE *is shoveling rapidly now.)*

SANTOUCHE: Eat shit. Eat dirt. Eat shit. Dirt... shit... dirt...

MAN: But I'll suffocate. You can't be serious.

SANTOUCHE: Mr. McKinley, sir, my name is Santouche,
and I am very serious.

MAN: You're a monster.

SANTOUCHE: I'm doing you a favor. Get your head
down or I'll shoot your ears off. Get down...

MAN: Help, a monster!

(SANTOUCHE *kills him with the shovel.)*

SANTOUCHE: You're part of nobody's show now, my friend.
(Finishes burying the MAN.*)*
Takes all kinds, my friend.
A man who fools with me hurts me,
and I'll be obliged to hate him. *(Pause)*
You started it, buster.

Won't go playing your tricks
on anyone else.... *(Pause)*
Guess I showed you. *(Pause)*
Wonder who the hell he was? *(Pause)*
Buried two presidents today!
First time I ever did that. *(Pause)*
...didn't mean no harm! My ass! *(Pause)*
...all part of the show. You are dead,
man, and I spit on your stiff, and
man, you can't do one blessed thing
about it! *(Pause)*
Wonder who the hell he was? *(Pause)*
...part of the show!

Scene Ten

(A circus wagon standing on an open plain. SANTOUCHE, *looking very exhausted, sits downstage. He takes off his boots and rubs his feet. The members of the* CHORUS *speak their lines in turn from their usual position just outside the main playing area.)*

FIRST CHORISTER: Guyanousa? I heard of it, but offhand
I can't recall what it was I heard.

SECOND CHORISTER: Never heard of it. You must be crazy.

THIRD CHORISTER: I heard of it, but there ain't no
such thing, of that I'm sure.

FIRST CHORISTER: Nope.

SECOND CHORISTER: Search me.

THIRD CHORISTER: Never heard of it.

FIRST CHORISTER: Guya-what?! You must be stewed!

SECOND CHORISTER: A story that's told by folks
'round here. Don't you pay it no nevermind.

THIRD CHORISTER: It's against the laws of nature for such
a creature to exist. Of that I'm sure.

FIRST CHORISTER: Somebody pulling your leg, fella!

SECOND CHORISTER: But that was all part of the show.
bud, they ain't nobody takes such things
serious anymore.

THIRD CHORISTER: I hear there's wonderful strange creatures
at the far end of the world. That's what I hear.
*(*CROWSFOOT *emerges from the wagon, walks downstage, and sits next to* SANTOUCHE.*)*

CROWSFOOT: My friend, mind if I sit down beside you?

SANTOUCHE: Nope.

CROWSFOOT: Crowsfoot's the name. What's yours?

SANTOUCHE: Santouche.

CROWSFOOT: You look beat.

SANTOUCHE: Yup.

CROWSFOOT: I bear good news.
(Pause)

SANTOUCHE: Go away.

CROWSFOOT: You're a fortunate man.

SANTOUCHE: Go away.

CROWSFOOT: I am the first ordained minister of the Church
of Christ Fornicator. No shit, it's true. And
I got my license right here. Now you, friend:
What woe has been your lot, who can tell? You
look like a disaster. What you need's a nice
little piece. Now you can get it, and get saved
at the same time. Ticket's only a quarter.
You don't want to miss out on a good thing, do you?

SANTOUCHE: Don't have no quarter.

CROWSFOOT: Come on, don't feel shy. It'd be
good for you. Buy your ticket. Climb
into my wagon there. My little madonna,
she's got fine moves, and my friend, it's
not every day you can get saved and laid
at the same time. Why, it's practically
miraculous. Only costs a quarter.

SANTOUCHE: Don't want no pussy.

CROWSFOOT: The Lord don't have much use for melancholia,
my friend.

SANTOUCHE: Don't want it.

CROWSFOOT: How do you expect to get it if you don't
want it?

SANTOUCHE: Fed up.

CROWSFOOT: You look like a fine, strapping man of god.
There is no point in all this down-and-out misery.
I'll tell you because I know from my own experience.
If you turn your heart to Christ Fornicator you
will find untold bliss. Satisfaction guaranteed.
Once you get enlightenment anything is possible.
No one ever gonna shove your face in shit, no one
ever gonna call you names! If you got it, friend, and
I mean get it, you're gonna get laid both in body and soul!
With the Lord doing it in your heart, you're gonna
have a big edge on the next man, friend, and in this
evil son-of-a-bitch's world, full of conniving wildcats,
you need every bit of edge you can get. Ain't it so,
friend? Don't matter where it come from. How about it?

SANTOUCHE: Had enough. Don't want nothing.

CROWSFOOT: Now I was as empty and bitter as you are once, before
I got religion. Then I put down my quarter, and all of
a sudden, I saw that all my former life was spent in
folly. And that squaring the circle of desire and completion
was a cinch. *(Pause)*
What it comes down to, my friend, is quite simple:
YOU CAN HAVE WHAT YOU WANT! IT'S YOURS FOR THE ASKING!
Myself, I was part of he show, I am ashamed to say.
You look like you know whereof I am speaking. I practiced
deception on my fellow man. Now that all seems like a nightmare
of some dark, grimy, brooding, sooty, barren, windswept country
full of liars, cheats, scoundrels, lunatics—monsters even—who all
look the same! The fools! And that nightmare was lit up only
by the fires of vengeance and hatred. Honestly, one could gag.
Why, the terrible things I done! And youknow, I never got laid!

SANTOUCHE: What was your con?

CROWSFOOT: I can see you're a child of darkness
still, my friend.

SANTOUCHE: Your con, what was it?

CROWSFOOT: Shameful, I cheated folk by pretending
to be a fabulous beast.

SANTOUCHE: I've done things like that. Are you for real?

CROWSFOOT: Do I not radiate gladness and
the joy of fulsome success?

SANTOUCHE: You smell like a bank of roses.

CROWSFOOT: My friend, why not let me enlist you right this
minute in our double-indemnified and wholly tax-
deductible Church of Christ Fornicator, and lead
you to consummation devoutly to be wished?

(SANTOUCHE gives a quarter to CROWSFOOT.)

SANTOUCHE: What kind of beast were you?

CROWSFOOT: Let us not dwell on the antediluvian,
my friend, let me lead you instead up...

SANTOUCHE: Just curious, that's all. I was a killer.

CROWSFOOT: I see. Well. If I can't interest you, young
man, I guess I'll be seeing you. Aha! Yes...
(He gets up and looks at the watch, which is still sprung.)
It's getting late. Nevertheless, I wish you well.
Our paths may be different, but our hearts....

SANTOUCHE: Where did you get that watch?

CROWSFOOT: What! Why? This watch?

SANTOUCHE: The watch. Where did you get it?

CROWSFOOT: You do ask questions.

SANTOUCHE: Where.

CROWSFOOT: Ah...

SANTOUCHE: I think we have some matters to discuss, my friend.

CROWSFOOT: Oh, I wouldn't want to detain you any further.

SANTOUCHE: No trouble, I'm sure. Your little presentation
has stirred up quite a commotion in my cynic breast.
and I am eager to learn more.

CROWSFOOT: I can tell by your bearing that you're a man
of eminence. My poor insignificant surmises could
be of no possible interest to one of your erudition
and mental prowess. Therefore...

SANTOUCHE: On the contrary...
(Pulls out his gun.)

CROWSFOOT: You want your quarter back?

Scene Eleven

(The same as the previous scene. The circus wagon is turned upside down, and one wheel is spinning. It is nearly dark. The FIRST *and* SECOND CHILDREN, *who cry out at* SANTOUCHE, *are hidden behind boulders. They dart from one place to another as he tries to catch them.* SANTOUCHE *and* ISLE OF MERCY *stand facing each other as the scene begins.)*

SANTOUCHE: You, look at you, fucking whore.

ISLE OF MERCY: Got the money. Had to get the money.

SANTOUCHE: You, look at you.

ISLE OF MERCY: Couldn't sell the watch.
It was busted. Lost the quarter.

SANTOUCHE: Shut up.

ISLE OF MERCY: Here's the money.

SANTOUCHE: How come you stayed with him?

ISLE OF MERCY: You didn't have to kill him.

SANTOUCHE: After what he done?

ISLE OF MERCY: None of your business.

SANTOUCHE: You and him in on it together?

ISLE OF MERCY: Things don't always work out right.

SANTOUCHE: Shut up.

ISLE OF MERCY: You shut up. I got my pride.

SANTOUCHE: You got nothing. Except me.
And I don't know if I want you anymore.
(Pause)

ISLE OF MERCY: Here's the money. I'm leaving.

SANTOUCHE: What?

ISLE OF MERCY: Going.

SANTOUCHE: Sit down.

ISLE OF MERCY: I'm leaving. Going. I'm finished
with people mad all the time. Sick of it.
Like you.

SANTOUCHE: Who'd take you in?

ISLE OF MERCY: Don't bother me.
Who'd treat me worse? I used to love

you. Santouche, but you're a killer
and I'm sick of that.

SANTOUCHE: Bitch. Sit down. I told you.

ISLE OF MERCY: You eat shit, Santouche.

SANTOUCHE: Don't talk to me that way.

ISLE OF MERCY: Now I'm getting mad, Jesus!

SANTOUCHE: None of 'em got killed, but
had it coming, I assure you.

ISLE OF MERCY: World's a bad place, I know.

SANTOUCHE: So leave me be. Sit down.

ISLE OF MERCY: No, I don't want to. Too much,
too late. You know, I can't stand
the sight of you, Santouche.

SANTOUCHE: Isle of Mercy!

ISLE OF MERCY: That's not my name.

SANTOUCHE: You're not going anyplace.

ISLE OF MERCY: Here's your stink money.

SANTOUCHE: Where would you go anyway? Stay.

ISLE OF MERCY: And do what?

SANTOUCHE: I got a reputation to maintain.

ISLE OF MERCY: Look at you.
You don't even look right.
You been taking drugs?

SANTOUCHE: I won't let you go.

ISLE OF MERCY: Santouche, I won't stay.

SANTOUCHE: You can't let me down.

ISLE OF MERCY: I'm going. Good bye.

SANTOUCHE: I won't let you.

ISLE OF MERCY: You gonna kill me?

SANTOUCHE: I can't let it happen.

ISLE OF MERCY: Why don't you kill me, too,
Santouche? You'd better, because
that's the only way I'm going
to stay here.

SANTOUCHE: You shut up.

ISLE OF MERCY: Yeah. I'll shut up. So long, Santouche.

SANTOUCHE: You stay.

ISLE OF MERCY: What are you going to do, Santouche,
shoot me in the back? Well, go right
ahead, if you want to. I don't give a crap.

SANTOUCHE: Hold on, Isle of Mercy.

ISLE OF MERCY: So long.

(He shoots her in the back.)

SANTOUCHE: I told you. *(Pause)*
Dumb thing to do. *(Pause)*
Everybody telling me what to do.
Got my pride. People won't leave you alone. *(Pause)*
Got no respect. That's the trouble. *(Pause)*
Who the hell you think you are, fancy lady?
(Pause)
Busted my watch, you did. *(Pause)*
People get what they deserve.
(Pause)

FIRST CHILD: Going to kill everybody, mister?

SANTOUCHE: Who's that?

FIRST CHILD: Going to kill everybody, mister?

SANTOUCHE: Who're you talking to?

SECOND CHILD: You gonna kill me, mister?

SANTOUCHE: Who're you, kid? Hey!
You! Where're you hiding?

FIRST CHILD: You gonna kill both of us, mister?

SANTOUCHE: You better shut your mouth, kid...

SECOND CHILD: You gonna kill everybody, mister?

SANTOUCHE: Little son-of-a-bitch...

FIRST CHILD: You gonna kill everybody, mister?

SANTOUCHE: SHUT UP, YOU LITTLE SHITHEAD!

SECOND CHILD: You gonna kill me, mister?

SANTOUCHE: Leave me alone, or I will!

FIRST CHILD: You going to kill me, mister?

SANTOUCHE: Fuck, how many of you are there?

SECOND CHILD: You gonna kill everybody, mister?

SANTOUCHE: Stop it!

FIRST CHILD: You gonna kill everybody, mister?

SANTOUCHE: LEAVE ME ALONE!

SECOND CHILD: You gonna kill everyone, mister?

SANTOUCHE: GODDAMN, COCKSUCKING, MOTHERFUCKING, SHIT HEADED...

FIRST CHILD: You gonna kill everybody, mister?

SANTOUCHE: Leave me alone, god damn it...

SECOND CHILD: You gonna kill everybody, mister?

SANTOUCHE: Hell.... What's the use? *(He sink to the ground.)*

CHORUS: You gonna kill everyone, mister?
You gonna kill everyone, mister?
You gonna kill everyone, mister?
You gonna kill everyone, mister?
You gonna kill everyone, mister?

END OF PLAY

7 DIFFERENT PLAYS

$12.95

THE BAD INFINITY
Mac Wellman

A BRIGHT ROOM CALLED DAY
Tony Kushner

DER INKA VON PERU
Jeffrey M Jones

IN A PIG'S VALISE
Eric Overmyer

IN HIS 80TH YEAR
Gillian Richards

KID TWIST
Len Jenkin

NO MERCY
Connie Congdon

PLAYS FROM PLAYWRIGHTS HORIZONS

$12.95

BABY WITH THE BATHWATER
Christopher Durang

COMING ATTRACTIONS
Ted Tally

HERRINGBONE
Book by Tom Cone, music by Skip Kennon,
lyrics by Ellen Fitzhugh
Production rights handled by Broadway Play Publishing

JUNGLE COUP
Richard Nelson
Production rights handled by Broadway Play Publishing

MARCH OF THE FALSETTOS
William Finn

THE TERRORISTS
Dallas Murphy
Production rights handled by Broadway Play Publishing

PLAYS FROM THE NEW YORK SHAKESPEARE FESTIVAL

$12.95

FOR COLORED GIRLS...
Ntozake Shange

THE LEAF PEOPLE
Dennis Reardon
Production rights handled by Broadway Play Publishing

NECESSARY ENDS
Marvin Cohen
Production rights handled by Broadway Play Publishing

SHORT EYES
Miguel Pinero

STREAMERS
David Rabe

THE TIME TRIAL
Jack Gilhooley
Production rights handled by Broadway Play Publishing

PLAYS FROM CIRCLE REPERTORY COMPANY

$12.95

THE DIVINERS
Jim Leonard Jr

DOWN BY THE RIVER...
Julie Bovasso
Production rights handled by Broadway Play Publishing

THE GREAT GRANDSON OF JEDEDIAH KOHLER
John Bishop
Production rights handled by Broadway Play Publishing

KNOCK KNOCK
Jules Feiffer

THE MOUND BUILDERS
Lanford Wilson
(revised in 1986)

SNOW ORCHID
Joe Pintauro
Production rights handled by Broadway Play Publishing

PLAYS FROM ACTORS THEATRE OF LOUISVILLE

$12.95

COUP/CLUCKS
Jane Martin

CRIMES OF THE HEART
Beth Henley

FOOD FROM TRASH
Gary Leon Hill
Production rights handled by Broadway Play Publishing

GETTING OUT
Marsha Norman

TALES OF THE LOST FORMICANS
Constance Congdon

THE UNDOING
William Mastrosimone

FULL LENGTH PLAYS BY WOMEN

BALLOON
Karen Sunde
$4.95

EMPRESS OF CHINA
Ruth Wolfe
$4.95

MOLLIE BAILEY...MOTHER JONES
Megan Terry
$4.95

...OMAHA MAGIC THEATER:
includes **AMERICAN KING'S ENGLISH FOR QUEENS, BABES IN THE BIGHOUSE,** and **RUNNING GAG**
Megan Terry and Jo Ann Schmidman
$9.95

WINDFALL APPLES
Roma Greth
$4.95

STARSTRUCK
Elaine Lee, Susan Norfleet Lee, and Dale Place
$9.95

Shipping is $2.00 for the first book ordered, and 25 cents for each book thereafter.

Prices subject to change.